CONFRONTING SEXUAL HARASSMENT

To my Mother, Sister and Father
and
To Richard

Confronting Sexual Harassment

The Law and Politics of Everyday Life

ANNA-MARIA MARSHALL
University of Illinois, Urbana-Champaign, USA

ASHGATE

Published by
Ashgate Publishing Company
Gower House
Croft Road
Aldershot
Hants GU11 3HR
England

Ashgate Publishing Company
Suite 420
101 Cherry Street
Burlington, VT 05401–4405
USA

Ashgate website: http://www.ashgate.com

British Library Cataloguing in Publication Data
Marshall, Anna-Maria
    Confronting sexual harassment : the law and politics of
    everyday life. - (Law, justice and power series)
    1.Sexual harassment - Law and legislation - United States
    I.Title
    344.7'3014133

Library of Congress Cataloging-in-Publication Data
Marshall, Anna-Maria.
    Confronting sexual harassment: the law and politics of everyday life / by Anna-Maria Marshall.
        p. cm. -- (Law, justice, and power)
    Includes bibliographical references and index.
    ISBN 0-7546-2520-6
    1. Sexual harassment--Law and legislation--United States. I. Title. II. Series.

    KF3467.M365 2005
    344. 7301'4133--dc22

                                                                            2004030677
ISBN-10: 0 7546 2520 6

Typeset by Saxon Graphics Ltd, Derby
Printed and bound in Great Britain by MPG Books Ltd, Bodmin, Cornwall

Contents

List of Tables

Acknowledgements

Many people have made important contributions to this book, from nurturing the original idea to bringing it to its final completion. I decided to study law and social change through the lens of sexual harassment in my first semester in Northwestern University's Political Science department. The members of my dissertation committee – Jonathan Casper, Dennis Chong, Ben Page, Jenny Mansbridge, and the late Herbert Jacob – fostered my interest in the subject, even though the topic did not fit squarely in the rigid boundaries of political science. I thank them for their creativity and encouragement. I am particularly grateful to Jonathan Casper and Shari Diamond for hiring me as a research assistant and bringing me to the American Bar Foundation, where I learned everything I know about research design.

The Sociology Department at the University of Illinois, Champaign-Urbana, has been a warm and hospitable place to finish this book and to develop a research agenda. My colleagues there have read drafts of chapters and provided much-needed moral support at critical times. I am particularly grateful to Ruth Aguilera, Michael Biggs, Zsuzsa Gille, Michael Goldman, Keith Guzik, Moon-Kie Jung, Catherine Kenney, Tim Liao, John Lie, Zine Magubane, Winnie Poster, Rachel Schurman, and Charis Thompson.

My membership of the Law and Society Association has provided inspiration and intellectual engagement for over ten years. I have found many mentors and friends there whose advice and guidance have influenced me as I finished this project. These friends and colleagues include Shari Diamond, Laurie Edelman, Howard Erlanger, Ben Fleury-Steiner, Meg Hobart, Beth Hoffman, Kathleen Hull, Michael McCann, Laura Beth Nielsen, Gerald Rosenberg, Austin Sarat, Stuart Scheingold, Vicki Schultz, Susan Shapiro, and Sandy Welsh.

Many colleagues and friends stuffed envelopes, read chapters, listened to rants, and offered advice and encouragement, including Kate Baldwin, Anita Bernstein, Jacob Corre, Steve Heyman, Dan Steward, and especially my friend and co-author Scott Barclay who has been a role model as I've navigated my path in academia.

And finally, I could not have completed this book without the love and support of my family. I grew up in a family that emphasized education and intellectual curiosity. My parents, Frank and Mary Marshall, and my sister, Cathy Marshall, all laid the foundation for this path. I got pushed along by my husband, Richard McAdams, who had the crazy idea that I go to graduate school. I dedicate this book to all of them.

1 The Legal Consciousness of Injustice: A Theoretical Framework

Inequality structures everyday life. Systems of stratification based on class, race, gender, sexual orientation, ethnicity, for example, shape such crucial aspects of daily life as the schools we attend, the jobs we hold, the neighborhoods we live in and the health care we receive. For the most part, our daily lives and routines are unquestioned and unexamined. Patterned by broad social forces, these routines seem inevitable and natural. Thus, inequality in life circumstances becomes an unfortunate but widely accepted aspect of social life.

Yet people do not always accept the oppressive conditions associated with inequality. At particular historical moments, challenges emerge. Indeed, these challenges are often mounted in public policy arenas, such as courts or legislatures. The civil rights movement of the 1950s combined a variety of strategies – direct action, legislative lobbying, coordinated litigation campaigns – all directed at developing policies that dismantled legalized segregation and other systematic inequalities (Kluger 1975; Tushnet 1987). Following in the path of the civil rights movement, women's organizations pursued similar strategies to promote women's equality in education and employment and to protect them from violence (Costain 1992). More recently, organizations advocating for the rights of gay, lesbian, bisexual and transgendered people are active in courts and legislatures at both the federal and state level, seeking protection from hate crime and support for their rights to form families (D'Emilio, Turner, and Vaid 2000; Cain 2000). These political and legal developments reflect a common strategy – one assuming that social change is ratified by changes to law and public policy.

Resistance is not confined to the public policy arena, but can also occur in everyday life (de Certeau 1984; Ewick and Silbey 1998; Scott 1985, 1990). "New" social movements, in particular, politicize the personal and explicitly encourage everyday resistance.

1

Movements focusing on gay rights or abortion, health movements such as …
anti-smoking, … and the women's movement all include efforts to change
sexual and bodily behavior. They extend into areas of daily life: what we eat,
wear and enjoy; how we make love, cope with personal problems, or plan and
shun careers. (Johnston, Larana, and Gusfield 1994, p. 8)

Based on new, oppositional interpretations of their experiences, people alter
their expectations, their desires, their needs, their grievances – the very
meaning of their daily lives. As people are emboldened to make demands for
better treatment, those demands can be opposed by spouses, children,
neighbors, co-workers, teachers – all those with whom they interact in their
normal routines. Thus, challenging inequality can create conflict in everyday
life, and these conflicts become the seeds of social change.

Law provides one arena for these conflicts. Law helps shape the meaning
that people make of their lives – the way that they understand the living
conditions created by structural inequality (Engel and Munger 2003; Ewick
and Silbey 1998; Merry 1990; Sarat and Kearns 1993; Nielsen 2000). People
may see in law and the legal system a set of traps that support systems of
oppression, but they may also find in law a set of tools to resist such
oppression (Merry 1995; McCann 1994; Thompson 1975). But law alone
does not determine people's interpretations of their experiences. Rather, it is
one of many frames and schemas – both hegemonic and subversive – that
promote or discourage the everyday conflicts that constitute social change.
So when African-Americans sought equal treatment by "trespassing" at lunch
counters (Morris 1984), when the collective abortion service, Jane, helped
women in Chicago obtain safe abortions before legalization (King 1993),
when battered women's shelters encouraged prosecutors to pursue criminal
charges against batterers (Schneider 1986), law was both guiding and
constraining those practices of resistance. In these cases, law supported
oppressive regimes at the same time that it represented the hopes and
aspirations of liberation, but it was always part of a larger social struggle that
touched everyday lives.

This book develops a theoretical framework for analyzing the role of law in
everyday resistance to inequality – what I call the legal consciousness of
injustice. It represents an effort to understand the relationship between law
and social change from the bottom up, where changing social, political, and
cultural values create conflict in everyday life. Law is important in this
analysis, but so are political debates and organizational practices that likewise
shape disputes. I rely on this framework to conduct an empirical study of
sexual harassment in a particular workplace. Specifically, I study the way that
women confront their experiences with unwanted sexual attention at work,
specifically how they interpret those experiences and how they respond. I
argue that the meaning that women assign to these experiences reflects not
just legal rules but broader political and social debates about equality and the
role of women in the workplace. Women rely on these meanings to decide

whether to complain or to ignore the behavior or even to participate in sexual joking and banter with co-workers. And the bundle of these women's decisions – and management responses – shape the meaning of sexual harassment laws in particular workplaces.

Law and Social Change: Top-Down or Bottom-Up

In spite of considerable skepticism, the "myth of rights" has been politically potent in social movement challenges to inequality over the past fifty years (Scheingold 1974). In the 1950s and 1960s, civil rights activists went to court to challenge state-mandated segregation. With other political institutions inaccessible, the courts seemed to be the most likely arena for obtaining relief (Tushnet 1987; Vose 1967). Moreover, the language of rights was symbolically powerful, appealing to American audiences who believed, in the abstract, in such values as freedom and equality (Polletta 2000; Williams and Williams 1995; Snow and Benford 1992). Thus, the National Association for the Advancement of Colored People (NAACP) and other civil rights attorneys made the law and litigation appear to be potent tools in liberation movements for oppressed minorities in the United States (Kluger 1975; Tushnet 1987; Vose 1967). Legal strategies continue to be popular among social movement organizations representing oppressed minorities, including gays and lesbians, women, and racial and ethnic groups (Eskridge 2002; Cain 2000).

The judicial impact study challenged this political faith in the courts. Designed to measure the success of these legal campaigns, the studies showed that impact litigation could not dismantle structural inequality and that, in some situations, litigation campaigns could actually be detrimental to a social movement's mobilization efforts. Using similar methodologies, the authors examined social conditions before a judicial decision, often from the Supreme Court, was handed down. Their data included survey results, as well as case studies and ethnographies of institutions and communities (Dolbeare and Hammond 1971, Muir 1973, Rosenberg 1991, Handler 1978, Tushnet 1987). Then, in the aftermath of the court's decision, the studies examined the responses of various groups of actors, such as lower courts, the actors and institutions charged with enforcing the decision, the intended beneficiaries of the decision, as well as the public itself. They also consulted the baseline measures of social conditions to detect whether the decision produced a change (Canon and Johnson 1999).

In *The Hollow Hope* (1991), Gerald Rosenberg offered a bleak assessment of impact litigation. Rosenberg surveyed a variety of Supreme Court decisions in politically controversial cases,[1] including *Brown v. Board of Education*. He argued that the Supreme Court had little effect on Southern state legislatures that engaged in serious delay tactics to avoid complying with the *Brown* decision. He also argued that while *Brown* itself captured a great deal of media attention, it did not seriously affect media attention to the issue of desegregation over time. Finally, he showed that many children still attended segregated schools, decades later. Rosenberg concluded, based on *Brown* and several other constitutional cases, that the Supreme Court could not bring about social change on its own. To have any effect at all, the Court needed the cooperation of other powerful institutional actors, such as Congress or state legislatures. Although his methods have been criticized,[2] Rosenberg's general conclusions about the limited capacity of the courts to bring about social change echo the skepticism of an earlier generation of judicial impact studies (Tushnet 1987; Handler 1978; Scheingold 1974; Muir 1973; Canon and Johnson 1999).

Rosenberg's *Hollow Hope* and other judicial impact studies have been criticized as being overly attentive to the courts in trying to assess the relationship between law and social change. Such studies begin at the top – the Supreme Court or other judicial decision-makers. Law is conceptualized rather narrowly as a product of official behavior, such as judicial decisions. Judges are the critical legal actors in this research; it is their decisions that theoretically produce the social change, and change is assessed against the goals of the judicial decision. This approach, however, ignores the more symbolic aspects of law, where legal cases place pressing issues on the political agenda and garner sympathetic publicity for social movements (McCann 1992, Feeley 1992). In this broader view, law is not simply a collection of judicial pronouncements that trickle down from the courts, but rather constitutes a powerful set of symbolic resources and everyday practices that shape politics, culture and social relations.

By contrast, dispute-centered approaches to studying the legal struggles surrounding inequality are more attentive to the social struggle itself before it ever reaches a courtroom (McCann 1992). Rather than judicial behavior, such studies focus on non-judicial actors – particularly social movement organizations and activists – that frame their grievances and demands in legal terms. Law is but one arena of conflict, although it is an important one because by shaping opportunities, constraints, and the meaning of experience, law constitutes ongoing social relations (McCann 1994, Ewick and Silbey 1998). In the midst of social, political, and cultural conflict, legal action can have "implications ... for issue agenda setting, movement building, negotiating and lobbying efforts, remedial program development, and even personal transformation" (McCann 1992, p. 735).

The first studies in this tradition analyzed social movements and their use of legal strategies, concluding that such strategies were of limited use in bringing about social change. First, litigation can oversimplify the complex social processes that constitute inequality and injustice by flattening structural problems into isolated disputes between parties that come to court in a lawsuit (Scheingold 1974; Handler 1978). In a legal proceeding, the dispute never turns on a vaguely identified social ill, such as poverty, unemployment, or the lack of adequate health care. Rather, a lawsuit must specify a tangible, legally-recognized harm, where the plaintiff has suffered some particular injury that violates a particular right or legal entitlement. Lawsuits also require identifiable defendants – some actor who has caused the injury and who may be held accountable for it. It is impossible to sue "society" or "an inadequate educational system" for one's grievances. In addition, this form of policy-making depends on judges who, by training and expertise, are rarely reliably on the side of oppressed groups (Scheingold 1974, Handler 1978, Rosenberg 1991).

Second, this reduction of structural social problems into simplistic disputes makes it less likely that courts can alleviate serious inequalities. Not every injury has a legal remedy, and even when available, those remedies are very limited. Courts mostly provide monetary compensation or issue injunctions, neither of which may be suitable to redress the injuries resulting from widespread inequalities. On occasion, courts provide extensive injunctive relief or administer complex consent decrees that require sweeping reforms in an institution or organization (Handler 1978). Yet these remedies can also be ineffectual because they are difficult to enforce. Judicial resources for oversight are limited, and social movement organizations may not have the capacity for monitoring compliance to make such remedies effective. Thus, judicial remedies are ill-equipped to make the kind of structural social change sought by many social movements (Handler 1978; Scheingold 1974).

Finally, litigation strategies are dominated by lawyers who may be elevated to inordinately powerful positions in social movements, thus displacing the grassroots in favor of elites and making political mobilization more difficult (Scheingold 1974). The language and procedures of a courtroom are fraught with jargon and can be inaccessible to members of oppressed groups who make up the movement. Moreover, the publicity and disruption that sometimes accompany social movement strategies can be inconsistent with a lawyer's desire to present a more conservative and less challenging picture to a judge. Lawyers themselves may be more interested in winning a particular case than in achieving the movement's broader goals. Thus, lawyers can occupy a troublesome role in movements, deflecting energy away from direct action and other strategies to less effective legal strategies (Scheingold 1974; McCann and Silverstein 1998).

However, paying attention to the struggle rather than judicial opinions reveals that litigation is one of many strategies that social movements use to challenge inequitable social conditions. This perspective places law in a broader context of other movement tactics, such as direct action, boycotts, lobbying – a perspective that sometimes illustrates how ineffective litigation is compared to these other methods (McCann and Silverstein 1998). A struggle-centered perspective also demonstrates the many uses of litigation in a challenge to inequality. For example, litigation is often used as a tool to bring public attention to a pressing social problem and to obtain concessions in negotiations (Olson 1984, McCann 1994, Silverstein 1996). And when a lawsuit is successful, it provides evidence that the system is vulnerable and subject to wider reform. When publicized among potential movement members, this widening of "political opportunities" becomes a way to empower and mobilize more activists to participate in other forms of action (McCann 1994, McAdam 1982).

But law also plays a more formative role in the development of social movements because legal concepts, particularly rights, are so important in the shape of movement grievances, demands, and collective identity. Many scholars have demonstrated the significance of rights in modern social movements, including those for civil rights (Polletta 2000, Morris 1984), comparable worth (McCann 1994), animal rights (Silverstein 1996), and gay and lesbian rights (Goldberg-Hiller 2002). Grounded in individualistic and liberal values, rights are well-respected in American culture and therefore constitute an appealing frame to garner sympathy from adherents, the general public, and public officials. Moreover, the invocation of rights can be empowering for members of oppressed minorities who use rights to make a claim for citizenship (MacKinnon 1979, Polletta 2000, Schneider 1986). According to Elizabeth Schneider, "[T]he assertion or 'experience' of rights can express political vision, affirm a group's humanity, … and assist in the collective political development of a social or political movement, particularly at its early stages" (Schneider 1986, p. 590).

By emphasizing social conflict over judicial decisions, the dispute-centered approach provides a complex picture of the role of law in bringing about social change. But studies of social movements that deploy legal norms and tactics are not necessarily at the "bottom" of a dispute. Social movement organizations are representing and formulating grievances and demands based on the experiences of their members, adherents, and other constituencies. As organizations and policy actors, they rarely confront the kinds of conflict they construct. While these studies analyze the rights consciousness of individual activists, those activists are already immersed in movement ideology, so it is not entirely surprising that they adopt movement frames in their daily encounters with inequality. Adopting a "bottom-up" perspective, then, requires an analysis of the way that ordinary people navigate the everyday conflicts that stem from conditions of inequality and oppression. Do social movement messages reach ordinary people? Or are people more attentive to messages from authority figures and counter-movements protecting the status quo? What role does law play in the many frames that are routinely available for interpreting daily manifestations of inequality? To build a framework that answers these questions, I turn to an analysis of law in everyday life that shows how people make sense of their quotidian encounters with inequality.

Getting to the Bottom of Disputes: The Study of Law in Everyday Life

Law and society research has always taken the ordinary person seriously as a legal actor (Jacob 1969; Zemans 1983; Felstiner, Abel and Sarat 1980–81; Sarat and Kearns 1993; Ewick and Silbey 1998; Marshall and Barclay 2003). Two prevailing law and society traditions – legal mobilization and legal consciousness – examine the role of law in everyday life. Defined as "the process by which legal norms are invoked to regulate behavior" (Lempert 1976, p. 173, quoted in Zemans 1983, p. 693), legal mobilization has been traditionally studied as the mechanism individuals use to enforce their legal rights. Adopting an instrumental perspective, this approach portrays law as a tool to resolve conflict when it arises. More recent work on legal consciousness has focused on the constitutive nature of law; that is, the way that law shapes how people make sense of their experiences (Sarat and Kearns 1993). In these studies, law does not simply resolve conflict – although that is always a possibility. Rather, law may be responsible for giving rise to the conflict in the first place. In this section, I describe these two different approaches to studying law in everyday life.

Legal Mobilization and the Disputing Process

Based in dispute-processing analysis, legal mobilization research has focused on how individuals navigate conflict in their daily lives and how they use law as a tool to resolve such conflict (Zemans 1983; Barclay 1999). In some of these early studies, legal mobilization was modeled as a form of political participation where ordinary people placed demands on state institutions for rights and privileges promised them by law (Zemans 1983; Jacob 1969). Even when simply invoking the law to resolve conflicts among private individuals, such legal mobilization involved bringing public norms to bear on private disputes, thus re-creating the law in a way that had broader significance for the next case (Zemans 1983). Compared to voting or joining a political party, this form of participation was a more direct form of democracy, although not necessarily egalitarian, since courts and other legal institutions are usually restricted to those who have access to material resources (Zemans 1983; Lawrence 1991a, 1991b). Still, in these early studies, legal mobilization was depicted as an important aspect of a democratic society.

Based largely on survey research, the studies in legal mobilization examined the everyday problems of ordinary people – coping with too much debt, seeking compensation for personal injuries, or facing discrimination at work, for example (Jacob 1969; Miller and Sarat 1980–81; Kritzer, Vidmar, and Bogart 1991). These surveys measured the number of problems people had and the ways that people resolved these problems, including the use of legal strategies. For example, the Civil Litigation Project (CLP) conducted a survey on a random sample of households and asked about experiences with eight different categories of problems, including divorce, consumer problems, and discrimination (Miller and Sarat 1980–81). The CLP found that conflict was endemic in American society but that people rarely turned to legal actors or institutions for remedies. The use of law was closely related to the type of problem involved. For example, divorces required the involvement of the courts so people were more likely to have hired lawyers and gone to court when having marital difficulty. However, people were much less likely to seek legal relief when they had problems with discrimination (Miller and Sarat 1980–81; Bumiller 1987, 1988). Thus, the type of law at stake in the dispute seemed to shape people's attitudes and practices with respect to the conflict (Miller and Sarat 1980–81; Curran 1977; Engel 1998, p. 123; Zemans 1983).[3]

While legal mobilization studies focused on individual behavior, they were grounded in a conceptualization of disputing as a social process shaped by a wide range of actors, audiences, institutions, and ideologies (Felstiner, Abel, and Sarat 1980–81). Felstiner, Abel, and Sarat outlined the stages of a dispute which they describe as transformations: "the way in which experiences become grievances, grievances become disputes, and disputes take various shapes, follow particular dispute processing paths, and lead to new forms of understanding" (Felstiner, Abel, and Sarat 1980–81, p. 632). The first stage, *naming*, consists of identifying an experience as harmful. This stage depends on the individual's definition of what is harmful, a definition often widely shared. For example, there is widespread consensus that breaking one's leg or having one's car stolen is an injurious experience. However, the authors noted that not all experiences carry such a consensus. They observed:

> For the most part, people agree on what is disvalued. But such feelings are never universal. Where people do differ, these differences, in fact, generate some of the most important research questions: why do people who perceive experience similarly *value* it differently, why do they *perceive* similarly valued experience differently, and what is the relation between valuation and perception? … Though hard to study empirically, naming may be the critical transformation; the level and kind of disputing in a society may turn more on what is initially perceived as an injury than on any later decision. (Felstiner, Abel, and Sarat 1980–81, pp. 634, 635, emphasis in original)

Thus, the authors recognized how difficult it would be for survey methods to capture the naming process since that particular transformation depended so heavily on individual perceptions and the meaning that individuals assigned to events.

After a person perceived themselves as being injured, the next stage of a dispute, *blaming*, occurs when a person "attributes an injury to the fault of another individual or social entity. By including fault within the definition of grievance, we limit the concept to injuries viewed both as violations of norm and remediable" (Felstiner, Abel, and Sarat 1980–81, p. 635). Thus, a grievance emerges in the aftermath of blaming. *Claiming* occurs when the injured party makes a demand for redress against the responsible party, and a dispute arises when that claim is rejected in whole or in part (Felstiner, Abel, and Sarat 1980–81). The dispute becomes a legal dispute when its terms implicate legal norms or institutions (Felstiner 1974).

Because of the instability and subjectivity of these stages, disputes rarely follow the smooth, linear trajectory suggested by this framework. Rather, some stages – such as naming and blaming – may occur all at once. In other cases, people may make repeated claims after the dispute arises (Felstiner, Abel and Sarat 1980–81). Moreover, the parties may abandon grievances, claims and disputes by avoiding each other or by "lumping it," where "the salience of the dispute is reduced not so much by limiting the contacts between the disputants, but by ignoring the dispute, by declining to take any or much action in response to the controversy" (Felstiner 1974, p. 81). These transformations and choices are subject to change based on new information or subtle changes of mood.

Felstiner, Abel, and Sarat also noted the importance of ideology in shaping dispute transformations: "The individual's sense of entitlement to enjoy certain experiences and be free from others is a function of the prevailing ideology, of which law is simply a component" (Felstiner, Abel, and Sarat 1980–81, p. 643). Although very basic, this conceptualization of ideology demonstrated an early sensitivity to the importance of politics in everyday disputing – that political debates can shape the demands that people place on others and on the state.

These early studies of legal mobilization emphasized that disputing was a social process, yet the survey-based research made it difficult to study the collective meanings that people gave their experiences or the specific social practices that constituted a dispute. The stages of the disputing framework were identified as interpretive phenomena where people, for example, might evaluate competing arguments for who was responsible or whether they were harmed at all, but surveys were ill-equipped to measure that evaluative process. Moreover, survey questions could not really capture the ways in which law influenced these interpretive processes. The CLP, for example, did not operationalize legal consciousness. Instead, it measured the respondent's previous experience with lawyers or familiarity with a legal worker and included those variables as specific resources, along with factors like income and education (Miller and Sarat 1980–81, p. 552). As a result, legal mobilization's conceptualization of law was limited to its instrumental role as a tool, similar to material resources or education, exogenous to the development of disputes.

The study of legal mobilization was a significant development in law and society research. These studies moved away from official law-making institutions, such as courts and legislatures, and demonstrated that law was present in the everyday lives of ordinary people. Limited by survey-based methods, legal mobilization studies could not probe the importance of law as a source of meaning, nor could it capture the complex relationships between law and other social structures as they manifested themselves in everyday life. Still, many insights generated in this line of research – such as the naming, blaming, claiming framework – remain useful for analyzing legal consciousness and the role of law in everyday life.

Legal Consciousness

Recent efforts to analyze the role of law in everyday life have moved away from the instrumentalist perspective inherent in the legal mobilization literature (Sarat and Kearns 1993; Sarat 1990; Merry 1990; Yngvesson 1993; Ewick and Silbey 1998; Nielsen 2000; Engel and Munger 2003). Adopting a constitutive approach, studies of legal consciousness have shown that people use law and legal concepts to interpret commonplace experiences, and that these interpretations themselves often give rise to conflict. Law, then, is an important source of symbolic and cultural influence in the social practices that give meaning to everyday events (Merry 1990; Ewick and Silbey 1998; Nielsen 2000; Engel and Munger 2003). Instead of survey methods, which relied on preconceived categories of respondents' experiences, researchers relied on ethnographic and narrative accounts of conflict. As Sally Engle Merry noted: "Consciousness is expressed in subtle and diverse ways, in the way people act and speak as well as in the content of what they say. It is embodied in the practical knowledge by which people do things" (Merry 1990, p. 5; Engel and Munger 2003).

The foundational studies in legal consciousness sought out the poor and working classes and analyzed how law structured their problems in their families, their neighborhoods, their workplaces, and their welfare offices. Researchers listened to people describe conflict in their daily lives and noted the ways that law shaped their understandings of their experiences. Yet most of these studies were situated in relatively formal legal institutions, like small claims courts (Merry 1990; Yngvesson 1993), welfare bureaucracies (White 1990, Sarat 1990), or lawyers' offices (Sarat and Felstiner 1995). By the time they reached these arenas, however, these people had already concluded that their problems had legal implications. More recent studies of legal consciousness have sought out individuals outside of formal legal arenas. These studies have asked individuals how they confront problems at work and school, in their families and neighborhoods, even on the streets (Ewick and Silbey 1998; Nielsen 2000; Levine and Mellema 2001; Engel and Munger 2003; Hoffman 2003; Hull 2003; Marshall 2003). This broader reach allows for a more complex picture of legal consciousness – one where law is just one of the many sources of cultural influence on people's lives.

Ewick and Silbey have offered the most theoretically elaborate treatment of legal consciousness in their book, *The Common Place of Law* (1998). In their framework, consciousness is more than a person's knowledge of or attitudes about the law. Nor is consciousness simply the by-product of the structural arrangements of social, political, cultural, and economic institutions. Rather, Ewick and Silbey conceive of legal consciousness as a cultural practice: "We develop a cultural analysis that integrates human action and structural constraint. We identify and specify the mediating processes through which social interactions and local processes aggregate and condense into institutions and powerful structures" (Ewick and Silbey 1998, p. 38).

This cultural analysis relies on frames and schemas – the rules and interpretative frameworks "that operate to define and pattern social life" (Ewick and Silbey 1998, p. 43; Sewell 1992):

> Through its organization, society provides us with specific opportunities for thought and action. Through language, society furnishes images of what those opportunities and resources are: how the world works, what is possible and what is not. These schemas ... include cultural codes, vocabularies of motive, logics, hierarchies of values and conventions, as well as the binary oppositions that make up a society's "fundamental tools of thought." (Ewick and Silbey 1998, pp. 39–40, quoting Sewell 1992)

Schemas depend for their power on individuals enacting those schemas. Ewick and Silbey argue: "At the same time that schemas and resources shape social relations, they must also be continually produced and worked on – invoked and deployed – by individual and group actors" (Ewick and Silbey 1998, p. 43). Thus, when people derive interpretations of their experiences from schemas and then act on those interpretations, they recreate the schemas.

While schemas impose constraints on the meanings available for particular experiences, they are by no means fixed, static or inflexible. Instead, they change through their repeated enactments by individuals and groups (Ewick and Silbey 1998; Sewell 1992). Because many schemas are available for similar events, individuals may have many different – and sometimes conflicting – interpretations of similar experiences. Moreover, schemas are "transposable" or generalizeable to many different situations: "They can be applied to a wide and not fully predictable range of cases outside the context in which they are initially learned" (Sewell 1992, p. 18). The possibility of social change, thus, emerges in this interaction between flexible schemas and the creative potential of human agency which generates alternative arrangements in the workplace, the family, and the community.

Law provides one source of these frames and schemas. In this view, law is not confined to the details of official rules and regulations – "the law on the books." Instead, Ewick and Silbey use the term "legality" to conceptualize the law. They describe legality as:

> ... the meanings, sources of authority and cultural practices that are commonly recognized as legal, regardless of who employs them or for what ends. In this rendering, people may invoke and enact legality in ways neither approved nor acknowledged by the law ... In sum, we conceive of legality as an emergent

structure of social life that manifests itself in diverse places, including but not limited to formal institutional settings. Legality operates, then, as both an interpretive framework and a set of resources with which and through which the social world (including that part known as the law) is constituted. (Ewick and Silbey 1998)

Legality can consist of broad legal concepts such as "property," "evidence," "fairness," and "entitlement" that look very different than their official formulations (Ewick and Silbey 1998, Mezey 2001, Polletta 2000). Thus, like other frames and schemas, law itself is re-created and re-shaped as people engage in social practices that reflect their interpretations of the law. Ewick and Silbey observe: "Every time a person interprets some event in terms of legal concepts or terminology – whether to applaud or criticize, whether to appropriate or resist – legality is produced. The production may include innovations as well as faithful replication. Either way, repeated invocation of the law sustains its capacity to comprise social relations" (Ewick and Silbey 1998, p. 45). Legal consciousness, then, is the individual's participation in this process (Ewick and Silbey 1998, p. 45).

Ewick and Silbey's conception of law is purposely broad to reflect the law's structural power. As an emergent structure, legality is malleable, polyvocal, not entirely dependent on the law on the books. In this framework, whether or not a person knows a specific legal rule is not important. The more important questions are when and to what purpose people invoke the law, whether or not they are "correct" in doing so. This flexibility is theoretically important in developing the possibility of people constructing law – just as they construct race and gender and class – through social practice. Through their invocations of the law – whether "right" or "wrong" – ordinary people are constructing the meaning of legal rules.

By situating legal consciousness in cultural analysis and in the relationship between structure and agency, this framework rejects a law-first perspective and insists that law must be understood as one of many possible schemas that might give meaning to an event (Ewick and Silbey 1998; Sarat and Kearns 1993; McCann and March 1995). Ewick and Silbey remark: "Law collaborates with other social structures ... to infuse meaning and constrain social action. Furthermore, because of this collaboration of structures, in many instances law may be present although subordinate. To recognize the presence of law in everyday life is not, therefore, to claim any necessarily overwhelming power for law" (Ewick and Silbey 1998, p. 22). Indeed, acknowledging the possibility of law's irrelevance – even where it should matter most – requires that we move out of the small claims courts and welfare offices where the original studies of legal consciousness were located. Instead, we should ask "how, where, and with what effect law is produced in and through commonplace social interactions within neighborhoods, workplaces, families, schools, community organizations, and the like" (Ewick and Silbey 1998, p. 20; Sarat and Kearns 1993; Nielsen 2000; Levine and Mellema 2001).

In their research, Ewick and Silbey identified three different types of legal consciousness. These categories were not mutually exclusive. Rather, they argued that people could exhibit all three types of legal consciousness in the course of recounting a single incident (Ewick and Silbey 1998, p. 50). The first form of legal consciousness they identified was "before the law" where people believed law to be an authoritative and predictable force outside of their everyday life (Ewick and Silbey 1998, p. 47). Another form of legal consciousness, "with the law," considered law a type of game or a set of tactics that people could use to advance or protect their interests (Ewick and Silbey 1998, p. 48). Finally, when people's legal consciousness was "against the law," they imagined themselves trapped by the law, powerless to resist its control over their lives (Ewick and Silbey 1998, p. 48).

Critics have challenged this framework from two seemingly contradictory positions – that there is both too much and too little law in existing theories and empirical studies of legal consciousness (Mezey 2001; Levine and Mellema 2001; McCann 1999). By analyzing everyday life, the legal consciousness approach promised to de-center the law. Examining social practices in neighborhoods, families, workplaces, and schools could illuminate how law interacts with other frames, social norms, beliefs, values, and emotions (Marshall and Barclay 2003; Sarat and Kearns 1993). But this analytical promise has gone largely unfulfilled as legal consciousness research continues to emphasize law over all other social forces. The narrative method used to study legal consciousness has been criticized, for example, for being insufficiently attentive to the structural bases of inequality, particularly race, class, and gender – social forces that are probably more powerful influences on everyday life (Seron and Munger 1996; McCann and March 1995, p. 220; Handler 1992). Moreover, only a few recent studies aim to systematically account for frames other than law that might help people make sense of their experiences (Engel and Munger 2003; Nielsen 2000; Levine and Mellema 2001; Hull 2003; Marshall 2003). Thus, even as it moves away from formal legal institutions, the existing legal consciousness framework nevertheless "prioritize[s] law above other forces and institutions" by self-consciously looking for legality, even in situations where law is virtually irrelevant to people's problems (Levine and Mellema 2001; Mezey 2001).

On the other hand, some argue that the conceptualization of law enshrined in the legal consciousness approach is so vague that it is barely recognizable as "legal" (Mezey 2001; McCann 1999). For example, Mezey argues:

Law in *The Common Place of Law* is paradoxical: it is everywhere and nowhere. Ewick and Silbey interviewed hundreds of people for their book, many of whom faced not-so-legal institutions and actors with concepts no more legal than the notions of contestation or authority. One wonders, then, what is legal about the consciousness they describe. (Mezey 2001, p. 153)

In fact, particular areas of law or legal institutions may shape legal consciousness in meaningful ways (McCann 1999; Nielsen 2000; Marshall and Barclay 2003). For example, Laura Beth Nielsen (2000) situated her study of legal consciousness in a particular problem – offensive public speech. She identified the ways that specific legal domains, such as the First Amendment and criminal law, shaped people's encounters with those experiences. Thus, legal consciousness research should begin to develop "mid-range theories" that "investigate the relationship between legal and cultural production in the context of particularized legal questions" (Mezey 2001, p. 154).

Contextualizing Consciousness: Politics, Institutions, and Organizations

In this section, I develop a mid-range theoretical framework for analyzing law and inequality from the bottom up – in the context of everyday conflicts that emerge out of broad social, political, and cultural debates. This theoretical framework contextualizes legal consciousness in a particular legal arena – in this case, sexual harassment and employment discrimination law – and at the same time de-centers legal rules by emphasizing the political and cultural debates surrounding sexual harassment. Drawing on an empirical study of women's experiences with unwanted sexual attention at work, I argue that in their efforts to make sense of their experience and in their interactions with employment policies, women re-create the meaning of sexual harassment laws that are designed to protect them.

Situating Legal Consciousness in Social Problems

Recent research has situated the analysis of legal consciousness in concrete types of social problems, asking individuals how they deal with these problems when they arise in everyday life. For example, studies have recently analyzed the legal consciousness of people with disabilities (Engel and Munger 2003); people who confront street harassment (Nielsen 2000); women who engaged in drug crimes (Levine and Mellema 2001); and gay and lesbian couples seeking alternatives to marriage (Hull 2003). Placing legal consciousness research in the context of everyday encounters with social problems provides a unique opportunity to observe social change in action. Structural inequalities are not mere abstractions. Rather, they generate concrete living conditions – crumbling schools, low-paying jobs, disrespectful treatment in public spaces, more severe criminal penalties, neighborhoods contaminated by hazardous substances, among others. When people question these conditions and challenge the sources of inequality, they may presage collective action (Ewick and Silbey 1998; McCann and March 1995), or they may reflect the success of social movement efforts to raise consciousness (Polletta and Jasper 2001). Moreover, these conflicts often implicate the law. The disputes can be transformed into legal disputes that are resolved in lawyers' offices or courtrooms. Sometimes, the disputes are articulated in terms of rights. Thus, studying these particular experiences provides a "bottom-up" perspective on the role of law in creating or impeding social change.

Situating these studies in these concrete social struggles can also develop the theoretical framework for legal consciousness. First, these studies have the potential to de-center the law because they are anchored in broader political and cultural debates that invoke all manner of cultural and symbolic schemas – those that defend existing power arrangements as well as those that challenge authority. Law is present in these struggles in many complementary and contradictory ways. Law may be one of the frames that protects the status quo, but law can also provide means of resistance (Merry 1995; McCann and March 1995; Engel and Munger 2003). By emphasizing the struggle over the law, the multivalent nature of legality becomes more apparent.

Focusing on particular social and political struggles also makes it possible to account for legal rules and the legal system. Struggles that emerge from everyday life implicate many familiar institutions, such as families, workplaces, and schools. These institutions are governed by legal rules, and the challenges to these institutions are often mounted in legal terrains (McCann and March 1995; Engel and Munger 2003). Legal rules operating in these environments hardly resemble the "law on the books." Rather institutions shape legality in meaningful ways that should be accounted for in any analysis of legal consciousness (Edelman, Erlanger and Lande 1993; Marshall 2003).

There are many prominent social, political and cultural issues that implicate the arrangements and practices of everyday life: environmental hazards disproportionately located in poor and minority communities (Faber 1998); disabled people denied educational and job opportunities (Engel and Munger 2003); African-Americans singled out for racial profiling by the police. Gays and lesbians confront a wide range of obstacles when they try to protect their families (Eskridge 2002; D'Emilio, Turner, and Vaid 2000). Without access to marriage, for example, gays and lesbians are denied such taken-for-granted privileges as inheritance and property rights, medical decision-making on behalf of an ailing partner, and parental rights with respect to children (Eskridge 2002; Robinson 2001). Moreover, for some gays and lesbians, being denied marriage means that they are marginalized and excluded from the privileges of citizenship (Robinson 2001).

These material and symbolic obstacles to gay and lesbian family life are the subject of widespread political debate, particularly in states that are considering changes to their family laws (D'Emilio, Turner, and Vaid 2000). Carried out in the courts, legislatures, the mass media, and in the battle for public opinion, this debate invokes a variety of schema – religion, morality, rights, families. Moreover, these schema do not emerge from any single side in this struggle. Supporters and opponents of gay and lesbian family rights often vie for the meaning of these varied symbolic resources. For example, in the political debate surrounding Vermont's recent passage of a statute authorizing civil unions, the Catholic Church opposed the legislation. On the other hand, leaders of the civil union movement called on more liberal clergy members to mobilize their parishioners in support of the statute (Barclay and Marshall 2004). Not all gays and lesbians are political activists, but in their everyday lives, as they create alternative rituals or enter into legal arrangements that re-create marriage, these political and legal debates shape their decision-making (Hull 2003).

Sexual harassment is another social problem that can be fruitfully studied by incorporating politics into legal consciousness. By most accounts, sexual harassment emerges from women's inequality in the workplace (MacKinnon 1979; Schultz 1998, 2001; Francke 1997). Men who feel threatened by women's increasing numbers in the workplace use sexual harassment to intimidate women and undermine their confidence. Women who are targeted by such behaviors often report diminished productivity as well as emotional and physical problems (Fitzgerald et al. 1997; Welsh 1999). Indeed, legal rules in the form of judicial opinions and EEOC regulations have prohibited sexual harassment since the mid-1970s. Yet the meaning of sexual harassment is a matter of extensive political debate (Saguy 2000a, 2000b). In the wake of well-publicized scandals, there has been considerable disagreement about what practices constitute sexual harassment and how women should respond. In response to legal liability, employers have adopted policies and grievances designed to redress problems as they occur (Grossman 2003; Bisom-Rapp 1999). These institutional developments and political debates shape the way that women evaluate their experiences, attach the label of sexual harassment to those experiences, and decide how to respond (Marshall 1998, 2003). The legal right to be free from sexual harassment may shape women's understanding of events at work, but analyzing the law's significance depends on this political and institutional context.

Putting Politics into Legal Consciousness

Studies of legal consciousness can seem de-politicized (Handler 1992; McCann and March 1995; Seron and Munger 1996). Like studies of everyday resistance (Scott 1985, 1990), legal consciousness emphasizes the personal stories of ordinary people. By focusing on these narratives, this research abstracts individuals from the broader social forces and structures that shape their opportunities and choices (Handler 1992; Seron and Munger 1996). Moreover, these analyses stress individual identities rather than the collective identities that emerge from participation in collective action and other confrontational challenges to existing power structures (McCann and March 1995; Handler 1992). Handler has been particularly critical about the dearth of politics in legal consciousness research:

> The ... stories are about individuals, in the most marginalized spaces, engaging in very small acts of defiance, and, for the most part, very little if anything happens. The authors, at best, are extremely reluctant to draw common connections, to talk about the possibilities of collective action in any concrete manner, or even to suggest middle-level reforms, let alone reforms at a more societal level. (Handler 1992, p. 724)

Ewick and Silbey, however, have insisted that everyday resistance and individual legal consciousness should be understood as political because the social and cultural practices that constitute such consciousness can reveal "the social organization of power:" "Through everyday practical engagements, individuals identify the cracks and vulnerabilities of organized power and institutions such as the law" (Ewick and Silbey 1998, p. 187). When engaged in resistance, individuals are making injustice claims. That is, they understand that they suffer from some disadvantage, that this disadvantage emerges from the exploitive behavior of more powerful forces, and that the resulting injustice must be redressed (Ewick and Silbey 1995, 1998).

To Ewick and Silbey, these injustice claims lay the groundwork for future collective action and are therefore not really removed from collective challenges to power. They observe:

> A consciousness of the structure of power, and an experience of its openings and lapses may be a necessary, if not sufficient, precursor of political mobilization. Minimally, research on everyday tactical resistance allows us to inquire whether such acts do prefigure or even provoke more collective contests of power. (Ewick and Silbey 1998, p. 188)

Thus, in this rendering, individual acts are politically significant because they are prior to political action.

But this relatively rigid demarcation between collective and individual acts of resistance is analytically questionable, especially in light of social movements whose chief purpose is to transform identity (Melucci 1989; Taylor 1996; Johnston, Larana, and Gusfield 1994).[4] These movements strive to convince individuals that they face the same troubles and struggles that other members of their group do and that they should challenge the sources of their oppression, wherever those sources may be found, especially in everyday life. This movement strategy requires that many individuals realign their personal identities to reflect group concerns (Taylor and Whittier 1992). Where personal identities become highly contested, individual choices about what clothes to wear, what jokes to tell at the office, and whether to carry a fetus to term can reflect broader political debates and concerns. Thus, individual resistance does more than simply prefigure collective action; it also enacts changing social values and practices (Johnston, Larana, and Gusfield 1994). These new enactments, in turn, are responsible for the changes in frames and schemas that structure meaning (Steinberg 1999).

In their recent book, *Rights of Inclusion* (2003), Engel and Munger elaborate the dynamic process in which rights can enlarge personal identities. In their analyses of disabled citizens' life stories, Engel and Munger observe that rights can transform self-perceptions, leading people "to reassess their own capabilities" and to imagine better lives for themselves (Engel and Munger 2003, pp. 94–5). Rights also contribute "to paradigmatic shifts in everyday thought, speech, and actions" (Engel and Munger 2003, pp. 94–5). In the course of everyday conversations among family, friends, and co-workers, rights become available to educate and to persuade others about the problems confronting oppressed people (Engel and Munger 2003, p. 95). Thus, "rights talk" is not simply whining but a form of consciousness-raising and political persuasion in everyday life.

The legal consciousness framework can embrace a more vigorous conceptualization of politics by explicitly incorporating an analysis of the processes that shape the development of collective identities. This analysis shows how politics as well as law can mold the meaning of everyday experience. "Collective identity is the shared definition of a group that derives from members' common interests, experiences, and solidarity" (Taylor and Whittier 1992, p. 105). To bring about their programs of social change, social movements must encourage individuals to link their experiences to the collective experiences of other members of the group. "Most collective actors do this by finding similarities in the biographies of a group of people and emphasizing them in such a way that the group's definition becomes a part of individual members' definitions of self" (Taylor 1996, p. 126). This process of generating and sustaining a collective identity requires interpretive frameworks that help group members "re-evaluate themselves, their subjective experiences, their opportunities, and their shared interests" (Taylor and Whittier 1992). These interpretive frameworks, in turn, bind individuals to the movement and encourage individuals to participate in movement activities. That participation can be either collaborative or confrontational, but it is guided by newly generated and fostered collective identities (Hunt, Benford, and Snow 1994).

Collective action frames are crucial for creating collective identities. Based on the same conceptual foundations as the frame for legality, collective action frames perform an interpretive function by simplifying and condensing the complexity of the world into categories of meaning (Snow and Benford 1992, p. 198). But the primary goal of collective action frames is to generate discontent and to create conflict. These frames challenge existing interpretive frameworks by providing oppositional meanings that can mobilize collective action (Gamson 1995). Using such frames, group members can develop "a shared understanding of some problematic condition or situation they define as in need of change, make attributions regarding who or what is to blame, articulate an alternative set of arrangements, and urge others to act in concert to affect change" (Benford and Snow 2000, p. 615).[5] By adopting these frames, individuals may begin to see harm in conditions that had previously seemed tolerable. Moreover, collective action frames can suggest solutions to these problematic conditions (Gamson 1995).

Also like legality, collective action frames emerge out of an interactive, constructionist process. Gamson argues: "Collective action frames are not merely aggregations of individual attitudes and perceptions but also the outcome of negotiated shared meaning" (Gamson 1992, p. 111). Using these frames, individuals can find their commonalities with members of oppressed groups, making it possible to come together for mutual support and resistance (Taylor 1996, p. 131). Social movement messages circulate in a competitive, contested ideological environment (Steinberg 1999; Ellingson 1995). First, movements rarely develop a single position on any given issue. Rather, movements are made up of many organizations and actors, all of whom may develop differing views of similar events. In addition, their oppositional messages vie for attention along with hegemonic frames justifying the status quo as well as counter-movements which might seek to roll back social reforms (Steinberg 1999; Ellingson 1995; Morris 1992). Thus, participants in these public debates mold their discursive strategies, anticipating and responding to their opponent's arguments even as they articulate their own frames for experience (Steinberg 1999; Ellingson 1995).

One important audience for this activity is the general public (McAdam 1996). Social movements often direct their frames to sympathetic bystanders and others outside the movement in an effort to persuade them to adopt oppositional interpretations of everyday experience and thus offer the movement general support for its goals (Snow et al. 1986). For example, the civil rights movement in the 1950s publicized the Southern segregationists' brutal repression of the African-American community in part to appeal to white liberals in the North, who might in turn persuade the federal government to intervene in the civil rights struggle (McAdam 1982, 1996). Thus, even the general public exerts an influence on the shape of social movement frames.

Law is an important component of many collective action frames. First, legal concepts like "rights" are powerful liberatory ideas and help people to identify injustice in previously acceptable conditions (Polletta 2000; Scheingold 1974; McCann 1994). Rights are an important part of the political and cultural "toolkit" in United States politics (McCann 1994; Swidler 1986). Social movements often deploy rights to educate the general public about the unfairness of some social problem and to justify their demands for relief. But rights can also help mobilize a movement as well. The "politics of rights" helps members of oppressed groups identify themselves as rights-bearers and encourages them to make claims and participate in actions that will help them vindicate those rights (Scheingold 1974; McCann 1994). Thus, law assists in the vital purpose of generating collective identity (Polletta 2000; McCann 1998). For example, McCann has shown that rights-based arguments about equal pay provided potent frames for mobilizing activists into the comparable worth movement (McCann 1994). In addition, high-profile litigation has provided political opportunities that social movements can exploit to advance their agendas (McCann 1998).

Of course, law also helps to construct hegemonic social and political arrangements and thus constitutes the very thing that oppressed groups are resisting. Studies of legal consciousness have demonstrated that people often perceive law as being a web in which they are trapped, unable to protect their daily lives from the overwhelming force of the legal system (Ewick and Silbey 1998; Sarat 1990). In this view, law resides with the powerful; it supports and fosters structural inequalities. Thus, law plays a complex and sometimes contradictory role in the competitive framing environment surrounding social movements and their struggles for social change.

Aside from its role in constituting political and social struggles, law can also be instrumental in resolving the everyday conflicts that stem from structural inequality. In their struggles against oppression and injustice, many social movements sought and won new legal rights to redress inequality. One of the central achievements of the civil rights movement, for example, was the passage of the Civil Rights Act of 1964. Title VII of that Act prohibited race discrimination in employment, but enforcement of that right was left largely to individuals who had to file complaints and lawsuits (Belton 1978; Engel and Munger 2003). Thus, a powerful civil rights collective action frame identifies employment discrimination as a serious injustice. Moreover, to think of oneself as having been discriminated against requires the adoption of a collective identity: a person must perceive that she suffered some negative experience because of her membership in a group rather than because of her individual characteristics or actions (Bumiller 1988). But the frame's proffered remedy requires individual rather than collective action. Thus, legal consciousness presents an interesting context in which to examine the sometimes tense relationship between individual and collective identities.

Researchers should examine the way that competing forces frame a social problem. Social movements and their ideological competitors mount fierce debates about the most intimate details of modern life, including whether or not personal experiences should be considered unjust. Movements, counter-movements, and established interests deploy religion, morality, equality, and justice, as well as law, to persuade people of the righteousness of their positions. These debates, these frames provide the interpretive packages that ordinary people use when trying to make sense of their lives. Thus, this contested ideological environment surrounding collective identity should be included in an analysis of the legal consciousness of injustice.

Sexual harassment is not just a legal category, but it is also a contested political and cultural concept. Feminists first identified and named sexual harassment as an obstacle to women's equality in the workplace (MacKinnon 1979; Farley 1978). Through its public education efforts, the women's movement has been largely responsible for raising consciousness about how sexual harassment undermines women's equality at work. But the feminist frame has not gone unchallenged. Instead, by appropriating and adapting feminist frames, employers and human resources professionals have rendered sexual harassment a problem for firms' efficiency and productivity rather than a violation of women's civil rights. In addition, an emerging critique of the feminist perspective – originating from both friends and foes of the women's movement – suggests that the harms of sexual harassment have been exaggerated and that excessive regulation may have the unintended consequence of censoring women's sexual expression. This broader political and cultural debate finds its way into women's everyday encounters with sex and work and shapes their reactions to it.

The Legal Environment: Rules and Institutions

The broad conceptualization of legality enshrined in legal consciousness studies captures the infinite malleability of legal meanings in the hands of ordinary people. Law blends with other frames and schemas, and indeed, this overlap – this transposability – is central to law's power as a structure (Ewick and Silbey 1998, p. 49). Still, the abstract rendering of legality fails to capture the distinctive nature of law's structural power (Mezey 2001, p. 153). For example, unlike other structural norms, legal rules are unusually specific, often carefully prescribing or prohibiting behaviors and practices. Enshrined in official texts, such as constitutions, statutes, and judicial opinions, legal rules are knowable but also interpretable. Moreover, they are widely accessible to a mass audience through mass media, employers, schools, not to mention through repeated interactions with legal actors, such as police and lawyers. The specificity and salience of legal rules may make them particularly potent schema.

Nielsen's study (2000) of responses to offensive speech demonstrated the significance of substantive legal rules in shaping legal consciousness. She showed that the First Amendment's guarantee of free expression was important to white men considering the possibility of a ban on hate speech. On the other hand, African-Americans asked about the same possible regulation were most concerned about the excesses of the criminal justice system in enforcing such a regulation. Nielsen suggests that these two groups emphasized different legal rules because of their different structural locations, but it is clear that these legal rules – and their accompanying institutions and political values – shaped people's legal consciousness about what was acceptable regulatory practice.

Examining legality in the context of specific legal rules also demonstrates the "polyvocal and broadly ranging" nature of law itself (McCann 1999). People invoke legal rules for a variety of purposes in many different contexts, especially when conflict arises and they are seeking a resolution. Invoking the law can occur both in and out of courtrooms. Inside courtrooms, advancing legal claims can lead to the growth and expansion of formal legal rules. Yet even outside of formal judicial proceedings, repeatedly relying on legal rules to advance one's interests – or repeatedly ignoring such rules – can shape the meaning of those rules (Zemans 1983).

This is particularly important in the context of legal reform movements to remedy inequality. Such movements often seek new legal remedies to redress the consequences of inequality and oppression. But to be useful, remedies must be known; they must be recognized as relevant to a particular problem; and they must be invoked (Zemans 1983). These responsibilities often fall to individuals or small groups who are already disadvantaged and may not have the resources necessary to develop or sustain this kind of rights consciousness. When people invoke particular legal rules – or when they decline to invoke them – their actions speak meaningfully to the power of law to govern their experiences. Invoking the law in novel situations can expand its reach; forgoing a legal right narrows the power of the law (Engel and Munger 2003; Bumiller 1988). In this way, the social practices of ordinary individuals can reshape the legal rules themselves. In fact, it is in this process of knowledge, meaning-making and mobilization that the distinction between legal consciousness and legal mobilization begins to collapse (Sarat and Kearns 1993; Marshall and Barclay 2003).

A study of the legal consciousness of injustice should include an analysis of the legal environment surrounding the particular social problem. Legal rules can create rights that create the tools that individuals deploy in resolving conflict. Also, people confronting their problems may try to mobilize existing law in creative ways, such as gay and lesbian couples who seek to invoke their parental rights to forge new forms of family. On the other hand, law can impose a set of obligations and burdens that emphasize and aggravate a person's subordination. In many states, courts and legislatures have acted to make it more difficult for gay and lesbian families to retain custody of their children. Moreover, legal rules are often transformed in their implementation, through the institutions and organizations that try to abide by and enforce them (Edelman, Erlanger, and Lande 1993). The structure of these legal rules can also be so familiar that they shape the meaning that people make of their experiences.

The legal rules surrounding sexual harassment emerged from the anti-discrimination model of the Civil Rights Act, characterizing unwanted sexual attention at work as a form of employment discrimination (MacKinnon 1979). These legal categories were largely created in the courts through judicial interpretations of Title VII in dozens of individual cases (Marshall 1998). The rules that emerged from these cases have defined prohibited forms of conduct and specified the available remedies for victims. And in the shadow of these laws, employers have adopted policies and grievance procedures that help them avoid liability (Edelman, Erlanger, and Lande 1993; Edelman, Uggen, and Erlanger 1999). Thus, within organizations, a complex legal environment consisting of both legal rules and the institutional practices enacts and enforces those rules. Those rules and policies are familiar to working women – the intended beneficiaries of sexual harassment laws – even though the employees are not necessarily familiar with all the details. Those rules, in turn, shape women's decisions about what to do when confronted by unwanted sexual attention at work (Marshall 2001, 2003).

Studying Social Practices: Bringing Institutions Back In

Finally, this framework for studying the legal consciousness of injustice emphasizes the analysis of social practices – the ways that ordinary people struggle with the problems generated by inequality in their everyday lives. In keeping with most work on legal consciousness, this framework does not inquire into abstract legal attitudes and beliefs. Rather, in addition to asking how people perceive their problems, this inquiry asks how they evaluate their options and what they do in response, thus demonstrating that legal consciousness is reflected not just in what people think but also in what they say and do (Engel and Munger 2003; Merry 1990). Further, by locating studies in particular organizations and institutions, such as workplaces, homes, and community organizations, this framework makes it possible to account for the prevailing routines and social norms that shape interactions of individuals living and working within their ambit (Engel and Munger 2003). In this analysis, we can see many of the social influences on the construction of legal consciousness.

In analyzing the legal consciousness of inequality, I propose disentangling legal consciousness by mapping its trajectory through the stages of a dispute, as outlined by Felstiner, Abel, and Sarat (1980–81) in their naming, blaming, claiming framework. Indeed, not all accounts of legal consciousness are conflictual. Some forms of legal consciousness, such as those working "with the law," imply that law can structure collaborative relationships where disputes do not exist. However, the legal consciousness of inequality presumes disagreements and conflict: injustices are perceived where they did not exist before; demands are made and rebuffed, giving rise to disputes.

In their outline of the stages of disputing, Felstiner, Abel, and Sarat noted that the first stage of the disputing process – the perception of harm – was the least examined but perhaps the most important. This stage is particularly crucial in the everyday manifestations of inequality, as previously tolerable experiences are reinterpreted as unjust (Piven and Cloward 1977). In these cases, the perception of harm is an evaluative process where people weigh competing arguments about whether some set of social conditions actually presents a problem. In this stage, people may deploy collective action frames or countervailing messages protecting the status quo or some combination of all these frames in determining whether or not they have been injured.

Naming and blaming are also evaluative processes where law and legal categories assume significance. Legal categories provide names for some types of injuries – crime, defamation, Superfund sites, employment discrimination, for example. Legal categories can also help deflect responsibility for injuries away from individuals and toward other more powerful social actors. Knowing that someone may be held legally responsible for an injury may make it easier to blame that party. Yet there is nothing automatic about transforming an injury into a violation of one's rights. Legal rules may be unfamiliar, and even if they are familiar, they may seem inadequate to describe the experience of oppression (Bumiller 1988).

Finally, researchers should examine the social practices surrounding "claiming" – making demands for redress. These demands may be articulated in legal terms. They may invoke rights guaranteed by law, or legal institutions designed to enforce such rights, or they may deliberately choose to ignore legal categories when making these demands. In any event, in analyzing the legal consciousness of injustice, claiming constitutes the acts of everyday resistance. Of course, this analysis should also account for the decision not to make any demands for relief – the decision to "lump it" – which may be the most frequent choice in the face of systematic inequality. Of course, this disputing process does not occur in a vacuum, nor do legal rules float from official policy-makers down to the ordinary citizens who are beneficiaries or the target of those rules. Instead, disputing is a profoundly social process influenced by social and cultural norms in addition to law (Engel and Munger 2003). For example, the institutional and organizational sites charged with enforcing the law layer the rules with their own interpretations that reflect their own interests. When Ewick and Silbey (1998) turned away from formal legal institutions in favor of the social locations of everyday life – neighborhoods, workplaces and schools – their research design asked individuals about their experiences in these places. But by examining individuals abstracted from their context, they ignored the fact that these social locations themselves are constituted by law (Suchman and Edelman 1996; Engel and Munger 2003).

Organizations and institutions often have their own agendas that lead them to interpret and to distort the law in ways that advance their own interests (Edelman, Erlanger, and Lande 1993). Moreover, those interpretations and distortions are a source of schemas for the people who interact with them and within the social spaces that they create. In the course of these interactions, legal rules are re-negotiated and re-formulated (Marshall 2003; Edelman, Erlanger, and Lande 1993). A more grounded approach to legal consciousness, then, would be to examine conflicts in their habitats – specific workplaces, for example. By focusing on particular problems as they are refracted through organizations, institutions, and other social locations, researchers can answer important questions about how law shapes social practices and how those social practices, in turn, shape the law.

In studying the social practices, researchers interested in the legal consciousness of injustice should trace the trajectory of disputes. Rather than making assumptions about harm, the researcher can treat the perception of injury as a matter of empirical inquiry. In these studies, ordinary people can describe their everyday encounters with inequality and describe whether or not they felt harmed by the experience, who was responsible for that injury, and whether they saw any legal implications. Their responses to these events

– their invocation of law or some other social harm or their decision to "lump it" – can have dramatic consequences for the power of law to shape social relations and create social change.

It is well-documented that while women have rights embodied in employment policies and procedures protecting them from sexual harassment in the workplace, they still rarely complain about their experiences with unwanted sexual attention at work (Fitzgerald, Swan, and Fischer 1995; Gruber and Smith 1995; Welsh 1999). But these policies and procedures are administered by employers who are generally more concerned with protecting themselves from liability than protecting employee rights. This bias in the procedures is well understood by employees who report being afraid of retaliation or who believe that their complaints would not be taken seriously (Welsh 1999). Moreover, women often perceive these procedures to be adversarial and geared toward protecting the powerful in an organization (Marshall 2001). These obstacles, then, narrow the protections the law offers in a particular workplace. It is these practices, rather than the policies or the legal rules on the books, that give meaning to the law.

Data and Research Methods

To illustrate this framework for studying the legal consciousness of injustice, I conducted an empirical study of women's experiences with sex at work. This study is based on a multi-method approach, drawing on a variety of data and methodological strategies, which I describe in this section. At the heart of the study are women's own accounts of their experiences with sex at work. These narratives are crucial for understanding the subtle and complex way that law shapes the meaning they make out of those experiences. Their understandings of everyday events are the result of deliberation and evaluation in which they weigh many factors – law, experience, emotional well-being, and principle. Narratives provide crucial insight into that deliberative process and the importance of context (Engel and Munger 2003; Fleury-Steiner 2002; Ewick and Silbey 1998). While survey responses may not capture the subtleties of meaning-making, they can nevertheless confirm general patterns suggested by the narratives and provide greater confidence in the findings.

The study was conducted in a single workplace – a university in the Midwest (the "University") in 1997 and 1998. The subjects were all female members of the administrative staff. I confined the study to working women because while it is true that men confront sexual harassment at work (Williams 1997; Francke 1997; *Oncale v. Sundowner Offshore Services Inc.* 1998), sexual harassment continues to be a problem faced mostly by women (MSPB 1995; Welsh 1999). In addition, I focused on members of the administrative staff, rather than faculty or students, on the grounds that these employees were most like employees at other firms. Setting the research in a single workplace has the tremendous advantage of being able to control for the type of sexual harassment policies and procedures and the manner in which they operated.

In-Depth Interviews with Working Women

I conducted a set of interviews with 25 female employees at the University. All the women worked in administrative or staff positions. While I did interview several graduate students, their experiences with sexual harassment did not occur in the context of their studies but in more traditional employment settings. I solicited their participation through an e-mail to a listserv sponsored by an organization of female employees at the University.[6] In my e-mail message to the listserv, I asked women to contact me if they had experiences with "unwanted sexual attention in the workplace." I used this phrasing to leave open the question of whether the women had been sexually harassed, a topic of the interviews. Using this method, I identified a group of women who varied in income and occupational status. Five of the women were low-paid clerical workers who administered budgets and performed clerical tasks. The rest were middle-management employees performing a range of administrative tasks, including supervising employees and developing workplace policies. Of course, using a computer-based method of communication limits the number of type of employees I reached – only women who had access to computers, only women in pink-collar and white-collar occupations – but my sample does reflect variation across occupations. One of the women interviewed was Latina; the remainder were white.

The interviews each lasted about an hour, during which I followed a semi-structured battery of questions. The interview schedule is reproduced in Appendix A. I departed from the schedule when the subjects wanted to elaborate about a particular topic. The women chose pseudonyms to preserve their confidentiality; they are identified by these pseudonyms in this paper. During the interviews, I asked the women about their experiences with unwanted sexual attention at work. I also asked them about all the things they did in response, including formal and informal methods to resolve the problem (if they thought of it as a problem). At the end, I asked them whether they thought this behavior was sexual harassment.[7] I also asked them about their views of sexual harassment in general.

In the course of each interview, I found that every woman had stories about encounters with sex at work that reached far back into their careers. These past experiences figured in their understandings of more recent events. As Engel and Munger (2003) have recently noted, focusing on life stories rather than a narrow time period reveals the way that rights and identity shape each other over time (see also, Fleury-Steiner 2002). Thus, I have included, where relevant, women's accounts of past encounters with sex at work, being careful to distinguish between prior experiences and those at the University.

Although my method of sampling will not allow me to make any generalizations about the incidence of sexual harassment or about how a typical woman responds to such harassment based on these interviews, the interviews are nevertheless useful to detect relationships between women's legal consciousness and their experiences with sexually harassing behaviors. These relationships are not well-established in the empirical literature and thus may be fruitfully explored using qualitative methods.

Quantitative Data: Questionnaire on Sexual Harassment

To confirm the findings of the interviews, I conducted a survey of working women at a single employer, the University. I obtained a list of all female support staff from the University's Women's Center and drew a random sample of 1000 subjects from the list. I sent a questionnaire through the campus mail to each of the respondents along with a cover letter briefly describing the goals of the research. They were asked to return it in an enclosed, postage pre-paid envelope. About one month after sending the questionnaires, I sent a follow-up letter to those who had not replied, asking them to complete the questionnaire. The response rate for the questionnaire was 35 per cent. This is an acceptable response rate for mail-back questionnaires, particularly on a topic as sensitive as sexual harassment (Arvey and Cavanaugh 1995, 46).[8]

The sample reflects the diversity in the range of occupations in a large university – clerical workers, administrators, research technicians, librarians, law enforcement personnel, and housekeeping staff. Thus, the survey reached a wide array of employees with diverse educational and income levels. The survey sample was also racially diverse: 11.5 per cent of the respondents were African-American, 4.4 per cent were of Asian descent, and 4.1 per cent were Latina. Still, a sample derived from university employees may limit the generalizability of the results. Universities may be different from other kinds of employers, and their employees may be more highly educated than other employees.

The survey was designed to obtain data on women's experiences with unwanted sexual attention at work. It presented women with a list of behaviors and asked how often they had confronted such conduct in the past 24 months. A series of follow-up questions elicited information about the context surrounding the respondent's most memorable experience: whether the harasser was her supervisor, whether the respondent was the only target of the conduct, how the experience made the respondent feel. It then separately asked the respondents whether they considered such conduct sexual harassment. The respondents were asked how they responded to these experiences and what effect that response had on the situation. Finally, an open-ended question allowed the respondents to offer their comments about these experiences. The complete survey instrument is reproduced in Appendix B.

Frame Analysis of Sexual Harassment

The framing of sexual harassment is receiving increasing scholarly attention (Saguy 2000a, 2002; Quinn 2000; Bingham 1994). Most prominently, Abigail Saguy has shown that French and American "cultural entrepreneurs" developed the concept of sexual harassment from available cultural materials, leading the American concept to be grounded in equal opportunity ideology. In her analysis, she focused on both feminists and their critics, such as Phyllis Schlafly and Camille Paglia.

For the analysis of framing in this study, I too examine the framing of sexual harassment by feminists and the critical counter-movement that emerged in the backlash. However, I center my analysis on the construction of an injustice frame by feminists, and the counter-arguments challenging that frame. I also include management discourse about sexual harassment. Employers have responded to the prospect of liability for sexual harassment with an outpouring of ideas about what harassment is and how to stop it. These ideas should be included in any discussion of the framing of sexual harassment.

To develop the sample of feminist frames, I began with the list of organizations that signed onto amicus curiae briefs in the Supreme Court cases on sexual harassment. This was a diverse group of organizations, many of which were large organizations committed to legal and policy issues, such as the National Organization for Women (NOW), the NOW Legal Defense and Education Fund (NOW-LDEF), and the Feminist Majority Foundation. Some of the other organizations focused on working women's issues, such as 9 to 5 and the Coalition of Labor Union Women. Finally, there were many smaller, grassroots groups, like Women Employed and Chicago Women in Trades, that offered direct assistance to working women on issues like sexual harassment.

I consulted the website of each organization that was still in existence, if such a site was available. I also collected the organization's pamphlets and brochures on sexual harassment. I focused on materials that addressed working women and the public in general. In the course of reviewing these materials, I also found repeated references to Martha Langelan's book, *Back Off!*, which is a feminist self-help book advising women how to deal with sexual harassment. I included Langelan's book for the analysis of feminist frames as well.

I used a similar method to collect materials for the counter-movement challenging the regulation of sexual harassment. Again, I began with the organizations that filed amicus curiae briefs in the Supreme Court. Feminists for Free Expression (FFE) wrote a brief in support of Theresa Harris in her lawsuit against Forklift Systems Inc. Yet upon examining its website, I found that FFE disagreed with most of the other feminist organizations in their articulation of the harm of sexual harassment. I also found that one of their members, Joan Kennedy Taylor, wrote a book entitled *What To Do When You*

Don't Want to Call the Cops: A Non-Adversarial Approach to Sexual Harassment. Through this book, I located other organizations – such as Phyllis Schlafly's Eagle Forum[9] and the Independent Women's Forum – that were critical of the regulation of sexual harassment. I included books and materials from these other organizations as well.

Finally, to generate the sample of management frames, I consulted trade magazines and publications that cater to human resources professionals. Many studies have shown that this literature provides a rich source of data on managerial ideals and ideology (Edelman, Fuller, and Mara-Drita 2001; Edelman, Uggen, and Erlanger 1999; DiMaggio and Powell 1983). To generate the sample of articles, I followed Edelman and her colleagues (2001) by consulting *Business Information Sources* (Daniells 1993). Checking under the headings "Management," "Organizational Behavior," "Human Resources and Personnel," and "Training and Development," I generated a list of 15 English-language magazines and journals published in the US. This list did not include journals intended for an academic audience. Using ABI-Inform for the years from 1990 to 1999, I conducted a search using the key word "sexual harassment." This generated a sample of 354 articles which formed the basis of the analysis for the management frames.

I relied on an inductive approach to these data by identifying recurring patterns in the advice and argumentation offered in all three basic groupings of the debate. I also searched for patterns across the different groupings to elaborate on the areas where the different sides agreed and disagreed. I had three primary areas of concern that corresponded to the basic elements of an injustice frame: (1) how the harm of sexual harassment was conceptualized in the materials; (2) who was responsible for those harms; and (3) how those harms should be remedied.

Outline of Chapters

This study focuses on the law and politics of everyday experiences with sexual harassment. The book traces the legal and ideological environment surrounding sexual harassment from the public debates down to the women who confront unwanted sexual attention in their everyday working lives and have to make sense of the experience. These women use law, injustice frames, and organizational routines when evaluating their options and making decisions about how to respond. Their choices about whether to challenge their harassers and demand redress from their employers re-shape the legal rights that are designed to protect them.

Beginning with the legal environment, Chapter 2 provides a brief history and overview of the laws surrounding sexual harassment. Based on analysis of judicial opinions, regulations of the Equal Employment Opportunities Commission (EEOC), in-depth interviews with both plaintiffs and lawyers, and secondary accounts of the lawsuits, this chapter describes the way that these plaintiffs and their attorneys drew on civil rights ideology and legal precedent to identify sexual harassment as a form of employment discrimination, then outlines the current state of sexual harassment law and describes various debates about the limits of a legal claim situated in civil rights logic. The chapter also situates this legal regime in a particular organizational context by describing the University's anti-harassment policy and grievance procedures which closely conform, on paper, to formal legal requirements. But the legal environment in action is far from settled: as I show at the end of the chapter, the beneficiaries of these policies and procedures – ordinary employees – are skeptical of their value in providing adequate protection against sexual harassment.

Although sexual harassment is a firmly established legal category, it is also a highly politicized concept, and in Chapter 3, I describe the ideological environment surrounding sexual harassment. I show that three predominant frames circulate in the public debate about sexual harassment. One frame mostly associated with the women's movement emphasizes sex discrimination and women's inequality at work, and specifies the ways that sexual harassment interferes with women's careers. This frame encourages women to challenge this form of discrimination with complaints and lawsuits. Second, counter-movements describe the negative consequences associated with regulating sex at work at all and urge employees, particularly women, to stop whining about trivial sexual conduct. Third, the professional human resources discourse stresses the damage sexual harassment does to employer productivity and efficiency and touts grievance procedures as a remedy for all problems associated with sexual harassment.

The remainder of the book maps out the way this legal and political environment shapes women's interpretations of and responses to sex at work, beginning with whether they feel injured by such conduct. Not everyone is harmed by sexual interaction at work. In fact, people have widely different reactions to sexual behaviors in the workplace, ranging from feeling humiliated to feeling flattered to actually seeking out such interactions. Drawing on survey data and in-depth interviews, Chapter 4 analyzes the competing frames that employees use to decide whether sex at work constitutes a problem on the job. In describing their experiences, some specifically articulate the ways in which sexual harassment damages their working conditions, mirroring feminist frames about sex discrimination. Others confronting similar experiences find sexual conduct at work empowering and engage in such behaviors themselves to challenge organizational hierarchies. These differences result from a number of factors, most notably the targets' occupational status and the gender composition of the working environment. But the perception of harm is a crucial first step to identifying and confronting sexual harassment: if it poses no threat or disruption to a woman's working life, she is much less likely to frame the experience as sexual harassment.

Even when they are bothered by the conduct, targets do not automatically describe their experiences with unwanted sexual attention as "sexual harassment." Previous research has shown that they use that label only for the most seriously intrusive encounters. In Chapter 5, I analyze the reasoning process employees use in deciding whether to call an experience "sexual harassment." The employees in the study understood that label to have legal content in addition to its oppositional meaning, and women would not use it in circumstances they considered inappropriate. They relied on a rough form of legal reasoning that closely resembled the subjective and objective components of the legal test for a hostile working environment. Specifically, they considered a behavior sexual harassment when they felt harmed and when the behavior met some external standard of unacceptably intrusive behavior. Thus, everyday understandings of the legal definition for sexual harassment limited the types of conduct they were willing to assign that name.

Law provides the remedy for sexual harassment – lawsuits. Before filing a lawsuit, however, the legal rules require targets to use the employer's internal grievance procedures to resolve such problems before turning to the courts. Yet these grievance procedures, administered by managers and human resource professionals, protect an employer's interests as much as employee rights. In Chapter 6, I show that targets of harassment are skeptical of grievance procedures on these grounds and are therefore reluctant to use them to redress problems with sexual harassment. Even in the absence of effective dispute resolution mechanisms, targets develop their own oppositional strategies for dealing with sexual harassment. For example, they join with others to circulate information about harassers and to confront harassers when possible. Thus, even though legal institutions may provide remedies of questionable effectiveness, legal schemas nevertheless inspire resistance.

In the final chapter, I offer observations about the value of developing models of legal consciousness that further the contradictory goals of both de-centering and particularizing the law. Incorporating frames and social practices other than law reveals both the power and the limits of law in shaping individual and institutional behavior. Moreover, situating studies of legal consciousness in specific legal arenas vividly illustrates the theoretical claim that people re-create the law when they invoke – and decline to invoke – their rights. I also argue that situating studies of legal consciousness in the context of everyday encounters with injustice provides a unique and valuable perspective on the relationship between law and social change.

Notes

[1] Rosenberg analyzed Supreme Court decisions on civil rights, abortion and women's rights, the environment, reapportionment, and criminal law (Rosenberg 1991).
[2] See, for example, McCann (1992), Feeley (1992), Flemming, Bohte, and Wood (1997), Canon (1998), and Schultz and Gottlieb (1998).

3   Frances Zemans provides an explanation for the relationship between the type of issue and legal mobilization: "There are at least two issue-related factors that weigh heavily on the decision-making process involved in legal mobilization. The first is the extent to which the goal sought *requires* the use of the state legal apparatus. The second, related factor is the availability of specialized structures, legal and extralegal, to facilitate the pursuit of particular goals" (Zemans 1983, p. 699).

4   For example, Ewick and Silbey describe Theodosia Simpson who replaced the buttons on her uniform with union buttons during a campaign to unionize the factory where she worked (Ewick and Silbey 1998, p. 182). They argue that the alterations she made to her uniform were oppositional practices – both collective and individual challenges to existing power arrangements. But they insist on separately analyzing individual and collective resistance. They argue: "Although motivated by a collective vision, at the moment Theodosia Simpson took her stand, tearing off the buttons of her uniform did not constitute a collective action. At that point, her opposition was individual. It did not openly challenge or question the authority it defied" (Ewick and Silbey 1998, p. 182). Indeed, the absence of other workers' participation rendered Simpson's action an individual rather than collective action. But Simpson's act advanced union goals by publicizing the cause in a novel and creative way. Moreover, her act was completely meaningless outside of the broader struggle between labor and management in her workplace. Thus, in this context, the line between individual and collective identity seems blurred.

5   The punctuation and attribution functions of injustice frames are similar to the stages of disputing identified by Felstiner, Abel, and Sarat in the "naming, blaming, claiming" framework (Felstiner, Abel, and Sarat 1980–81). Thus, both disputing and social movement theories are concerned with the generation of grievances and the attribution of responsibility.

6   A listserv is a selected e-mail grouping, hosting discussions and making announcements of common interest to members. This particular group organized social, cultural and career programs for its members, arranging outings to museums and concerts and other social gatherings. In addition, the organization sponsored workshops to give women career advice and networking opportunities. Although not an advocacy group or a union, the organization arranged talks and lunchtime discussions on such topics as managing stress, the glass ceiling and violence in the workplace.

7   The women were primarily interviewed about their experiences with unwanted sexual attention at the University. However, in the course of the interviews, almost all the subjects revealed that they had had similar experiences at previous jobs, and we discussed those incidents as well.

8   In a summary of studies using mail-back questionnaires to assess the prevalence of sexual harassment, Arvey and Cavanaugh (1995) noted that such studies often have response rates falling below 50 per cent.

9   Saguy (2000a, 2000b) identifies Phyllis Schlafly as one of the "cultural entrepreneurs" on the issue of sexual harassment in her study of French and US law and activism.

2 The Legal Environment of Sexual Harassment: Law, Policies, and the Women Who Use Them

Legal innovation, particularly in the areas of civil rights and civil liberties, emerges from the clash of complex social forces. Notably, social movements are often responsible for initially advancing these novel claims that create new legal rights. However, social movements do not exercise complete control over the process or pace of legal innovation, particularly in the judicial arena. Litigation is inherently conflictual, consisting of a dispute between two or more opposing parties. First, the defendants being sued are advancing their own arguments resisting the new rights and legal claims. Of course, judges and juries bring their own perspectives to the conflict and can shape the outcome of the litigation. Out of this mix emerge judicial opinions that give form to the legal rights. Then, once the innovation takes hold and becomes well-established, non-activist lawyers representing paying clients can begin to use it, which may further expand or contract the scope of the right (Zemans 1983).

These efforts create a legal environment that has the potential to re-shape social relations, although probably never in the way anticipated or even hoped for when social movements begin their law reform efforts. As individuals become informed about their rights, they may mobilize them or they may choose to ignore them, both of which can affect the power of the right to constitute social relations. On the other hand, in the face of this new right, the entrenched interests that initially resisted its creation have to adapt. They develop strategies for avoiding liability, and those strategies further shape behavior. This competitive legal environment is filled with specific rules that must be accounted for in any analysis of how law shapes behavior; we need to know what the rules are before we assess the ways that they actually work.

The legal claim for sexual harassment follows this path of legal innovation. Original cases brought by feminist legal activists and civil rights attorneys grounded the claim in equal employment and educational opportunity protected by Title VII (rather than sexual violence, for example). Judicial opinions in the 1970s and 1980s provided definitions of prohibited conduct, beginning with *quid pro quo* harassment and gradually expanding to the hostile working environment. Moreover, the efforts of human resources professionals and employment lawyers and a series of Supreme Court opinions made sexual harassment policies and procedures virtually mandatory in the US workplace. As I will show in later chapters, these legal definitions, policies and procedures all shape the way that women evaluate and respond to unwanted sexual attention at work.

In this chapter, I map out the layered legal environment surrounding sexual harassment in a particular workplace – the University. After summarizing the origins of sexual harassment as a social problem and a legal claim, I outline the legal rules regulating sexual harassment, including the legal definitions of prohibited behavior and the rules governing employer liability. I show that these rules have generated an incentive for employers to adopt procedures to deal with sexual harassment. Second, I describe the sexual harassment policy that the University had in place at the time this study was conducted in 1998, showing that the policy represents a textbook example of formal compliance with legal requirements. Yet the law on the books – and the institutions responsible for enforcing those laws – rarely resemble the law in action. I examine this policy from the perspective of its intended beneficiaries – women working at the University, who were skeptical about the real purposes of the policy. I argue in the rest of the book that these legal standards are woven into women's experiences with and responses to sexual harassment.

The Legal History of a Social Problem

The emergence of sexual harassment as a social problem coincided with the development of the legal claim. Feminist lawyers were prominent among the original activists responsible for naming and publicizing the barriers that sexual harassment imposed on working women (MacKinnon 1979; Saguy 2000a; Cahill 2001; Elman 1996). Lawyers provided the movement with access to courts, whose favorable decisions eventually laid the groundwork for the bulk of US policy on sexual harassment (Saguy 2000a). Moreover, their involvement ensured the law and politics would be closely linked in the conceptualization of sexual harassment.

Political struggle around sexual harassment emerged from the feminist commitment to equality and the strategy of consciousness-raising. Through their involvement in the civil rights movement, female activists acquired "a language to name and describe oppression; a deep belief in freedom, equality, and community – soon to be translated into 'sisterhood'; a willingness to question and challenge any social institution that failed to meet human needs; and the ability to organize" (Evans 1980, p. 100; Allen 1970). The feminist movement developed unique strategies to realize this goal of equality. Rooted in women's experience, the practice of consciousness-raising consisted of small groups of women, coming together in their homes, their workplaces, their schools and discussing their lives. An early text on the process of consciousness-raising described the process:

> Through experiencing common discussion comes the understanding that many of the situations described are not personal at all, and are not based on individual inadequacies, but rather have a root in the social order. What we have found is that painful "personal" problems can be common to many of the women present. Thus, attention can turn to finding the real causes of these problems rather than merely emphasizing one's own inadequacies. (Allen 1970, p. 26)

As part of this endeavor, feminists studied many institutions, including family, religion, education, law, and the workplace, identifying the blatant and subtle practices that produced inequality (Allen 1970; Groch 2001).

One such group at Cornell University was at the center of the early movement against sexual harassment (MacKinnon 1979; Elman 1996; Farley 1978). Lin Farley was teaching a field seminar on Women and Work at Cornell. In keeping with feminist pedagogy, Farley used consciousness-raising in her class, whose students were diverse in both their racial and class backgrounds. As the group shared their work experiences, they detected a common theme: "Each one of us had already quit or been fired from a job at least once because we had been made too uncomfortable by the behavior of men" (Farley 1978, p. xi). They used the phrase "sexual harassment" to describe these behaviors. Farley later interviewed other working women and then wrote *Sexual Shakedown* (1978), one of the first accounts of women's experiences with sexual harassment.

Lin Farley's consciousness-raising group at Cornell provided the foundation for Working Women United (WWU), a small women's organization. WWU was a working group of activists studying the relationships between women and work in Cornell's Human Affairs Program. Sexual harassment became one of its priorities and its members developed a grassroots movement with a multi-pronged strategy to challenge harassment. First, WWU established a separate research branch – Working Women Institute (WWI) – that conducted some of the first surveys of working women documenting the pervasiveness of sexual harassment in the workplace. Second, WWU drew public attention to sexual harassment by sponsoring events like the first Speak-Out, where women told an audience about their experiences at work. Sympathetic reporters attending these events wrote widely syndicated articles that gave national attention to the problem (Elman 1996; Cahill 2001; Weeks et al. 1986). Finally, WWU engaged in advocacy efforts, offering advice and support to ordinary women who contacted them to tell them about their own encounters with sexual harassment.

In the late 1970s, larger, multi-issue women's organizations, such as NOW, the National Women's Political Caucus, and 9 to 5, also began to include sexual harassment in their agendas. They used their resources to reach a wider audience, both in the public and among policy-makers. Their involvement further linked sexual harassment to a broader set of problems women face at work. They developed and distributed materials that urged women to resist such treatment at work and that provided women with options for challenging these behaviors (Weeks et al. 1986). In addition, these organizations targeted large employers, trying to convince them that sexual harassment was a serious problem and that they should adopt sexual harassment policies (Saguy 2000b). According to Weeks and her colleagues, these large-scale groups provided "support through publication of pamphlets and position papers, testimony of their leaders in government hearings, and filing of amicus curiae briefs. Also through their basic ideological solidarity with the single-issue groups [like WWU], an image was presented to policy-makers of a broad constituency expecting action" (Weeks et al. 1986, p. 436).

Still, in spite of the research and publicity, legislative and administrative policy-makers were slow to take an interest in protecting women from sexual harassment. Because of limited political opportunities, women found the best access to policy-makers was through the courts (Saguy 2000a, 2000b).[1] But the legal strategies against sexual harassment were not the product of a planned campaign, like the NAACP's challenge to state-sponsored segregation. Rather, the legal claim emerged from dozens of individual lawsuits filed by individual women. Some of these plaintiffs were represented by feminist activists, who were part of a loose network of feminist attorneys, academics, and law students. These lawyers drew support and advice from each other, but did not engage in the kind of planning associated with test case sponsorship. Indeed, many of the attorneys were civil rights litigators and private practitioners who had little or no political commitment to dismantling sexism at work. But through the work of all these attorneys in developing the law in this area, it can fairly be said that the oppositional concept of sexual harassment is thoroughly enmeshed with the legal category.

Catharine MacKinnon's contribution to the development of sexual harassment law is by now well-known (MacKinnon 1979; Saguy 2000a, 2000b; Cahill 2001; Elman 1996). As a student at Yale Law School, MacKinnon wrote a paper that would later become the book *Sexual Harassment of Working Women*. In that paper, she argued that sexual harassment was a form of employment discrimination because it imposed undue burdens on women and created adverse working conditions that men did not have to endure (MacKinnon 1979; Saguy 2000a). She sent a copy of the paper to the law clerks for the appellate judges deciding a sexual harassment case in 1977, and some of her reasoning from the paper reached the final opinion (Saguy 2000a). In addition, MacKinnon was active in feminist legal circles. She attended Women and Law Conferences held in the 1970s and 1980s where she met many other prominent feminist attorneys and academics. At these conferences, activist legal professionals made contacts with each other, shared ideas, and formulated legal strategies for promoting women's rights. MacKinnon's paper was circulated through these networks (Marshall 2001).

These feminist legal networks generated attorneys of record in some of the original sexual harassment cases (Marshall 1998, 2001). For example, Nadine Taub was the director of the Women's Rights Litigation Clinic at Rutgers University School of Law when she handled the *Tomkins v. PSE&G* (1976) case, and Mary Dunlap was working for Equal Rights Advocates (ERA), a public interest law firm concerned with women's legal issues, when she took on *Miller v. Bank of America* (1976). Like MacKinnon, Dunlap and Taub were deeply committed to dismantling women's social and economic inequality using legal strategies. By participating in feminist networks, these attorneys received much-needed support for the creativity that allowed them to translate women's experience into a legal claim and to persist in the face of the initial negative judicial decisions. Taub described the experience: "I have to say that this is the example of how wonderful it was to work together with [other women] … We were women sitting around trying to figure out how to explain to somebody that this was wrong, and how to fit it into the legal requirements" (Marshall 2001).

The involvement of feminist litigators in these cases was basically accidental. The feminist activists did not go looking for cases with suitable facts. Instead, the plaintiffs often sought out private practitioners who, in turn, referred the plaintiffs to feminist lawyers. For example, Margaret Miller hired a lawyer who knew that Dunlap worked on litigation for women. Miller's first lawyer then referred Miller to Dunlap and ERA.

Some civil rights attorneys held on to the cases and thus played an important role in bringing these initial sexual harassment cases. Although these attorneys shared the feminist activists' conviction that women's inequality was a serious problem, they pursued a broader ideological agenda of assisting all subordinated groups, including racial and ethnic minorities. And having attended law school in the 1960s, they largely believed that law and legal strategies were good tools for fighting discrimination. Although they saw their work as being political, they nevertheless sought to support their private practices by collecting statutory-mandated attorneys' fees or contingency fees when they won their cases. Thus, their political goals were occasionally tempered by their view of whether they would be successful.

For example, Diane Williams found her attorney, Michael Hausfeld, through a list of cooperating attorneys maintained by a civil rights organization in Washington DC, the Lawyers' Committee for Civil Rights Under Law (LCCRUL). Other attorneys on that list were unwilling to take her case because the legal claim for sexual harassment did not yet exist. But Hausfeld and his law partners welcomed the challenge to take on the case and make new law. Hausfeld's familiarity with race discrimination cases made the legal analysis of Williams' complaint straightforward.

It was basically, at least in my mind, and that of my two partners who discussed this with me, it was a natural and logical outgrowth of the intention of Title VII to create a workplace that provided for equal employment opportunities for persons of whatever race, sex, or color. And you were not being given an equal employment opportunity if, because of your sex, you were being denied promotions and/or tenure because you refused to provide sexual favors or accede to sexual stereotypes.

For Hausfeld and other attorneys familiar with the basic structure of employment discrimination, sexual harassment may have been a stretch, but it represented a challenge for an ambitious, young lawyer (Marshall 1998, 2001).

Finally, one group of attorneys handling these initial cases were simply trying to earn a living. They had small private practices where they represented individuals on a variety of matters, such as employment disputes, police brutality complaints, and even divorces. Like many people embroiled in everyday disputes, the plaintiffs came to them seeking help after being fired, but the plaintiffs did not necessarily know what kind of legal problem they had or what kind of lawyer they should hire. Neither the clients nor their lawyers were pursuing political goals.

Even in the absence of ideological commitments, however, these attorneys absorbed civil rights and feminist frames circulating through the culture and the law. For example, Warwick (Bud) Furr III represented Paulette Barnes in the trial court proceeding of her sexual harassment case. Although Barnes lost at trial, it was Furr's idea to proceed using a sex discrimination theory. He got the case from an office mate who had gotten the case from LCCRUL but did not have the time to pursue it. Although Furr himself was not affiliated with LCCRUL, he occasionally got advice from its staff about how to pursue the case. Another attorney, Thomas Mauro, had only recently left law school when he represented Norma Rogers against Loew's L'Enfant Plaza in 1981.[2] Mauro was working on the case when he was browsing in a bookstore and came across MacKinnon's *Sexual Harassment of Working Women*. Mauro said of the book: "It was very helpful. You know, and it educated me to the problem. Which a lot of people, you know, didn't understand at the time. Clearly, it was something that most people didn't think was a problem" (Marshall 1998, 2001).

As sexual harassment lost its novelty as a legal claim, private practitioners brought more of the cases. Information about pleading and proving sexual harassment cases became widely available among lawyers specializing in employment and civil rights law. And because decisions about sexual harassment were being published, even general practitioners could file a sexual harassment complaint by doing basic legal research. Thus, much of the growth of sexual harassment law described in the following section has occurred outside of the scope of social movement activity.

The Legal Regulation of Sexual Harassment

American policy-making on the issue of sexual harassment has emerged mostly from the judiciary. Title VII of the Civil Rights Act of 1964 prohibits sex discrimination in the terms and conditions of employment but does not specifically mention sexual harassment. In fact, it was the federal judiciary that first recognized sexual harassment as a form of discrimination in the mid-1970s. Since then, the Equal Employment Opportunity Commission (EEOC) has adopted regulations on sexual harassment, and Congress has amended Title VII to broaden the available remedies. But these contributions have been slight compared to the overwhelming influence of the courts in defining sexual harassment. In this section, I briefly describe the legal standards for defining and evaluating sexually harassing behavior and the procedures employers must adopt to avoid liability.

Quid Pro Quo Sexual Harassment

In 1972, Paulette Barnes began working as an administrative assistant in the equal opportunity division of the Environmental Protection Agency (EPA). Soon after she took the job, the supervisor who hired her made sexual overtures and promised her job benefits if she complied with his sexual demands. After she repeatedly refused his advances and offers, he belittled her, took away job responsibilities, and finally abolished her job. When she went to file a complaint against this supervisor, EPA officials told her to file a race discrimination complaint, even though both she and her supervisor were black. After a lengthy hearing process, an administrative law judge rejected her race discrimination claim.[3] When she appealed that ruling to the district court on new grounds of sex discrimination, the judge rejected her request for a new trial, stating:

> The substance of plaintiff's complaint is that she was discriminated against, not because she was a woman, but because she refused to engage in a sexual affair with her supervisor. This is a controversy underpinned by the subtleties of an inharmonious personal relationship. Regardless of how inexcusable the conduct of plaintiff's supervisor might have been, it does not evidence an arbitrary barrier to continued employment based on plaintiff's sex. (*Barnes v. Train* 1974)

Barnes' case was the first time, but certainly not the last, that a federal district court would reject a woman's claim of sexual harassment against her supervisor. In *Corne v. Bausch & Lomb Inc.* (1975) decided one year later, Jane Corne and Geneva DeVane reported that their supervisor had given preferential treatment to women who submitted to his sexual advances. His behavior became so intolerable that they were forced to quit. The trial court also rejected their claim for sex discrimination, observing that their supervisor's behavior was no more than a "personal proclivity" and did not advance a company policy. Employers could only be liable for their discriminatory *official* policies. The court also fretted about the potential flood of litigation that might be caused by allowing this type of claim:

> An outgrowth of holding such activity to be actionable under Title VII would be a potential federal lawsuit every time any employee made amorous or sexually oriented advances toward another. The only sure way an employer could avoid such charges would be to have employees who were asexual. (*Corne v. Bausch & Lomb* 1975)

Two other trial courts soon dismissed women's claims for sexual harassment in decisions that would later be taken to appeal. In *Miller v. Bank of America* (1976), Margaret Miller's supervisor wondered what it would be like to have sex with a "black chick," and fired her when she refused his advances. The court emphasized the company's policy of discouraging sexual relations between employees, but also relied on biological explanations for the behavior at stake: "The attraction of males to females and females to males is a natural sex phenomenon, and it is probable that this attraction plays at least a subtle part in most personnel decisions." The court concluded that it would be best to protect this "subtle" process from judicial consideration. Finally, in *Tomkins v. PSE&G* (1976),[4] the court rejected the plaintiff's claim for sexual harassment, again citing the inevitability of sexual attraction among men and women at work:

> If the plaintiff's view were to prevail, no superior could, prudently, attempt to open a social dialogue with any subordinate of either sex. An invitation to dinner could become an invitation to a federal law suit if a once harmonious relationship turned sour at some later time. And if an inebriated approach by a supervisor to a subordinate at the office Christmas party could form the basis of a federal lawsuit for sex discrimination if a promotion or a raise is later denied to the subordinate, we would need 4,000 federal trial judges instead of some 400. (*Tomkins v. PSE&G* 1976)[5]

These first judicial opinions framed sexual harassment as a personal problem between men and women, emerging from biological urges, rather than as a systematic social problem between employers and employees based on unequal economic power. The judges regarded the supervisors' conduct as reflecting personal idiosyncrasies, certainly crude but not discriminatory because no official policies were at stake. Attributing sex at work to the "natural" attraction of the opposite sexes, these judges were unwilling to commit judicial resources to resolving "personal" problems between supervisors and employees (MacKinnon 1979, pp. 83–99).

Judicial resistance to sexual harassment claims finally ended in 1976 in the case of *Williams v. Saxbe*. As in the other cases, Williams' supervisor at the Department of Justice (DOJ) had repeatedly asked her out and had left her notes and cards professing his attraction to her. When she declined his advances, he began belittling her in front of colleagues and giving her negative performance evaluations. He finally fired her in 1972. As a federal employee, she filed an internal complaint in the DOJ, which was rejected by an administrative law judge. In reinstating her claims, a federal district court held that "the conduct of the plaintiff's supervisor created an artificial barrier to employment, which was placed before one gender and not the other" (*Williams v. Saxbe* 1976, p. 657). Instead of assuming that the supervisor's conduct was "an isolated personal incident," the district court gave Williams the opportunity to prove that the conduct was an impermissible condition of employment (*Williams v. Saxbe* 1976, pp. 660–661).

In 1977, three appellate courts, the Third, Fourth and DC Circuits, recognized a cause of action for sexual harassment as sex discrimination. In all these cases, *Garber v. Saxon Business Products* (1977), *Barnes v. Train* (1977), and *Tomkins v. PSE&G* (1977), federal circuit courts of appeal reversed the decisions of the district courts below and held that employees who had been fired for refusing their supervisors' advances could sue their employers for employment discrimination under Title VII. The judges in these cases reasoned that such sexual demands were a condition of employment imposed on women but not on men and therefore constituted sex discrimination. The appellate courts were careful, however, to limit their holdings to *quid pro quo* sexual harassment – those situations where the supervisor explicitly made a promotion, salary or the job itself contingent on sexual favors. They reserved judgment on whether employers had to provide a working environment free of sexual conduct or conversation when such conduct was not tied to compliance with sexual demands (*Tomkins v. PSE&G* 1977: 1046).[6]

After the Third, Fourth and DC Circuits recognized the cause of action for sexual harassment in 1977, courts in other parts of the country took notice. For example, in the next case to be decided, *Munford v. James T. Barnes & Co.* (1977), the trial court relied on the DC Circuit's reasoning in *Barnes* to recognize Munford's claim of employment discrimination, even though the court sat in Detroit and was not bound by the *Barnes* decision. Similarly, the trial court in *Heelan v. Johns-Manville* (1978) surveyed the growing body of sexual harassment law before recognizing Heelan's claim for employment discrimination.[7] Thus, by 1978, the cause of action for *quid pro quo* harassment seemed well-established in most federal trial and appellate courts.

The Hostile Working Environment

By the late 1970s, women were filing lawsuits with more expansive claims. In these new lawsuits, women described working environments rife with sexual jokes and banter and unwanted physical contact that in some extreme cases constituted sexual assault. Unlike women making claims for *quid pro quo* harassment, however, these women did not lose their jobs or suffer any tangible job-related detriment like loss of a raise or promotion. Nevertheless, they argued, the working environment imposed a substantial burden on their ability to perform their jobs. For example, in 1977, Roxanne Smith filed a complaint for sex discrimination against her employer. In one of the counts of the complaint, she told the court that she had been "subjected to sexual advances and remarks" but conceded that her rejection of these demands did not affect any specific working condition (*Smith v. Rust Engineering Company* 1978). The court dismissed this count of the complaint.[8]

Although courts were reluctant to recognize this form of sexual harassment, the EEOC had been following the legal issue closely. Catharine MacKinnon and other feminist legal activists consulted with the EEOC to help shape regulations advising employers about how to comply with the growing body of case law (Elman 1996). In November 1980, the EEOC issued regulations including conduct such as jokes, threats and demands in its definition of sexual harassment. According to the EEOC, sexual harassment should include "such conduct [that] has the purpose or effect of unreasonably interfering with an individual's work performance or creating an intimidating, hostile or offensive work environment" (29 C.F.R. §1604.11). However, while courts give great deference to the regulations issued by administrative agencies, regulations are merely advisory and do not have the force of law until adopted by a court (*Meritor Savings Bank v. Vinson* 1986).[9]

The first federal case acknowledging a sex discrimination claim for a hostile working environment was decided in 1981. In *Bundy v. Jackson* (1981), Sandra Bundy described sexual advances made daily by her supervisors and co-workers. For over three years, they constantly asked her out to lunch, invited her to go on vacations, made sexual jokes and even physically molested her by pinching her or caressing her. Once, when she complained about this conduct to a supervisor, he told her he would investigate but then justified his co-workers' actions by observing: "Any man in his right mind would want to rape you." Although the DC Circuit found that Bundy did not suffer any adverse job consequences as a result of her refusal of these offers, the court still held that the hostile working environment itself was sex discrimination. The court asked: "How can sexual harassment, which injects the most demeaning sexual stereotypes into the general work environment and which always represents an intentional assault on an individual's innermost privacy, not be illegal?" (*Bundy v. Jackson* 1981, 945). Shortly thereafter, the Fourth Circuit acknowledged a claim with similar facts but no physical acts of harassment, thus acknowledging that a hostile working environment could consist of verbal harassment alone (*Katz v. Dole* 1983).

It was not until 1986, when sexual harassment cases had been in the federal courts for almost 15 years, that the Supreme Court issued a decision that put to rest any question that sexual harassment – in *quid pro quo* or hostile working environment situations – constituted sex discrimination in employment. Mechelle Vinson's supervisor at Meritor Savings Bank had made sexual demands on her, including sexually assaulting her in the bank vault. Although her job was never explicitly threatened, Vinson complied with the supervisors's requests because she feared he would fire her. In *Meritor Savings Bank v. Vinson* (1986), the Court endorsed the EEOC's regulations defining a hostile working environment as a workplace where employees faced "unwelcome sexual advances, requests for favors, and other verbal or physical conduct of a sexual nature" (*Meritor Savings Bank v. Vinson* 1986, p. 65, quoting 29 C.F.R. §1604.11a). The Court continued: "For sexual harassment to be actionable, it must be sufficiently severe or pervasive 'to alter the conditions of [the victim's] employment and create an abusive working environment'" (*Meritor Savings Bank v. Vinson* 1986, p. 67, quoting *Henson v. Dundee Police Department* 1982). Thus, even as it recognized a cause of action for a hostile working environment, the Court placed restrictions on that claim. The plaintiff, it declared, must show that the conduct was unwelcome, which allows the trial to address issues such as the plaintiff's dress and manner. This inquiry can deflect attention away from the harasser's behavior (MacKinnon 1987; Pollack 1990).

In 1993, the Supreme Court further elaborated the definition of a hostile working environment. The Court held that to state a claim for sexual harassment, a plaintiff does not have to demonstrate that she experienced psychological distress (*Harris v. Forklift Systems, Inc.* 1993). On the other hand, to constitute a hostile working environment, the behaviors must also interfere with the employee's performance of her job duties. The Supreme Court in *Harris* observed: "If the victim does not subjectively perceive the environment to be abusive, the conduct has not actually altered the conditions of the victim's employment, and there is no Title VII violation. But Title VII comes into play before the harassing conduct leads to a nervous breakdown" (*Harris v. Forklift Systems, Inc.* 1993).

The legal definition of sexual harassment has gradually expanded to include more types of conduct. For example, a hostile working environment can now consist of same-sex harassment. Early in the legal history of sexual harassment, perplexed courts pondered how the legal framework would deal with the case of a bisexual supervisor who harassed an employee of the same gender. For example, the trial court in *Corne* observed: "It would be ludicrous to hold that the sort of activity involved here was contemplated by the Act because to do so would mean that if the conduct complained of was directed equally to males there would be no basis for suit" (*Corne* 1975, p. 163). In 1998, the Supreme Court resolved this question by holding that same-sex sexual harassment violated Title VII as long as the plaintiff could prove the statutory requirements: that the harassment was severe and pervasive and that it was discriminatory (*Oncale v. Sundowner Offshore Services, Inc.* 1998). The Court observed:

> In same-sex (as in all) harassment cases, the inquiry requires careful consideration of the social context in which particular behavior occurs and is experienced by its target ... Common sense, and appropriate sensitivity to

social context, will enable courts and juries to distinguish between simple teasing or roughhousing among members of the same sex, and conduct which a reasonable person in the plaintiff's position would find severely hostile or abusive. (*Oncale v. Sundowner Offshore Services, Inc.* 1998)

The flexibility of the category of sexual harassment is also apparent in the debate surrounding the appropriate legal standard for determining what constitutes an "unreasonable interference" with an employee's working conditions. This debate asks whether judges and juries should evaluate the working environment through the eyes of a reasonable person, a reasonable woman, a reasonable victim, or someone else (Bernstein 1997).[10] Most circuits follow the traditional "reasonable person" standard. The most famous – and most criticized – articulation of this standard came in *Rabidue v. Osceola Refining Company* (1986). Vivienne Rabidue was the only female manager in the company, and one of her co-workers routinely treated her with contempt, using vulgar language to address her. In addition, men posted in their offices pictures and calendars of naked women in demeaning positions. The trial and appellate courts denied that this conduct constituted sexual harassment. Citing the prevalence of near-naked women in magazines and television, the court observed that Rabidue could not have been offended by her co-workers' behavior. The court stated: "The sexually oriented poster displays had a *de minimis* effect on the plaintiff's work environment when considered in the context of a society that condones and publicly features and commercially exploits open displays of written and pictorial erotica at the newsstands, on prime-time television, at the cinema, and in other public places" (*Rabidue* 1986, p. 622).

However, several courts since *Rabidue* have adopted the different "reasonable woman" standard. In the leading case in this area, *Ellison v. Brady* (1991), a woman received notes from a co-worker, asking her out on dates and expressing his hope for a physical relationship with her. Ellison was "shocked" and "frightened" by his notes. In considering whether her harasser's conduct was sufficiently severe, the Ninth Circuit adopted the "reasonable woman" standard, which attempted to account for the different reactions of men and women to sexual attention.[11] The court argued that the reasonable person standard "would run the risk of reinforcing the prevailing level of discrimination" (*Ellison v. Brady* 1991, p. 878). In another case, a female welder working in a shipyard was confronted with pornographic pictures, sexual jokes, and threats every day. The trial court's opinion, documenting every picture, poster, and comment, went on for pages. Admitting that men might not be offended by this environment, the court found that "a reasonable woman would find that the working environment was abusive" (*Robinson v. Jacksonville Shipyards, Inc.* 1991).

Although the Supreme Court has not yet weighed in on the appropriate standard for evaluating a hostile working environment, it has made some suggestive comments in its most recent sexual harassment cases. For example, in *Harris*, the Court used the phrase "reasonable person" while also emphasizing that the plaintiff also had to show subjective harm. According to this ruling, then, the plaintiff has to prove both that she herself was bothered by the behavior and that most people would find the working conditions offensive. Most recently, in *Oncale*, the Court stated that the environment "should be judged from the perspective of a reasonable person in the plaintiff's position, considering all the circumstances" (*Oncale v. Sundowner Offshore Services* 1998, p. 81). Some have suggested that this formulation amounts to a reasonable victim standard, but the Court's cryptic treatment of this issue does little to clear up the confusion since being "in the plaintiff's position" could also include being a woman, thus indirectly importing the reasonable woman standard (Shoenfelt, Maue, and Nelson 2002). Thus, because the Supreme Court has not yet issued a clear statement on the test for reasonableness, the circuit courts of appeal remain divided about the appropriate standard to use in hostile environment cases (Shoenfelt, Maue, and Nelson 2002).

Employer's Liability and Sexual Harassment Policies

An employer's liability for the harassing acts of its supervisors and employees has been a recurring issue in the development of sexual harassment law. Employers have argued that they should not be held responsible for supervisory conduct that they neither authorized nor knew about, and sexual harassment is the paradigmatic example of such conduct.[12] Courts have responded to this argument by holding that employers must adopt grievance procedures that will both protect employees and employers by providing a mechanism for the identification and resolution of problems before they require litigation. In turn, this judicial endorsement of sexual harassment policies has made them proliferate in US work-places (Grossman 2003; Bisom-Rapp 1999; Edelman, Uggen, and Erlanger 1999).

In its first case on sexual harassment, *Meritor Savings Bank v. Vinson* (1986), the Supreme Court suggested that an appropriately designed policy could protect an employer from sexual harassment. The Court observed:

> If the employer has an expressed policy against sexual harassment and has implemented a procedure specifically designed to resolve sexual harassment claims, and if the victim does not take advantage of that procedure, the employer should be shielded from liability in the absence of actual knowledge of the sexually hostile environment (obtained, e.g., by the filing of a charge with the EEOC or a comparable state agency). In all other cases, the employer will be liable if it has actual knowledge of the harassment or if, considering all the facts of the case, the victim in question had no reasonably available avenue for making his or her complaint known to appropriate management officials. (*Meritor Savings Bank v. Vinson* 1986, p. 26)

Although Meritor had a grievance procedure, the Court found that it was unacceptable because it required employees to lodge complaints with their supervisors. The Court noted that such a procedure put employees being harassed by their supervisors in an untenable position and would therefore not protect the employer from being sued (*Meritor Savings Bank v. Vinson* 1986, 72–73).[13]

During its 1997–1998 term, the Supreme Court elaborated the rules governing an employer's liability for sexual harassment. In *Faragher v. Boca Raton* (1998), Faragher was a life guard where her supervisors subjected her to sexual comments and unwanted physical contact on a daily basis. Moreover, because they were working at a beach, they were far away from the city's offices and did not come in regular contact with human resources personnel. Although the city had a sexual harassment policy, neither the life guards nor their supervisors were aware of it. Noting that lower courts had been struggling since *Meritor* to come up with manageable standards governing employer's liability, the Supreme Court in *Faragher* and its companion case, *Burlington Industries v. Ellerth* (1998), articulated a new set of standards. First, the Court rejected the argument that employer liability revolved around the distinction between *quid pro quo* and hostile working environment sexual harassment. Instead, under the new rule, courts must ask whether an employee suffered a "direct, negative job consequence." The Court observed that this job consequence could be the result of either form of sexual harassment: the loss of a job benefit from refusing to comply with a sexual demand or a tangible job-related injury resulting from the hostile working environment.

Second, the harasser's authority in the workplace was an important element in the Court's clarified rule on liability. If the harasser was a supervisor, the employer could be held liable for the damage done to the employee, even if the employer did not know about the harassing behaviors. Employers resisted this rule, arguing that the harassing acts were outside the scope of a supervisor's employment duties and did nothing to further the firm's interests. Therefore, employers could not be held responsible for the supervisors' actions. But the Court rejected this position, reasoning:

> When a person with supervisory authority discriminates in the terms and conditions of subordinates' employment, his actions necessarily draw upon his superior position over the people who report to him, or those under them, whereas an employee generally cannot check a supervisor's abusive conduct the same way that she might deal with abuse from a co-worker. When a fellow employee harasses, the victim can walk away or tell the offender where to go, but it may be difficult to offer such responses to a supervisor, whose "power to supervise – [which may be] to hire and fire, and to set work schedules and pay rates – does not disappear ... when he chooses to harass through insults and offensive gestures rather than directly with threats of firing or promises of promotion." Recognition of employer liability when discriminatory misuse of supervisory authority alters the terms and conditions of a victim's employment

is underscored by the fact that the employer has a greater opportunity to guard against misconduct by supervisors than by common workers; employers have greater opportunity and incentive to screen them, train them, and monitor their performance. (*Faragher v. Boca Raton* 1998)

On the other hand, the Court held that when the harasser took no "tangible employment action," employers could not automatically be held liable. Accepting in part the employers' rationale that employees themselves could handle co-worker harassment that did not directly harm them, the Supreme Court endorsed a negligence standard for employer liability and created an affirmative defense for employers seeking to rebut sexual harassment claims:

> When no tangible employment action is taken, a defending employer may raise an affirmative defense to liability or damages, subject to proof by a preponderance of the evidence. The defense comprises two necessary elements: (a) that the employer exercised reasonable care to prevent and correct promptly any sexually harassing behavior, and (b) that the plaintiff employee unreasonably failed to take advantage of any preventive or corrective opportunities provided by the employer or to avoid harm otherwise. (*Faragher v. Boca Raton* 1998, p. 807; *Burlington Industries v. Ellerth* 1998, p. 765)

This new standard for liability thus creates new obligations for both employees complaining about sexual harassment and their employers.

Obviously, the new standard articulated in *Faragher* and *Ellerth* required employers to adopt new policies and procedures addressing sexual harassment in the working environment (Grossman 2003; Bisom-Rapp 1999; Edelman, Uggen, and Erlanger 1999). In fact, the decisions set off a feeding frenzy among human resources professionals and consultants who filled magazines and journals with articles outlining possible policies that would fulfill employers' obligations (Bisom-Rapp 1999; Grossman 2003; Edelman, Uggen, and Erlanger 1999). Although the Court was vague about the details of such policies, the professionals basically agreed on the bare minimum. First, the policy should define prohibited conduct, provide a list of specific examples, and be widely and regularly distributed to all employees (Grossman 2003). The procedures should provide multiple avenues for pursuing grievances; employers were advised to designate several managerial positions that could officially receive complaints about sexual harassment. In addition, the policies should not require targets to confront their harassers. Once a complaint has been lodged, managers must investigate by interviewing the parties involved and possible witnesses. Many commentators urge employers to be proactive and pursue these investigations even if the complainant is reluctant to file a formal grievance. Finally, employers were advised to respond promptly to complaints and to take corrective action to redress the problem.

The Supreme Court and human resources literature have suggested that an employer would have to do more than just adopt such policies to establish the affirmative defense that it had "exercised reasonable care" to prevent and redress sexual harassment. Both the courts and human resources experts urged employers to be proactive in monitoring harassment and in responding to complaints promptly and effectively. To demonstrate this proactive concern, some employers now implement training programs in an effort to educate employees about the limits of acceptable work behavior and to teach supervisors about how to handle complaints brought to their attention. In addition to the ameliorative effects on the workplace, such training programs are considered evidence that employers are taking the initiative in preventing sexual harassment, although courts have not yet held that training was (or is) mandatory (Grossman 2003).[14]

The courts have been notably generous in their interpretation of employers' obligations under the affirmative defense outlined in *Faragher* and *Ellerth*. A study published in 2001 found that in the overwhelming majority of sexual harassment cases following the decisions, employers satisfied this part of the affirmative defense when they showed that they had circulated a sexual harassment policy to their employees and that the policy allowed employees to bypass their harassers in lodging a complaint (Sherwyn, Heise, and Eigen 2001). In fact, commentators have noted that, under the defense, employers have an interest in designing policies that discourage complaints:

> When a victim complains, the employer, at least theoretically, cannot prevail on the affirmative defense because the second prong requires the plaintiff employee to have unreasonably failed to take advantage of corrective opportunities provided by the employer to avoid harm. Thus, employers may have an disincentive to undertake any employer measures that go beyond the minimum requirements if those additional measures actually *induce* victims to complain. (Grossman 2003, p. 14; see also Sherwyn, Heise, and Eigen 2001)

On the other hand, the new standard imposes an obligation on targets of harassment to complain using the employer's grievance procedure or lose their right to sue. Theoretically, employees have an opportunity to show that they had a good reason for not coming forward, but the study of lower court sexual harassment opinions also showed that no court has accepted any such reason. Every time a plaintiff failed to invoke a grievance procedure, the trial court dismissed the complaint (Sherwyn, Heise, and Eigen 2001).

In effect, the Supreme Court has placed the burden of exposing and eradicating sexual harassment squarely on the shoulders of the victims. By requiring women to come forward and lodge internal complaints, the Court ignored extensive empirical data that overwhelmingly established that women file complaints only as a last resort (Grossman 2003, pp. 51–52; Welsh 1999). Moreover, while there is some evidence suggesting that anti-harassment policies, complaint procedures, and training programs have some positive effects, these are not a cure-all for the problem of sexual harassment and may actually distract from finding real solutions (Grossman 2003).

The legal rules governing sexual harassment have shaped the US workplace in meaningful ways. Most obviously, employers have complied with their legal obligations and adopted grievance policies and procedures that define sexual harassment and provide targets with means for redressing their complaints. Yet by itself, law cannot dictate how these policies actually work. For example, the legal definitions of harassing behaviors remain ambiguous, depending on both objective standards of conduct and a target's subjective experience. Policies will not become relevant, therefore, until a target perceives an experience as sexual harassment. And although the policies theoretically play an important role in employees' ability to vindicate their rights, the procedures are administered by management employees who are chiefly concerned with protecting the employer's interests. In the section that follows, I examine the way that the University responded to the legal regime by describing its sexual harassment policies and procedures.

Legal Adaptation: The University's Anti-Harassment Policy and Procedures

In the aftermath of the passage of Title VII and subsequent judicial interpretations of that statute, employers adopted a wide range of personnel practices and grievance procedures that reflected symbolic commitments to fairness and due process (Dobbin et al. 1993; Sutton et al. 1994; Edelman 1990). These managerial innovations have been the product of human resources and management professionals who use the occasion of legal developments to market their services (Edelman, Abraham, and Erlanger 1992; Bisom-Rapp 1999). In the 1970s and 1980s, as the claim for sexual harassment became increasingly well-established, personnel administrators began writing articles urging employers to adopt such policies as a means of monitoring their workplaces for harassing behaviors and of preventing sexual harassment before it ripened into a lawsuit. In these articles, they suggested that having a policy in place would protect employers from liability in sexual harassment litigation, particularly if they could show that plaintiffs had not filed an internal complaint (Edelman, Uggen, and Erlanger 1999). This suggestion reflected a "rational myth" prevalent in organizations that policies and procedures provide evidence that employees receive fair treatment and due process when their rights are at stake (Edelman, Uggen, and Erlanger 1999). Although the claim that these policies would provide insulation from liability had no meaningful legal support until *Meritor*, many employers nevertheless adopted them.[15]

At the time this study was conducted, the University had a written sexual harassment policy ("Written Policy") that conformed to the basic legal rules governing the definition and redressing of sexual harassment. It applied to all members of the University community – students, faculty, administrators, and support staff. In the preamble to its policy, the University offered an expansive view of the harms of sexual harassment. It stated that the prohibition was part of its commitment "to the maintenance of an environment free of discrimination and all forms of coercion that impede the academic freedom or *diminish the dignity* of any member of the University committee" (emphasis added). In addition to this broad endorsement of worker dignity, the University's definition of prohibited conduct expanded on the legal definition of sexual harassment:

> Sexual advances, requests for sexual favors, and other verbal or physical conduct of a sexual nature constitute harassment when: (1) submission to such conduct is made or threatened to be made either explicitly or implicitly a term or condition of an individual's employment or education; (2) submission to or rejection of such conduct by an individual is used or threatened to be used as the basis for academic or employment decisions affecting that individual; or (3) such conduct has the purpose or effect of substantially interfering with an individual's academic or professional performance or creating an intimidating, hostile or offensive employment, educational or living environment.

The first two conditions are essentially *quid pro quo* sexual harassment where working conditions depend on submission to sexual demands. However, the third provision expands on the legal definition of a hostile working environment. According to the Supreme Court, a target of such harassment must "subjectively perceive the environment to be abusive" (*Harris v. Forklift Systems, Inc.* 1993). Yet Section 3 of the Written Policy's definition also prohibited conduct that had the *purpose* of interfering with other employees and their working environments. Thus, while the Written Policy tracked the legal definitions, it also gave managers the discretion to intervene with a harasser even in the absence of harm to employees when the harasser seemed to be trying to cause trouble.

The Written Policy also outlined a flexible process for resolving complaints. First, employees could bypass their supervisors and take their complaints to one of many specified University officials, including the Deans of the colleges, the Human Resources department, the Women's Center, and the Staff Advisory Committee (SAC).[16] In fact, supervisors were not even specified as an option, thus perhaps suggesting that the policy was directed mostly at preventing and punishing harassment by supervisors. The Written Policy also directed officials receiving complaints to "immediately seek to resolve the matter by informal discussions with the persons involved," but it explicitly recognized a complaining employee's right to pursue additional review if not satisfied with the informal resolution. The policy therefore anticipated that managers would handle problems before the more formal grievance procedure was ever invoked.

Along with the flexibility, however, the Written Policy also included provisions that imported due process protections into the proceedings by promising fairness to the parties, especially the accused harasser. For example, an official could initiate an investigation of the employee's charges but only after finding "probable cause" to believe that the policy had been violated. The Written Policy offered very little guidance on the breadth and depth of these investigations except to require the complainant to support the claims with "clear and persuasive evidence." Thus, managers and supervisors had wide discretion under the Written Policy to take complaints very seriously or very lightly as circumstances dictated. Moreover, the Written Policy promised that "the University also will take appropriate steps to ensure that a person against whom such a complaint is brought is treated fairly and has adequate opportunity to respond to such accusations." In addition, the investigations and other proceedings were confidential.

If a complaint was found to be "substantiated," the University could discipline and even discharge the harasser. On the other hand, the Written Policy also anticipated appeals by dissatisfied employees. It provided that if this process did not produce a satisfactory outcome, employees might also file "formal complaints" within the University's formal employment grievance procedure. The University also promised to "take appropriate steps to ensure that a person who in good faith brings forth a complaint of sexual harassment will not be subjected to retaliation."

The University made significant efforts to publicize its sexual harassment policies. All employees were handed a copy of the policy on their first day of work. The University also circulated a copy to all employees every two years and kept the policy posted on its website. In addition, the University offered workshops and training programs to supervisors, administrators, and faculty members who might be called upon to enforce the policy and conduct investigations. These training sessions consist of information about what constitutes sexual harassment and how to investigate complaints. Finally, the Women's Center at the University sponsored talks about sexual harassment by various speakers.

Like most internal dispute resolution mechanisms, the University's Written Policy promised protection to complaining employees and accused harassers while also preserving a supervisor's flexibility in investigating and resolving sexual harassment complaints. While on paper the policy conformed to the legal requirements, and therefore satisfied the University's legal obligations, the policy's mix of formal and informal processes and the expansive discretion enjoyed by management implementing it created considerable ambiguity in the meaning and operation of the grievance procedure. In Chapter 6, I provide an extensive analysis of employee practices in the shadow of the University's sexual harassment policy, but in the next section, I show that employees, the intended beneficiaries of these policies and procedures, were skeptical of the power of any policy to protect their rights.

Perceptions of the Policy

While many studies document the widespread adoption of sexual harassment policies and procedures in the wake of judicial rulings (Grossman 2003; Bisom-Rapp 1999; Edelman, Uggen, and Erlanger 1999), we know less about how employees receive and understand those policies. Female employees were familiar, for the most part, with the University's sexual harassment procedures. Almost all of the women interviewed remembered receiving a copy of the policy at some point during their employment. Some women knew the details of the procedures: because they were supervisors or members of employee advisory committees, they themselves handled complaints about sexual harassment and were therefore expected to understand the policy itself. While others may not have had this detailed familiarity with the Written Policy, most women were simply aware that it existed and knew that they could find the details if they had to. For example, Nora observed:

> I think I've probably heard about [the procedures for complaining about sexual harassment]. There are these flyers that come out now and then, which I nicely file in my file drawer. It hasn't come up – it comes under the category of things that I don't remember. I put them somewhere so that if I have to, I can go to the file and pull it out, and find out what it is.

Some women in the study reported being satisfied with the University's sexual harassment policy. One survey respondent, for example, stated: "[The University] has a very good policy for dealing with sexual harassment to my knowledge. The HR office sends info regularly (two or three times a year) to employees re. policy and what to do if sexual harassment occurs at work." This respondent reported experiences with sexual attention at work, but represented those experiences as consensual: "Pictures, jokes, emails of a crude nature are only passed through a closed circle of friends/co-workers. Everyone is a willing participant – we only send material to people who have sent us similar stuff. Overall it's a friendly atmosphere and there are no negative feelings associated with it." Another employee who worked with student athletes observed: "I think [the University] does a good job about informing its employees about the issue."

These views, however, reflected a minority opinion. Most women in the study were skeptical of the University's sexual harassment policies. Many women suggested that the University's efforts to prevent sexual harassment, specifically its training programs, were either unavailable or ineffectual.

Moreover, most women believed that when complaints arose, the University would take the side of the more important employee – usually the harasser.

While the University trained supervisors about what to do when they received a complaint about sexual harassment, ordinary employees did not received training about what sexual harassment was or what to do about it. As a result, even women familiar with the Written Policy felt unsure about their options when confronting harassing behaviors. One survey respondent was the frequent target of crude sexual remarks and discussions of her sex life. Although she knew there was a special procedure for handling sexual harassment complaints, she nevertheless felt she needed additional guidance:

> Women need workshops on what actions constitute harassment and the action we can take. The circumstances for me were the most horrible of my life. It was the lowest point I've ever had regarding self-esteem. We need education because throughout the whole process (verbal only) I was in self-denial that it was actually happening (a definite coping strategy) and the men aware of the situation intimidated me every time I brought it up.

Similarly, Erna believed that circulating a statement was not enough to communicate the University's anti-harassment policy to employees. She observed:

> I think sometimes there's too much to read, and people don't read it, and so maybe it's clear in a certain paragraph, and by that time you're so mixed up ... I mean, I have an office where I can close the door, and I can read it, or I can take it home. But a lot of people don't want to take it home because they find it embarrassing, or they think that they might get a comment, and then reading it out in the open people don't do. And I'm not sure – and I mean, I don't think that I've ever heard of any program here that they teach supervisors at upper levels and then filter it down to what is acceptable and not acceptable. I think they kind of just put this statement out and say, "Okay. That's what you should be doing and we're behind it," but then what do you do.

Even when such training was available, however, many women believed that it did not have its intended effect. One employee working with student athletes complained of "inappropriate comments and touching" by the students. She observed: "They have all been given sensitivity training during orientation, but it doesn't seem to have tempered the aggression shown by a handful of the worst apples."

Women were also generally skeptical of the way the University handled sexual harassment complaints when they arose. Women interviewed thought that highly-charged problems like sexual harassment were too complex for human resources to untangle. Describing the complaint procedures, Erna noted: "You could go to Human Resources. And that seems to have been a very negative thing because Human Resources doesn't ... has never come through with any *other* problems that people have had. So people don't do that." Observing several times during the interview "I don't trust Human Resources," Dallas reflected critically on advice she herself gave to a young woman sexually propositioned by the chair of a department: "I told her 'Why don't you go to SAC or to Human Resources?' But the thing was, okay, SAC is there, but it really isn't a strong arm. Human Resources – that's a joke." To Dallas, women complaining of sexual harassment had very few options for obtaining relief from their problems.

Several women echoed the concerns of legal commentators that the Written Policy and the grievance procedures were created to protect the employer's interests and not the employees. As a manager, Rose felt that the University's primary concern was avoiding lawsuits rather than protecting employees:

> But if you get involved with Employee Relations, invariably everything is colored and tinted by the question of risk management. Everything is colored and tinted by, "Where does this fall in terms of the University's liability, and will we ever come to suit on this?" And so all the information you're given as a manager, at least my experience has been, has been about "CYA." Cover your ass. And "make sure you put it in writing," and all the rest of it that goes along with that – and a much less clear emphasis on the practicality of dealing with the situation.

Siena said, quite simply, "I think the University would have taken the University's side and not the employee's side."

Women also believed that in the course of protecting the University's interests, Human Resources would inevitably side with the person who was most valuable to the University, and that person tended to be the harasser. Matilda observed:

> I think they normally don't stand up for the staff anyhow. If a faculty member wants something, they usually get it. So are you going to go to them with this problem? I don't think so. I don't think they're impartial. I don't at all. I think there's too much interest in 'Well, he makes a lot of money for the University, we have to appease him.' I see it every day.

Dallas stated it more bluntly: "Staff are peons. [The University] is not going to get much money out of us. He is generating money for the University so whatever he does [they] are going to overlook."

Like many employers, the University adopted a flexible policy designed to prevent sexual harassment before it occurred and to handle problems after they arose. But based on their experiences and the experiences of others, the female employees in this study questioned the value of those policies. In particular, they questioned the loyalties of the staff who implemented the grievance procedures, recognizing that they would almost inevitably choose the employer's interests over those of the employers.

Summary

In this chapter, I have outlined the legal environment surrounding sexual harassment in a particular workplace. This environment consists of specific legal rules, enshrined in judicial opinions and EEOC regulations. The legal environment also includes the employment policies and practices that have emerged to comply with those rules and regulations. Yet, as I will show in later chapters, sexually harassing behaviors have not disappeared at the University in spite of these efforts. As Joanna Grossman has observed (2003, p.70): "[A] near-perfect state of rule compliance can peaceably co-exist with an uncomfortably high level of harassment."

Thus, this summary of the legal environment also provides a first glimpse of the gap between the law on the books and the law in action in the area of sexual harassment. While the University's policy closely maps the legal obligations placed on the employer, this analysis shows that those policies may not work precisely in the way intended. As I will show, employee skepticism and doubt interferes with the implementation and the effectiveness of anti-harassment policies mostly because that skepticism discourages women from lodging complaints even in the face of severe and intrusive behaviors. Thus, the right to be protected from sexual harassment may be seriously eroded.

Establishing the legal environment is central to the analysis of the legal consciousness of injustice. New legal rights, like those protecting women from sexual harassment, represent efforts to dismantle unjust social conditions. Yet those rights must be invoked to remain salient and powerful enough to reshape social relations. The legal environment, therefore, provides the necessary context for assessing the way those legal rules work in practice. But these legal rules are not the only sources of meaning when ordinary people confront injustice in their daily lives. Indeed everyday resistance can also be grounded in the debates challenging inequality. The next chapter will de-center the law by examining the competing frames and schemas in the political debates surrounding sexual harassment.

Notes

[1] Some feminists testified before congressional committees, but those committees were conducting investigations of sexual harassment in various governmental agencies; they were not necessarily considering legislation against sexual harassment.

[2] In *Rogers v. Loews L'Enfant Plaza* (1981), the court held for the first time that sexual harassment could also constitute the tort of intentional infliction of emotional distress.

[3] Unlike employees working for private employers, federal employees did not begin the litigation process in the EEOC. Rather, they pursued complaint procedures within their respective administrative agencies.

[4] Adrienne Tomkins was a secretary for PSE&G when her boss took her out to lunch. During the meal, he told her that if she wanted to keep her job, she would have to have sex with

him. When she tried to leave, he physically restrained her and threatened to fire her. When she complained about the incident, she was transferred to a series of worse positions and was finally fired (*Tomkins v. PSE&G* 1976).

5   At around this time, another plaintiff lost her case in federal district court, but since only a *per curiam* appellate opinion is available, we know less about the district court's reasoning for dismissing her claim (*Garber v. Saxon Business Products, Inc.* 1977).

6   Also in 1977, a federal district court recognized for the first time that sexual harassment could constitute sex discrimination in education in *Alexander v. Yale University*. The court relied on the appellate opinion in *Barnes* to recognize a private cause of action under Title IX of the Civil Rights Act, prohibiting discrimination in education. The only plaintiff remaining in the lawsuit after the other plaintiffs were dismissed in pre-trial motions, Pamela Price, alleged that her professor had given her a bad grade in a class after she refused to sleep with him. Although her claim was allowed to go forward, she lost at trial. While still a law student at Yale, Catharine MacKinnon assisted the attorneys who represented Pamela Price and the other attorneys (Marshall 1998, 2001).

7   See also the cases of *Brown v. City of Guthrie* (1980) and *Henson v. Dundee Police Department* (1982), where the plaintiffs both filed their complaints with the EEOC in 1977.

8   Courts dismissed similar claims against employers in *Marino v. D.H. Holmes Co.* (1979) and *Neeley v. American Fidelity Assurance* (1978).

9   In *Meritor*, Justice Rehnquist, writing for the Court, observed of EEOC regulations: "As an administrative interpretation of the Act by the enforcing agency, these guidelines, while not controlling upon the courts by reason of their authority, do constitute a body of experience and informed judgement to which courts and litigants may properly resort for guidance. [Citations omitted.]" (*Meritor v. Vinson* 1986, 65).

10 Bernstein suggests, in the alternative, a standard of "respectful person" (Bernstein 1997).

11 Other cases that have adopted the "reasonable woman" standard are *Andrews v. City of Philadelphia* (1990); *Yates v. Avco Corp.* (1987); *Burns v. McGregor Elec. Indus.* (1993).

12 According to the legal principles of agency, employers are only legally responsible for the acts of employees when those acts benefit the employer. However, when a supervisor engages in sexual taunting or threats but never takes any action against the target, the employer derives no benefit from this conduct. In addition, harassers often try to conceal their behavior, leading employers to argue that they are often unaware of the harassment until they are sued and therefore have no opportunity to remedy the problem outside of court (*Faragher v. Boca Raton* 1998; *Burlington Industries v. Ellerth* 1998).

13 Justice Rehnquist, writing for the Court, observed: "Moreover, Meritor's grievance procedure apparently required an employee to complain first to her supervisor, in this case Taylor. Since Taylor was the alleged perpetrator, it is not altogether surprising that respondent failed to invoke the procedure and report her grievance to him. [Meritor's] contention that respondent's failure should insulate it from liability might be substantially stronger if its procedures were better calculated to encourage victims of harassment to come forward" (*Meritor Savings Bank v. Vinson* 1986, p. 73).

14 Grossman (2003, p. 13, n.50) points out that the EEOC strongly recommends training for all employees, particularly supervisory staff. In addition, Connecticut, Vermont, and Illinois require some employers to offer some employees training. But these requirements have not yet been enshrined in federal law, either by Congress or by the courts.

15 Edelman and her colleagues use the promulgation of sexual harassment policies as an example of the endogeneity of law. They argue that law is not exogenous to the organization; it does not operate as an external force that imposes constraints on or opens up opportunities for organizational actors. Rather, law may be produced first within organizations and institutions, and then can later be officially ratified by courts, legislatures and administrative bodies (Edelman, Uggen, and Erlanger 1999).

[16] The University's staff employees were not unionized, but each year, they elected fellow staff members to represent them in SAC. SAC did not engage in collective bargaining but did offer the University advice on employment policies. For example, at the time the study was conducted, there were several much-discussed incidents of violence – pushing and shoving – directed at staff members, and SAC was encouraging the University to adopt a policy of zero-tolerance for on-the-job violence. In addition to this policy role, SAC was also authorized to process employee complaints on a range of workplace issues, including sexual harassment.

3 Equality, Sex, and Productivity: The Competitive Framing Environment of Sexual Harassment

Apart from its legal significance, sexual harassment is an example of a powerful oppositional frame that has transformed the way that women think about their working lives. Women have been dealing with sexual demands from supervisors and colleagues since they entered the workforce (Farley 1978). Such attention was supposed to be flattering, and if it ever got to be too much to handle, women would simply quit and move on to the next job. Through efforts described in the previous chapter, the women's movement re-framed sexual behavior at work, characterizing it as an obstacle to women's enjoyment of equal opportunity in employment and education and naming it sexual harassment. Now, by virtue of highly-publicized lawsuits and scandals, that oppositional name is widely circulated and available to millions of working women.

But the feminist framing of sexual harassment does not dominate the ideological environment. Instead, there is a vigorous political debate surrounding the limits of and remedies for sexual harassment. For example, counter-movements endorsing traditional gender roles argue that the harms of sexual harassment have been exaggerated to further the radical feminist goal of censoring heterosexual sex (Patai 1998). Moreover, the oppositional concept of sexual harassment has been mainstreamed by human resources and personnel professionals who have turned sexual harassment training into a profitable industry. Sexual harassment has many different meanings in these different sides of the debate.

Indeed, law appears in all these strands of the public discussion of sexual harassment. For feminists, legal rights are a source of empowerment for women who might otherwise struggle for equality on their own. To conservative activists, on the other hand, sexual harassment regulation represents the state's unreasonable intrusion into personal, professional, and sexual relationships. Law also provides potentially costly sanctions to persuade employers to change their behavior. Yet as this chapter shows, while law runs through the debate, it does not necessarily dominate it. Instead, the politics of sexual harassment revolve around the ongoing struggle for women's equality in US society. These political struggles are crucial for analyzing the legal consciousness of injustice. These broader political debates, where law is one of many themes, are important sources of frames and schemas for ordinary people facing inequality in their daily lives.

Injustice Frames

Changing social, cultural, and political values create tension in the everyday decisions of ordinary people who face unwanted pregnancies, sexual advances from supervisors, and race-based traffic stops. In fact, social movements have devoted considerable resources to making these everyday events controversial (Taylor and Whittier 1992; Johnston, Larana, and Gusfield 1994). Movements rely on collective action frames to generate discontent and to mobilize activists (Snow and Benford 1992; Gamson 1995). According to Snow and Benford (1992), collective action frames are "action-oriented sets of beliefs and meanings that inspire and legitimate social movement activities and campaigns." Yet frames also circulate beyond the boundaries of the movement and become available to others who may be sympathetic, apathetic or even hostile to the movement and its goals (Snow and McAdam 2000; Marshall 2001). Thus, ordinary people may rely on these frames to re-interpret their everyday experiences as unjust, even if they are not necessarily motivated to become activists (Snow and McAdam 2000; Katzenstein 1998; Taylor 1996; Whittier 1995).

To generate discontent among target audiences, a movement's collective action frames must perform three functions. The first, diagnostic framing, punctuates the harmful nature of existing social conditions by taking experiences and events that had previously seemed acceptable and translating them into examples of grave injustice (Piven and Cloward 1977; Gamson 1995; Snow and Benford 1992). Diagnostic framing attributes responsibility for these injustices to particular social actors or institutions. Social movements often generate frames that assign blame to external forces and away from individuals; blaming the victim can be demobilizing and lead people to "lump" their problems (Gamson 1995; Snow and Benford 1992; Felstiner 1974). For example, Snow and Benford argue that in the civil rights frame: "blame is externalized in that unjust differences in life circumstances are attributed to encrusted, discriminatory structural arrangements rather than the victims' imperfections" (Snow and Benford 1992). To inspire action, such attributions should also include concrete social actors or institutions rather than abstract structural forces that are less susceptible to change (Gamson 1995).

In the second framing task, prognosis, collective action frames prescribe a course of action to ameliorate these unjust social conditions. Generally, this prescription consists of participation in social movement activities. In the social movement literature, participation in collective action is generally restricted to non-institutional political strategies, such as protests, sit-ins, boycotts and rioting. Recently, however, researchers in "new" social movement theory have begun to focus on cultural movements where "the personal is political." These movements do not emphasize changes in existing state and economic structures; "activists" are more likely to be ordinary people who identify with the movement and who pursue social and cultural change through "lifestyle" politics (Taylor and Whittier 1992; Buechler 1995).

The third and final framing function, motivational framing, "provides a 'call to arms' or rationale for engaging in ameliorative collective action, including the construction of appropriate vocabularies of motive" (Benford and Snow 2000, p. 617). As Gamson notes, "Most of us, even those with political activist identities, spend most of our time and energy on sustaining our daily lives" (Gamson 1995, p. 95). Thus, movements must inspire activists to believe that by participating in political action, they can bring about change (Gamson 1995; Benford 1993). Motivational frames provide a variety of messages, emphasizing the severity or the urgency of the problem, for example (Benford 1993).

Although they provide oppositional interpretations of experience, collective action frames are nevertheless based in existing cultural material (Johnston and Klandermans 1995; d'Anjou and Van Male 1998; Platt and Fraser 1998; Taylor 1999). Social movements draw on meanings, narratives, beliefs, values and ideologies that constitute the cultural "tool kit" (Swidler 1986). Thus, movements are "both consumers of existing cultural meanings and producers of new meanings" (Tarrow 1992, p. 189). Movements therefore face the difficult task of devising "interpretive packages that both challenge and correspond with the extant culture" (d'Anjou and Van Male 1998, p. 208).

Instead of concentrating exclusively on the articulation and circulation of collective action frames, social movement researchers have recently developed a more constructionist approach to frame analysis. This constructionist approach emphasizes the interactive, often conflictual ideological environment from which frames emerge. This perspective acknowledges that social movements have a variety of audiences and tailor their messages to the different interests of these audiences. Thus, social movements cannot exert complete control over their messages. Rather, they compete with other forces that can be extremely hostile to the movement's program for social change. These opposing forces disseminate their own frames that challenge the movement's claims of injustice and that defend existing social, political, economic, and cultural arrangements. In response, movements adapt their frames in what becomes a dialogic process of framing and re-framing (Steinberg 1998, 1999; Ellingson 1995). Writing about English cotton spinners who were trying to organize unions in the early 19th century, Marc Steinberg noted the way that the spinners and mill owners mutually constructed the discursive terrain of that particular struggle: "The spinners' case demonstrates the multivocal nature of discourse ... 'Property,' 'rights,' 'freedom,' 'slave,' and other key signifiers passed back and forth between the mouths of workers and employers, and in transformative processes of meaning" (Steinberg 1998, 1999).

Sympathetic bystanders may also help shape a movement's frames. Once a movement has emerged, groups must be able to mobilize broader public awareness and support by appealing to popular culture and social norms (McAdam 1996, p. 349). In reaching out to the general public, however, movements may dilute their message and lose the support of more committed activists (Kubal 1998). McAdam has shown that public support for the civil rights movement was instrumental in persuading the federal government to intervene on the side of protestors (McAdam 1996, p. 350). But beyond basic measures of public opinion, there has been little effort to investigate how social movement frames are received and interpreted by ordinary people.

The concept of sexual harassment is at once culturally significant and deeply contested both in women's everyday working lives and in public debates among policy-makers, employers, the women's movement and its ideological opponents (Saguy 2000a, 2000b). When sexual harassment was first recognized as a social problem in the 1970s, feminists had competing views about the nature of the problem. Some in the women's movement framed sexual harassment as a form of sexual violence against women. Others, however, emphasized the problems it presented to women in the workplace, a perspective that came to dominate both the public debate and policy-making (Saguy 2000a, 2000b; Weeks et al. 1986). More recently, feminists have questioned the wisdom of relying on liberatory strategies that invoke state power to regulate women's sexuality (Schultz 1998). Still, the feminist interpretation of unwanted sexual attention at work as a form of employment discrimination is a powerful and resonant injustice frame emphasizing the harms of sexual harassment and demanding justice.

But that injustice frame competes with other frames that emphasize management logic, freedom of sexual expression, and freedom of speech. The feminist challenge to patriarchal assumptions about male dominance at work and in sexual relationships provoked a response from social conservatives who insisted that sexual harassment was mostly harmless flirtation and that legal protection constituted a form of special rights for women who claimed to want only equality. Moreover, when sexual harassment was recognized as a legal claim, it threatened to disrupt the workplace, so employers had to adapt. Rather than deny sexual harassment was harmful, employers instead have claimed that the real harm is to economic efficiency and productivity.

In this chapter, I sketch the polyvocal framing of sexual harassment. In particular, I examine the feminist diagnosis of the problem as well as employer and counter-movement challenges to that diagnosis. I also examine the curious convergence on a prognosis for the problem of sexual harassment. Although they disagree on whether sexual harassment is harmful and what kind of harm it is, the different sides in this debate largely agree that the best solution is to file a complaint through the use of an employment grievance procedure.

The Harms of Asking: Feminist Injustice Frames

According to the feminist frame, sexual harassment consists of a set of sexualized behaviors ranging from sexually explicit jokes and gestures and the display of pornographic images to sexual assault or coercion. Often directed at women, sexual harassment imposes undue burdens on women's working lives. Like other injustice frames, the feminist frame denies that the practice occurs because of the personal idiosyncrasies of the harasser or the target. Rather, sexual harassment is a systematic practice that contributes to women's economic and sexual subordination. Interestingly, the remedy most often recommended in feminist literature takes the form of individual resistance: confronting the harasser, filing complaints, going to court. Collective action is almost never prescribed.

Defining Harm

The women's movement has expansively defined the set of practices that can constitute sexual harassment. Emphasizing dimensions of the legal definition, many feminist organizations stress that sexual harassment is unwelcome or unwanted sexual conduct (Feminist Majority Foundation 2003; Langelan 1993). These organizations also provide the outlines of prohibited behaviors falling into the general legal categories of *quid pro quo* and hostile environment harassment. For example, the Feminist Majority Foundation (FMF) identifies three types of sexually harassing conduct:

> Direct sexual advances or propositions, including higher-ranked employees asking for sexual favors.
>
> Intimidating or excluding women employees to jeopardize their employment status.
>
> Creating a hostile workplace for women by using sexist jokes, remarks, or pinning up sexually explicit or pornographic photos. (Feminist Majority Foundation 2003)

These broad definitions highlight sexualized behaviors that have adverse consequences on the conditions of women's employment.

To illustrate these broad categories of conduct, feminist materials on sexual harassment often provide specific examples of prohibited behaviors. In her book, *Back Off!*, Martha Langelan observes: "Sexual harassment is not some vague, abstract concept, impossible to define. It is a pattern of behavior with a long and ugly history" (Langelan 1993, p. 25). She provides a list of examples taken from women's experiences reported in self-defense classes: wolf whistles, leering, sexual innuendo, sexually explicit gestures, sexist jokes and cartoons, displaying pornography in the workplace, unwelcome touching and hugging, pressure for dates, discussion of one's partner's sexual inadequacies, indecent exposure, and sexual assault. Langelan states: "There is no excuse for any of this behavior. But for generations, this is what women have been expected to tolerate, in shame and silence, as the price for holding a job ..." (Langelan 1993, p. 26). In this rendering, these behaviors are reinterpreted. Instead of being conduct that – while unpleasant – women could reasonably anticipate at work, these behaviors are translated into offensive and inexcusable intrusions on a woman's working life.

In the feminist frame, these behaviors are not harmful simply because they offend women's sensibilities. Rather, this frame specifies the negative impact that sexual harassment has on women's equal opportunities at work. The FMF observes: "Sexual harassment affects women's mental and physical health as well as their social and economic status." Activists have identified a wide range of negative effects associated with sexual harassment that take a toll on women's working lives, including emotional problems, anger, stress, and anxiety. Women experiencing sexual harassment report that their job performance suffers, they take sick days, and may transfer or quit rather than continue to endure harassing behaviors (Welsh 1999; MacKinnon 1979). The FMF reports: "According to the National Council for Research on Women, women are 9 times more likely than men to quit their jobs, 5 times more likely to transfer, and 3 times more likely to lose their jobs because of harassment."[1]

In keeping with injustice frames, feminists reject the notion that women are personally responsible for the distress they feel when they confront unwanted sexual attention at work. In this framing, such distress is "not the product of an overactive, 'hysterical' imagination" (Langelan 1993, p. 41). Instead, feminists place the blame squarely on the harassers. Challenging the common argument that sexual harassment is nothing more than misunderstood flirtation, Langelan observes:

> [M]en who claim that harassment is simply a friendly sexual game are deluding themselves (at best) about the real meaning of their behavior ... [H]arassment is not courtship behavior of any kind. It is not clumsy courtship, or rude courtship, or joking courtship, or "misunderstood" courtship. It is not meant to appeal to women; it is behavior that serves another function entirely. Like rape, sexual harassment is designed to coerce women, not to attract them. (Langelan 1993, pp. 39–40).

Thus, the feminist frame characterizes sexual harassment as an abuse of power, reflecting male aggression against women (Feminist Majority Foundation 2003, NOW 2003, Langelan 1993). Langelan explains:

> Men are able to harass because they have three types of concrete power: (1) straightforward economic power over women on the job; (2) status or role-based social power over women, in the case of ministers, teachers, coaches, and other authority figures; and (3) gender-based social power on the part of almost all men. (Langelan 1993, p. 41)

This diffuse male power has therefore shaped the boundaries of acceptable conduct in the workplace and has justified predatory sexual practices. As Catharine MacKinnon noted: "[S]exual harassment at work undercuts woman's potential for social equality in two interpenetrated ways: by using her employment position to coerce her sexually, while using her sexual position to coerce her economically" (MacKinnon 1979, p. 7). Sexual harassment is therefore one of the systematic forces that contributes to women's economic and sexual subordination.

The feminist frame also emphasizes that sexual harassment is mostly a women's problem. By characterizing sexual harassment as a form of discrimination, feminists have stressed that these behaviors are most often directed at women and impose the most serious burdens on women's working lives. MacKinnon has argued: "Sexual harassment limits women in a way that men are not limited. It deprives them of opportunities that are available to male employees without sexual conditions. In so doing, it creates two employment standards: one for women that includes sexual requirements, one for men that does not" (MacKinnon 1979, 193; Francke 1997; Saguy 2000a). Comparable to the damage that race discrimination has done to African-Americans, sexual harassment constitutes a group-based injury that systematically puts women at a disadvantage in the workplace. This bridge to race discrimination and the civil rights master frame has provided a resonant cultural image that feminist activists have used in circulating their messages about sexual harassment.

As the concept of sexual harassment has become institutionalized in US law and employment practice, feminists have begun to re-visit and debate its meaning for women's lives. For example, some have argued that by emphasizing sexual practices and behaviors, the current understanding of sexual harassment is too narrow to protect women from the worst abuses they face in the workplace. The current concept excludes other forms of gender-based harassment that denigrate women's competence on the job. Vicki Schultz argues that gender hostility, as long as it is not sexualized, is both pervasive and legally permissible in the workplace, even though such behaviors effectively bar women from male-dominated occupations and relegate them to low-status employment (Schultz 1998). Others have argued that the discrimination frame assumes heterosexual harassment and that same-sex harassment fits into the frame only uncomfortably (Francke 1997; Saguy 2000a).

Another strand in the feminist debate challenges the use of state power to regulate women's sexual expression (Schultz 1998, 2001; Cornell 1995; Francke 1997). In this view, sexual behavior at work is not harmful in and of itself. Many people report that they met their spouses and partners while at work. To cordon off working environments and bar sexual behavior creates artificial obstacles to sexual expression (Schultz 1998; Cornell 1995). Moreover, sexual expression at work can be a source of empowerment for women. Vicki Schultz has argued:

> Even if all sexual interaction could be eradicated from the work world, this would not necessarily be desirable. Sexuality should not be conceptualized solely as a sphere of gender domination, but also as a potential arena of women's empowerment. If some men use sexual behavior as a weapon of gender struggle at work, one solution is for women to refuse to cede sexuality as a source of male domination to use it to turn the tables on oppressive men. History provides examples of women who successfully mobilized sexual conduct or expression as a way of undermining authoritarian male control in the workplace. (Schultz 1998, pp. 1794–95)

This feminist critique of current sexual harassment frames comes from skepticism about judges and legislators who are called on to regulate women's sexuality (Schultz 1998; Cornell 1995). Schultz notes: "Rather than emphasizing the use of harassment law to promote women's empowerment and equality as workers, [the current standard for sexual harassment] subtly appeals to judges to protect women's sexual virtue or sensibilities." In turn, this paternalism protects only women who conform to conservative sexual norms – that is, those who don't engage in sexual banter, wear tight-fitting clothes or otherwise "ask for it."

In challenging the existing discrimination frame for sexual harassment, feminist critics have suggested alternatives. For example, Vicki Schultz (1998) has proposed de-emphasizing sexuality and broadening the conceptualization of harmful practices to include many more forms of gender hostility, including sexist remarks and the purposeful sabotage of women's work. Others have suggested de-coupling sexual harassment from discrimination frames. These commentators encourage adopting alternative values, such as enforcing respect and workers' dignity in the workplace (Bernstein 1997), values that are relatively marginal to the current understanding of sexual harassment.

Prognosis

The feminist prognosis for sexual harassment urges individual women to confront their harasser and tell him to stop his behavior. According to 9 to 5 materials, women should "say no clearly." The FMF tells women: "If possible, and if the harassment is not too severe or violence, directly confronting the harasser may be useful. Also, although having protested is not necessary for a claim, it would strongly strengthen a claim" (Feminist Majority Foundation 2003). The FMF reprints a list of steps women should take from *Back Off!* Six of the nine steps provide advice about handling a direct confrontation with a harasser, including "Demand that the behavior stop," and "Name the behavior. Whatever he's done, say it and be specific." This list also includes advice about how a woman should carry herself during the confrontation:

"Make honest, direct statements. Speak the truth (no threats, no insults, no obscenities, no appeasing verbal fluff and padding). Be serious, straightforward, and blunt." It further urges women to adopt "strong, self-respecting body language: eye contact, head up, shoulders back, a strong, serious stance. Don't smile. Timid submissive body language will undermine your message." (Feminist Majority Foundation 2003; Langelan 1993)

This advice is clearly designed to empower women to take control over events and to make demands on others for better treatment.

When confrontation does not work or is not feasible, the feminist frame urges women to pursue complaints either through internal grievance procedures or through the legal system. In its materials, 9 to 5 suggests that women "explore company channels" or "consult with an attorney." The Feminist Majority Foundation describes employers' legal obligation to provide a workplace free from sexual harassment and outlines what a sexual harassment policy should look like. FMF also provides advice about finding an attorney and encourages women to choose one who has successfully handled sexual harassment cases or at least employment discrimination cases.

Feminist organizations also urge women to prepare for complaints by documenting every harassing incident. FMF tells women to "photograph or keep copies of any offensive material at the workplace; keep a journal with detailed information on instances of sexual harassment. Note the dates, conversation, frequency of offensive encounters, etc." Careful documentation creates evidence that can be used in a proceeding against the harasser, either in court or in a grievance procedure.

In support of individual resistance against sexual harassment, feminist frames propose local forms of collective action. Specifically, these frames direct women to seek out others and share their experiences. For example, 9 to 5 tells women to "get emotional support" from friends and co-workers. Apart from its therapeutic value, talking to others holds the harasser accountable for his actions. Exposing harassers to others creates the potential for shaming them. Langelan tells women to let "other women and men know what he did (finding allies and using the pressure of public condemnation against the harasser)." She adds: "Privacy protects harassers. Visibility undermines them" (Langelan 1993, p. 117). Talking to others also has an instrumental value. In the process, targets may find witnesses or other victims who might be willing to come forward and support a confrontation or a complaint (Brady, 2003; Feminist Majority Foundation 2003). Feminist frames endorse group complaints because they bolster the victims' credibility, convey the seriousness of the problem, and make it more difficult to retaliate against the complainants.

Langelan links these individual and collective strategies of confrontation and complaint to stories about individual resistance to oppression in the context of the civil rights movement. Comparing sexual harassment to poll taxes and Jim Crow laws, Langelan suggests that sexual harassment stems from unjust cultural norms supporting male sexual domination, norms that amount to unwritten laws (Langelan 1993, p. 86). She observes that "because sexual harassment is a pervasive social practice, it is a political as well as a personal problem" and states:

> No right exists in the abstract. If current social conditions prevent significant numbers of people from freely exercising a right, that right has effectively ceased to exist … [S]exual harassment – one man at a time, one incident after another – costs women their most basic human rights today. Jobs, education, housing, religion – no aspect of women's lives is immune to destruction when harassers strike. (Langelan 1993, p. 81).

In the face of such systematic subordination, Langelan urges women to engage in "civil disobedience" in their everyday lives. Just as civil rights activists used non-violent direct action to protest Jim Crow, Langelan argues: "A woman who confronts harassment is doing much the same – using direct action to protest an unjust social norm and to change the unwritten, but equally powerful, standards of socially accepted sexist behavior" (Langelan 1993, pp. 85–86). Thus, to Langelan, confrontations and complaints about sexual harassment should not invoke personal feelings or sensitivities but should stand on principle. Emphasizing the group-based nature of the injury, she urges women to "Make it clear that all women have the right to be free from sexual harassment. Women who confront can strengthen their statements considerably by speaking up on behalf of women everywhere. Objecting to sexual harassment is a matter of principle" (Langelan 1993, pp. 119–20).

To Langelan, each individual confrontation or complaint that challenges sexual harassment in a particular workplace comprises a larger effort to disrupt systematic sexism and to bring about social change: "We can confront individual harassers until they find harassing women so risky and unrewarding that they simply give it up. We can begin to multiply our successes, bringing to bear the cumulative impact of thousands of lawsuits and individual and group confrontations" (Langelan 1993, p. 331). In this view, social change occurs when increasing numbers of people re-name experiences and feel empowered to resist in their daily lives.

The women's movement has engaged in direct action around the issue of sexual harassment, but the demonstrations and protests have generally targeted either policy-makers or the politicians and corporations that have become the subject of highly publicized scandals. When Anita Hill's allegations against Clarence Thomas were revealed, NOW sponsored demonstrations in cities across the US to stress the seriousness of sexual harassment in women's working lives and to protest the Senate's treatment of Hill (Kong 1991; Levy 1991). Protestors followed and heckled Senator Robert Packwood in his home state of Oregon and elsewhere after revelations that he had propositioned and groped dozens of women working for him (Egan 1993; Graves and Shepard 1993; Phillips 1993). NOW joined forces with Operation PUSH (People United to Serve Humanity) and the Rainbow Coalition to boycott Mitsubishi Motors after the EEOC filed a lawsuit against the automobile manufacturer because of unchecked sexual harassment in its plant in Normal, Illinois. Such forms of direct action draw additional media attention to the scandals, re-framing them as political and not just prurient stories (Saguy 2002).

Finally, women's organizations also engage in institutional strategies geared toward law reform. Much of the feminist prognostic frame depends on women's filing complaints and lawsuits. To make this a viable option, women's organizations have an interest in making the legal environment as hospitable as possible. First, they lobby federal, state, and local legislatures and regulatory agencies to strengthen existing laws against sexual harassment. For example, NOW's "Initiative to Stop Sexual Harassment" includes elements that seek to have states criminalize *quid pro quo* harassment, lengthen the statute of limitations for sexual harassment claims, and increase funding for the EEOC's enforcement efforts.

Second, because so much policy-making on sexual harassment has been conducted in the courts, women's organizations pursue legal strategies. As described in the previous chapter, feminist legal activists have not actively pursued test case litigation in the area of sexual harassment, but they have assisted private attorneys at the appellate level and coordinated amicus curiae briefs when sexual harassment cases have reached the Supreme Court. For example, Mechelle Vinson was represented at trial and in the court of appeals by Patricia Barry, a solo practitioner. By the time the case reached the Supreme Court, the Women's Legal Defense Fund (WLDF) and the NOW Legal Defense and Education Fund (NOW-LDEF) had taken notice. Apart from coordinating the writing of amicus curiae briefs, these organizations arranged to have Catharine MacKinnon write the brief before the Supreme Court. They also sponsored several moot courts so Barry could practice her oral argument before she appeared in the Supreme Court.

Similarly, Irwin Venick represented Teresa Harris in her sexual harassment claim against Forklift Systems, Inc. Venick was first notified that the Supreme Court accepted the case by one of these women's litigation organizations, although when interviewed, he could not remember which one it was. WLDF and NOW-LDEF were both anxious to help Venick with the Supreme Court brief and oral argument because they were concerned about the reasonable woman standard, an issue that the Court never addressed. However, Venick had already enlisted the help of Robert Belton, a professor specializing in employment discrimination at nearby Vanderbilt Law School. Still, the WLDF consulted with Venick and Belton about the main brief, coordinated the amicus effort, and helped Harris to deal with media interviews.

The women's rights organizations have been most active on the issue of sexual harassment when they sponsor and coordinate the filing of amicus curiae briefs before the Supreme Court. There has been a strong although declining level of amicus curiae participation in sexual harassment cases. When the hostile working environment was still a relatively novel claim in the *Meritor* and *Harris* cases, over 50 organizations contributed amicus briefs. This number included women's organizations engaging in research (such as Working Women's Institute and the Center for Women Policy Studies), organizations concerned about gender and racial justice (such as the Mexican-American Women's National Association and the National Council of Negro Women), as well as larger women's rights organizations that concentrated on law reform projects.

Three organizations filed amicus briefs in all five Supreme Court cases on sexual harassment: ERA, NOW-LDEF, and the WLDF. They often joined with other groups when filing these briefs. Their co-sponsors reflect the ability of women's rights organizations to build coalitions within both the civil rights community and the working women's movement. For example, in the first Supreme Court case, *Meritor*, the WLDF, NOW-LDEF, and ERA all joined a single brief with groups such as the Center for Constitutional Rights, the Mexican-American Women's National Association, the National Institute for Women of Color, and Women Employed, a small organization promoting the interests of women working in non-traditional jobs, such as construction and the trades.

In later years, the coalitions filing amicus briefs narrowed. Most briefs were filed by legal rights organizations rather than the smaller groups dedicated to women's employment or racial justice. In the *Faragher* case, ERA and the WLDF filed a brief together with the National Women's Law Center. In the companion case of *Ellerth*, they were joined by NOW-LDEF. Neither case attracted the same level of interest from women's organizations as they did from the law reform groups.

The predominant remedy for sexual harassment in the feminist frame is individual confrontation and complaint – practices that vindicate a woman's right to a workplace free from sexual intimidation and coercion. To the extent that the frame prescribes collective action, it is mostly local action in support of the complaint. These remedies do not resemble consciousness-raising, encouraging women to develop continuing bonds, to use this contact to identify more sources of oppression, to be creative in making the workplace more friendly for women. Although women's organizations have pursued both direct action and institutional strategies, those tactics have generally been designed to enhance women's individual rights.

Fitting In and Having Fun: Challenges to Feminist Notions of Harm

The most vocal critics of current conceptualizations of sexual harassment come from a variety of positions on the ideological spectrum. Identifying themselves as feminists, these critics articulate concerns about how current understandings of sexual harassment actually undermine women at work. Some are libertarian, deeply concerned about freedom of expression. Some resist any restriction on sexual freedom. Some are aligned with employers in their fear of costly lawsuits brought by deceptive plaintiffs. What they have in common is skepticism about whether hostile working environments, as currently defined in the law and in the public's understanding, are actually a serious problem for women. In addition, they challenge feminist arguments that women's subordination is responsible for sexual harassment.

The critics largely agree that some forms of predatory sexual behavior can constitute a serious threat to women's working lives. For example, sexual assault and threats or comments directed at a particular person could amount to sexual harassment according to the critics. In an amicus curiae brief outlined on their website, Feminists for Free Expression (FFE) describe a hostile environment as one where "an employee suffers physical abuse such as unwanted touching and *quid pro quo* pressures. Words alone may constitute a hostile work environment when an employee suffers a pattern of targeted and/or intentional abuse." Joan Kennedy Taylor, a founding member of FFE, has observed:

> Women have long been tormented on the job with demands for sexual favors and hostile remarks disguised in the language of sexual attraction, which often turn into overt actions that could be called assaults. Often, too, women have felt they would lose their jobs if they didn't put up with gross behavior on the part of their office superiors. (Feminists for Free Expression)

However, the legal and cultural representation of sexual harassment is no longer restricted to these blatant forms of serious abuse, and critics argue that women have actually suffered as the concept has expanded.

A common complaint in this critical literature is that sexual harassment has come to include many innocuous and innocent behaviors that do not undermine women on the job. In her book, *Heterophobia*, a former Women's Studies professor, Daphne Patai argues: "[I]t seems as though the establishment of sexual harassment as a major category of illegal behavior is taking us into a future in which sexuality itself – as innuendo, as allusion, as a vital part of life – will increasingly be viewed as corrupt and illegitimate"

(Patai 1998, pp. 28–29). She claims that the right to be free from sexual harassment has been diluted into a demand for "comfort" in the workplace – a demand she derides: "How did we get from clear examples of sexual discrimination in school and workplace to a preoccupation with 'comfort' levels, dirty jokes and passing innuendoes" (Patai 1998, p. 21).

According to these critics, the trivialization of sexual harassment has had several adverse effects. First, it has de-sexed the workplace, a place where flirtation and joking can be mutually satisfying for both men and women. Diane Furchtgott-Roth of the American Enterprise Institute and Christine Stolba of the Independent Women's Forum have written:

> For better or worse, American women are spending more time than ever before at the office. Although some workers experience harassment on the job, many more meet their future spouses there. The workplace now serves as the site for a large part of our social interaction – whether in the form of friendships, romances, or animosities. (Furchtgott-Roth and Stolba 2001, p.89)

In this view, the category of sexual harassment has come to embrace the kinds of behaviors that people rely on to find partners, and ruling the workplace off-limits curtails employees' opportunities to enjoy these possibilities.

But a more serious side effect of trivializing sexual harassment is the poisonous gender relations that emerge between men and women. According to some critics, by characterizing every joke or comment as sexual harassment, women grow to view all men as potential rapists, and men begin to think of every woman as a potential false accuser.[2] Patai claims that the "Sexual Harassment Industry" (SHI) – the scholars and activists who write about sexual harassment – purposely try to scare women:

> If it genuinely sought to protect women from the proclaimed harm of sexual harassment, the SHI would first of all strive to separate serious from trivial offenses. It would not set out to frighten women into believing that all public-sphere environments are "hostile" to them. Nor would it wish to see precious resources squandered on investigating flimsy allegations. But the SHI appears unwilling to make such distinctions or to give up its tendency to conflate all cases of "uncomfortable" reactions relating to sex and gender. (Patai 1998, p. 39)

Thus, until it becomes "serious," threatening more than women's comfort level at work, sexual harassment in this view does not constitute a serious harm to most women's working lives.

In addition to downplaying the harm of sexual harassment, critics also dispute the feminist theory that male sexual and economic dominance make sexual harassment possible. Instead, most sexual harassment is the result of a failure of communication between men and women – a failure for which women bear equal responsibility. Indeed, the critics of sexual harassment are generally tolerant of the cultures that have developed in male-dominated workplaces. Although they acknowledge that such cultures are characterized by sexualized practices, the critics accept this condition as naturally occurring when men routinely interact with one another over long periods of time. Rather than disrupt these cultures, women should, according to the critics, simply try to fit into them.

For example, Taylor argues that, rather than reflecting widespread misogyny, sexual harassment reflects two trends in the US workplace. First, women have begun working in a wide-range of non-traditional occupations and professions where they used to be a minority. Second, women have developed an unrealistic expectation that the definition of sexual harassment depends on "their *feelings*: anything that makes them uncomfortable is sexual harassment" (Taylor 1998, p. 24). This expectation ignores the fact that the workplace was, up until women's appearance, a "world that men create for themselves together ... a world of shared action rather than shared inner life" (Taylor 1998, p. 91). Taylor argues that this "world of shared action" has some common characteristics. She observes that "men alone together use vulgar language that they're sure women won't like;" "men tell dirty jokes and anti-female jokes among themselves;" and "men haze newcomers to the group, whether these newcomers are equals or superiors" (Taylor 1998, pp. 92, 103, 129). Elements of the social process commonly referred to as "male bonding," these practices have both negative and positive consequences:

> The idea that we are all guys together and that's all we need to know is in many ways very positive, as it searches for commonalities that transcend class and education. It can also, of course, isolate and exclude the person whose differences are hard to overlook – the religious fundamentalist, the effeminate gay, the woman. (Taylor 1998, p. 91)

Although the practices of male-dominated workplaces are exclusionary of others, especially women, Taylor argues that they are not necessarily discriminatory:

> When a woman comes into a workplace, especially one with few women there before her, and encounters some of these aspects of male group culture, it is very easy for her to assume that the behaviors are targeted at her, as a woman. But they are not especially aimed at the newcomer because she is a woman if they were routine before she got there. (Taylor 1998, p. 91)

In this view of the workplace, men treat each other horribly, so women should not be surprised when they too come in for mistreatment.

Moreover, critics argue that there is rampant hostility between men and women in the workplace over the issue of sexual harassment. Taylor argues that the hostility runs in both directions. She claims:

> The polarizing hostility brewing in the workplace comes from both sides, male and female. While men may want to keep their old-boy territory from being invaded, women are sometimes vocal about their scorn for all things masculine and may take advantage of the fact that they have a favored position under some interpretations of sexual harassment law. (Taylor 1998, p. 25)

On the one hand, men resent women who, Taylor argues, enter the workplace through affirmative action. Then, once the women are there, men feel restricted in the things that they can do or say lest they spark a lawsuit. Women, on the other hand, are too sensitive, anxious to see a discriminatory slight in every gesture or joke. They would rather challenge and complain about the workplace than try to adapt to its culture.

In this view, the real cause of the problem of sexual harassment is the women's movement itself. Critics argue that feminists have been so successful in imposing the sexual harassment frame on employers, educators, men, and the culture as a whole that an entire generation of women has the inflated expectation that they are entitled – as a matter of right – to feel comfortable in their workplaces. Taylor argues that women are:

> … made angry by their own expectations. Just as the grapevine has encouraged men to feel that workplace *rules* violate their rights, women are encouraged to expect that the workplace *climate* will violate their rights … Some feminist spokespersons publicly deplore the permissiveness of young women towards male behavior; feminist groups sometimes encourage women to think of themselves as constant victims of male aggression. In general, women are encouraged in many ways to feel that they are underhired, underutilized, underpromoted, and denigrated by 'the patriarchy' in the workplace … .
> (Taylor 1998, p. 54, emphasis in original)

Although she argues that there may be some truth to this assessment, Taylor urges women to not to adopt this way of thinking: "it is not empowering" (Taylor 1998, p. 55).

Patai goes further and argues that, through their frames for sexual harassment, feminists have introduced a contradictory paradigm of victimhood that clashes with the feminist agenda of autonomy and independence. According to Patai, to claim to have been sexually harassed, a woman must turn herself into a dupe who fell prey to the sexual advances of a predatory male. When targets of harassment describe their experiences, their "characterizations of woman-as-victim and man-as-predator are astonishing recapitulations of traditional, pre-feminist stereotypes about men and women, according to which women have been socialized into passivity and weakness" (Patai 1998, p. 69). Feminists and researchers who study sexual harassment have an interest in circulating these frames, Patai argues, because the frames keep the Sexual Harassment Industry thriving. She states:

A more moderate vocabulary, in which "victims" did not swiftly pass into "survivors," might suggest that too much is being made of tactless remarks, tasteless jokes, and witless insinuations. But even to speak of tact, taste, or wit is to evoke the pre-SHI consciousness in which women had not yet been turned into perpetual victims. And it is precisely the function of the SHI to oversee this process of transformation. (Patai 1998, p. 80)

In their counter-framing activities, critics of sexual harassment laws challenge the broad definitions of harassing conduct. They argue instead that feminists have exaggerated the risks and dangers that sexual harassment poses to women's careers. Arguing that women should aim to fit unobtrusively into male working environments, these critics ignore or deny women's structural disadvantages in such contexts. Moreover, these critics emphasize the importance of women's sexuality and urge women to learn to feel comfortable with sex at work to advance their careers.

Harming the Company: Management Frames for Sexual Harassment

By now, human resources and personnel experts are resigned to the legal reality that corporations can be held liable for sexual harassment. Rather than challenge the legitimacy of these claims in their professional publications, they instead advise each other on how to protect corporations from the costs of such lawsuits. The advice in the pages of these magazines and journals sometimes even endorses feminist values and slogans, although these values are usually reflected through a management lens. So while consultants may argue that sexual harassment "is not about sex, it's about power," the power in question is executive authority, not male dominance. Moreover, preventing sexual harassment is a good business practice requiring adequate training and simple common sense, not systematic changes making the workplace more hospitable for women.

Defining Harm

Costly judgments in lawsuits and attending legal fees are, not surprisingly, the most prominent harm of sexual harassment reflected in the human resources literature. Some articles focus on the problems plaguing a single organization, such as this *Business Week* article about sexual harassment litigation against Ford Motor Company:

In early September, Ford Motor Co. reached a $17.5 million deal with the feds to settle ugly sexual harassment allegations at two Chicago-area factories. Civil rights leaders hailed the accord as a model for Corporate America. The carmaker agreed to set aside $7.5 million to compensate victims of harassment and $10 million more to train managers and male workers to stop what women alleged to be a years-long pattern of groping, name-calling, and parties with strippers and prostitutes. (Muller 1999, p. 94)

Many other articles describe huge jury awards in notorious cases, warning managers that their companies could suffer such losses. In an article appearing in *Management Review*, the author provided a parade of horrible cases:

> As a result of the Civil Rights Act of 1991, jury trials are now available in federal harassment cases, and the remedies available to plaintiffs in such cases have expanded to include not just equitable relief, such as reinstatement and back pay, but also compensatory and punitive damages. Last year, a federal jury awarded nearly $5.7 million to the family of a former U.S. Postal Service engineer who complained of sexual harassment prior to committing suicide. A male dude ranch wrangler was awarded $300,000 by a federal jury based on his claim that he was sexually harassed by his female supervisor. In California, the average jury verdict in employment cases in 1998 was $2.5 million. Equally important are the intangible damages associated with harassment claims, such as absenteeism, employee turnover, low morale and low productivity. (O'Blenes 1999, p. 49)

One of the more costly aspects of liability is the gradually expanding definition of sexual harassment. Articles warned managers about the expansion of employer liability to include the conduct of customers and clients:

> Most employers know by now that they may be held liable for the sexual harassment of an employee committed by a co-worker and/or supervisor. But many employers may not understand that this same liability is extended to harassment of an employee from a customer or client. This is known as third-party sexual harassment and many claims have resulted in lucrative lawsuits brought by aggrieved claimants. Third-party sexual harassment is on the rise, according to employment law attorneys, and it can be very costly to employers who fail to take proper action when such behavior is brought to their attention. (Brady 1997, p. 45)

For example, several magazines informed their readers about the case where Pizza Hut was held liable for a customer's sexual harassment of a food server. *Workforce* summarized the impact of the case for readers: "Employers are advised that when they have knowledge of customer harassment and the means to prevent it, they may be held liable" (Hatch 1999, p. 108).

Other themes included the increasing number of men who brought sexual harassment complaints:

> It should have come as no surprise. Yet the increase in the number of sexual-harassment cases in which men are the victims and women are the harassers has business scrambling to make sure that its managers and supervisors understand that regardless of who the victim – or who the harasser – may be, sexual harassment is sexual harassment. (Verespej 1995, p. 64)

Authors also warned employers that high-profile sexual harassment scandals inflate the number of complaints that the employer will hear. For example, during Paula Jones' highly-publicized lawsuit against Bill Clinton, *Industry Week* reported:

> "Now that sexual harassment is back on the front pages, it wouldn't surprise me if there were an increase in claims," says Ann Elizabeth Reesman, general counsel, Equal Employment Opportunity Council, a group of 500 large employers. Indeed, less than two weeks after the Supreme Court ruled that sexual harassment can apply to workers of the same sex, a New Jersey man filed a same-sex harassment lawsuit against his former employer, alleging that his former boss at a chemical manufacturer taunted him for over five years about his sex life with his wife. (Verespej 1998, p. 7)

In at least one account, the courts were to blame for this state of affairs. Because of their generosity to plaintiffs, employers were left in a permanent state of confusion – which itself was costly – about what behaviors were prohibited. *Fortune Magazine* chided the Supreme Court's holding in 1994 that plaintiffs need not show they had a nervous breakdown to prevail in a sexual harassment claim:

> In the latest expansion of sex-discrimination law, our High Court overruled a number of district courts about what it was that a plaintiff had to show to prove a hostile-environment case. The new ruling is that one need not claim to have been damaged. One need not point to signs of psychological distress or impaired work ability – only to an environment that is uniquely unpleasant to women or to any of those other protected groups. Sounding utterly defeated, Justice Scalia glumly signed onto the new decision (*Harris v. Forklift Systems Inc.*), noting that past Court decisions combined with the "inherently vague statutory language" left him no choice. (Seligman 1993, p. 195)

One article among all those reviewed, however, questioned this prominent theme of dramatically expanding sexual harassment verdicts. Criticizing the circulation of this "myth," *Training and Development* provided the "truth" about jury awards:

> In many harassment programs, facilitators talk about the cost of sexual harassment. They say that more and more multimillion-dollar suits are being filed and that juries are awarding millions. That's true, but it's not the whole truth.
>
> In fact, plaintiffs lose about half of the cases that are decided in trial courts. When they win, they usually get a small award. If they get a huge award, inevitably it is reduced …
>
> In 1998, there were 16 state and federal sexual harassment jury verdicts that were appealed to US higher courts. (Yes, 16 in the entire United States.) The average jury award in the federal cases was $92,000. The range was from one dollar to $225,000. There was one reversal and one reduction, but the average award on appeal was a bit higher, $96,300 …

> One hundred thousand dollars is still big money, and the employers pay the attorneys' fees. But let's be honest: multimillion-dollar verdicts are rare, and million-dollar awards are almost nonexistent. Sure, there are million-dollar settlements, but they're often not paid in the end.
>
> Harassment cases are expensive and should be prevented. But the way to do that is not by exaggerating the magnitude of the risk. (Risser 1999, p. 21)

The exception that proves the rule, this article reveals the practices of "inflating the threat" of sexual harassment liability.

Yet jury verdicts are not the only costs of sexual harassment. Indeed, management and personnel publications contain an often-repeated mantra that sexual harassment on the job results in lower productivity, absenteeism, poor morale, and high turnover – all matters of grave concern for employers. Several magazines cited a study described in detail in *Industry Week* showing that corporations "spent an average of $6.7 million a year in sex-harassment related costs (based on absenteeism, low productivity, and employee turnover)" (Moskal 1991, p. 37). Losing female employees because of harassers is obviously a problem: "If she quits, the harasser will continue to harass other employees – and the company loses a valuable person in whom time and money have been invested. In either event, the employer loses" (Bohren 1993, p. 61). Moreover, sexual harassment can contaminate the workplace for all employees, even men. Quoting an employment lawyer, *Management Review* observed: "Studies show that men are also less comfortable, less secure, and less productive in an atmosphere of sexual harassment" (Hickens 1998, p. 6).

Sexual harassment cases also bring bad publicity to a corporation, which may, in turn, trigger protests and consumer boycotts. Every magazine had detailed coverage of the sexual harassment case at the Mitsubishi Motors factory in Normal, Illinois. The articles described the allegations and offered theories for the management failures that allowed the harassment to occur. But the Mitsubishi case was particularly notable because it triggered outrage in the civil rights and women's movement, whose organizations organized demonstrations outside of Mitsubishi dealerships and who called for consumer boycotts of Mitsubishi products. Although the boycotts and protests did not dramatically hurt Mitsubishi's bottom line, the adverse publicity was embarrassing to an already-hurting company.

Aside from these specific problems, sexual harassment reflects a broader, more serious problem with the management practices of a company, according to human resources experts:

> New York City attorney Christensen says that complaints of sexual harassment may be symptoms of a much more widespread problem. She cites cases in which "the individual was charged with specific acts of sexual harassment, but when you investigated the general perception of this individual throughout the workplace, you'd get a very negative response: that the person was a bully, was

a yeller, would insult and humiliate employees, and was generally disliked."
(Barrier 1998, p. 14)

Business Week provided extensive coverage of the scandal-ridden
pharmaceutical company, Astra, where the CEO, Lars Bildman, presided
over company functions where women were harassed by drunken executives
and Bildman himself openly groped and propositioned female executives.
Women also reported that Bildman and other top corporate officials told
women that they should be sexually inviting to important clients and
purchasers. But after these allegations of sexual harassment surfaced, more
information emerged about Bildman's militaristic management style and his
misappropriation of corporate funds (Maremont 1996a, 1996b, 1997). In
Business Week's coverage, sexual harassment was simply one of the many
things going wrong in Astra's business practices – a symptom of other more
serious problems.

Feminist explanations of sexually harassing behaviors are reflected in the
human resources literature. For example, some authors cite sexism and sexist
attitudes toward women that are prevalent in corporate America. In the wake
of Anita Hill's testimony before the Senate, a writer for *Industry Week* offered
these observations:

> During the last few months, there has been ample hand-wringing and group
> apologies for blatant insensitivities, some reforms about language at the water
> cooler, and a lot fewer close encounters at Xerox machines. But little has been
> said or done about the real issue: basic respect. A lot more men may be
> watching their workplace behavior, but there is little evidence that there are any
> heartfelt changes in attitudes. Some women say that the remarks that used to be
> spoken loudly are now merely whispered. (Fulcher 1992, p. 22)

In this article, the author also offers differences in the way men and women
are socially conditioned, which in turn produces changes in the way they
think: "Even those who support Ms. Hill's position have neglected the most
basic reason of all: women in general are simply more patient, more
understanding, more considerate, and more forgiving than men are and,
unfortunately, more used to being victimized" (Fulcher 1992, p. 22).

A few authors writing for the personnel publications even suggested that
there might be structural explanations for sexual harassment. One such article
quoted representatives of women's organizations – experts rarely appearing
in management publications – linking sexual harassment to other sex
discrimination issues.

> "When it comes to workplace issues important to women, sexual harassment,
> discrimination in hiring and promotion, pay equity health and safety and the
> glass ceiling are all related," argues Barbara Otto, national program director for
> 9 to 5, the advocacy group representing office and clerical workers. Otto, and
> other leaders in the women's movement, feel the Hill-Thomas hearings have

given them a boost. "It galvanized the women's movement. Sexual harassment is something that crosses racial, economic and class barriers. It's a topic that has united all working women," Otto says. (Reynolds 1992, pp. 36–38)

At least one author argued that sexual harassment was caused by these sexist business practices:

Actually, pay equity is relevant to this entire issue. It's well known and commonly accepted that one's worth in the workplace is based on how much one gets in his or her paycheck. If women were paid equally for equal work, their status in general and their respect level among their male peers would rise, making them less susceptible to degrading insults and behavior. (Fulcher 1992, p. 22)

It should be noted that these explanations were still couched in articles that characterized the principal harm of sexual harassment as a problem for employers rather than women.

However, most human resources explanations of sexual harassment appropriated feminist values but gave them a management twist. For example, articles appeared in several magazines that endorsed the feminist observation that sexual harassment is not about sex but about power. For example, discussing the increase in female harassers who target male employees, *Industry Week* quoted a lawyer: "We forget that more than half the time there is no romantic component to sexual harassment – that it is mostly an intentional power play by a man or a woman trying to assert authority." Thus, these abuses of authority are simply a symptom of poor management.

According to the human resources literature, sexual harassment is primarily a business problem. In addition to the costs of litigation from liability and legal fees, sexual harassment does damage to a business because it distracts and harms employees. But authors make efforts in this literature to suggest sexual harassment is a problem for all employees, not just women. Thus, the management literature de-politicizes the harm of sexual harassment.

Prognosis

Among human resources professionals, sexual harassment is the result of misunderstandings and lapses in effective management practice. There is a prevalent view in these publications that sexual harassment will wither away once a good training program is in place to educate employees about prohibited practices and their consequences. As one commentator noted: "Most people want to do the right thing and create a respectful workplace" (Risser 1999). When problems do arise, policies and procedures should be in place to process grievances and protect both accusers and harassers before they end in litigation. Thus, the remedy for sexual harassment is providing grievants with an outlet for their complaints with swift, fair discipline for harassers.

Taking advantage of Supreme Court developments and scandals involving prominent companies, human resources professionals pointedly sell training programs as a means to end sexual harassment at its source. In the wake of the Supreme Court's 1998 decisions in *Faragher* and *Ellerth*, one author quoted an employment lawyer on the importance of educating employees:

> And she adds that companies are scrambling to get training programs together. "At many companies, especially if they're having a bad financial year, training may be one of those things that goes. But I've heard some HR pros say, 'I'm going back to my boss and tell him or her we really need to put training about sexual harassment back in the budget, given what's occurred with these Supreme Court decisions." Those who've already been vigilant on this issue remain convinced they need to stand firm in their actions. "Essentially, the rulings have no immediate effect on us because we've had a long-standing policy in place," says DuPont's Hamilton. (Laabs 1998a, p. 34)

Authors and experts are sometimes divided about who should be trained – supervisors or all employees – but agreed on the general goals. Programs should primarily define "what lawful social-sexual behavior is and is not" (Moore, Gatlin-Watts, and Cangelosi 1998, p. 12). Beyond providing definitions, though, training is a way of inculcating management values among employees who are either targeted by sexual harassment or who are handling complaints: "Trainers can use coaching to help clarify procedures and policies. They can illustrate and encourage appropriate behavior, while preparing employees to confront alleged perpetrators. That helps reduce the liability from unlawful workplace behavior, overcome the negative influence on productivity and morale, and enhance an organization's image" (Moore, Gatlin-Watts, and Cangelosi 1998, p. 13). In this view, in addition to informing employees about the employer's policies, training can provide models of minimally disruptive behavior.

Indeed, there are risks associated with sexual harassment training. Seminars, role-playing, and video-taped presentations all may raise the salience of sexual harassment. Summarizing the risks and the benefits, one author wrote:

> In every regard, the survey found that respondents in companies which sponsor training programs are more likely to identify the behaviors listed in the survey as examples of sexual harassment. In other words, training increases sensitivity. And though companies providing such training had a higher level of reported incidents, a markedly lower percentage of those incidents rose to the level of a legal claim, which made them less likely to end up in court. Simply put, companies operating without a sexual harassment policy and without training were found to be more vulnerable to lawsuits. (Laurenzo 1996, p. 5)

Most companies, however, cannot afford a full-scale training program. To prevent sexual harassment complaints from ripening into lawsuits, they must settle for anti-harassment policies and procedures. Every publication provided general articles describing the general parameters of what such a policy should contain. It should define harassing behaviors and provide a grievance procedure for handling such complaints. Employers should communicate the policies to their workers. Supervisors should investigate complaints promptly, confidentially, and fairly, and should take remedial action as soon as harassment is discovered. This excerpt from *Workforce* is a good example of what these articles advised:

> Have a state-of-the-art policy that clearly says your organization won't tolerate harassment, including harassment between members of the same gender.
>
> Widely disseminate the policy at regular intervals (annually or more often is ideal), post the policy on your intranet, keep records of when the policy was disseminated and keep signatures on file that employees received the policy.
>
> Make at least two reporting venues available to employees – one must be someone other than employees' supervisors (HR, an ombudsperson, supervisors, managers, 800 number, open-door policy, internal review procedure or others).
>
> Conduct training for employees, supervisors and managers on anti-discrimination and anti-sexual harassment policies and practices. Ideally, have the firm's leader introduce the sessions to nail down the point that senior management is serious about non-discrimination. Make sure everyone understands what constitutes discriminatory behavior and why it won't be tolerated.
>
> Investigate all reports of sexual harassment promptly (including harassment between members of the same gender) and ensure that employees who report such misconduct aren't retaliated against.
>
> Take swift and appropriate action against employees who are found to have violated company policies on sexual harassment and anti-discrimination.
>
> Hold supervisors, managers and executives accountable for communicating anti-discrimination and anti-sexual harassment policies and practices to their work groups, and dealing appropriately with any misconduct. (Laabs 1998b, p. 41)

Human resource professionals have developed highly specialized institutional mechanisms that are supposed to protect employees but that really shield employers from liability. For example, many articles endorse a "zero-tolerance" policy as a panacea for all sexual harassment problems. Yet there is surprisingly little understanding of what a zero-tolerance policy is or how it should work. Employers also encourage the use of ombudsmen who can develop informal, trusting relationships with employees but who have the direct ear of the CEO of the firm. Thus, they can act as advocates for employees with problems.

But employers are warned to exert care in conducting investigations of sexual harassment or risk aggravating an already delicate situation. For example, human resources professionals repeatedly caution employers to include anti-retaliation provisions in their policies and to make sure they are enforced, even if it takes additional resources after the complaint is resolved:

> After filing a charge of harassment or discrimination, employees often perceive any adverse actions as related to their complaint. Therefore, a human resources officer or other appropriate manager should carefully monitor a complainant's work environment and work with his or her supervisor to avoid even the appearance of retaliation. Further, ensure that the complainant is not shunned by his or her co-workers, and counsel managers to make a conscious effort to include complainants in appropriate workplace meetings or events. (O'Blenes 1999, p. 49)

Human resources professionals argue that good corporate communications is central to both preventing sexual harassment and resolving problems when they occur:

> Progressive, best-practice organizations combine several aspects for an effective overall plan. First is an open-door policy that encourages employees to communicate their problems so they can have help in solving them. Secondly, some companies have confidential hotlines. This voluntary process allows people to talk to a supervisor or person in senior management who will answer questions without any fear of retaliation. This can be part of a dispute resolution program in which one individual is responsible to oversee all legal questions and help resolve them before they fester. (Solomon 1998, p. 52)

But they also encourage good communication among employees themselves. Lamenting the decline of civility in the US in general, one author wrote: "One thing that distresses me about this problem is that it shows just how immature some people can be or, at the very least, how lacking in judgment. After all, treating one's co-workers with respect and being courteous, decent, and principled isn't rocket science" (Koonce 1998, p. 16). One even suggested that old-fashioned peer pressure would help enormously:

> An in-house lawyer told me what typically happens on his company's email bulletin boards. He said, "If people post For Sale on the wrong bulletin board, they get 10,000 flames, and they never do it again. But if people post tasteless jokes, HR gets 10,000 complaining emails. If people just flamed [sexual] offenders, they'd stop immediately. Peer pressure is much more effective than a warning from HR." (Risser 1999, p. 21)

In the end, though, human resources experts acknowledge that employers will never be able to prevent sexual harassment and that lawsuits are almost inevitable. Those employers who despair of finding a solution in the workplace are encouraged to purchase employment practices insurance:

Companies have been hit with a hail of sexual-harassment and racial-discrimination lawsuits in recent years, and the litigation has spawned a new industry: specialized insurance against discrimination and harassment claims. In the mad scramble to protect against rising awards, many companies have snapped up the specialized coverage, called employment practices liability, or EPL. (Holyoke 1997, p. 26)

Summary

Sexual harassment is a deeply contested concept. Although feminists first named the problem in the 1970s, they have not exercised complete control over its dimensions. While a vocal counter-movement has resisted the notion that sex is harmful or that women are at a structural disadvantage in the workplace, human resources professionals have gradually transformed sexual harassment into bad management practice.

Although these competing forces have different perspectives on the nature of the harm, there is an interesting consensus on what women should do when confronting unwanted sexual attention at work. Indeed, feminist frames urge women to pursue legal remedies, while management frames and conservative frames scorn or at least discourage such methods. Still, most participants in this political debate agree that women should directly confront their harassers and demand that they stop. If that fails, women should pursue complaints through available grievance procedures. Thus, even for feminists, collective action is not a prescription for sexual harassment.

Notes

[1]   Although feminists have emphasized sexual harassment at work, they have not ignored other possible sites for sexual harassment. For example, Legal Momentum (formerly NOW Legal Defense and Education Fund) provides extensive information to the public about sexual harassment in housing and all levels of education (Legal Momentum). In addition to this, Langelan's book provides strategies for confronting sexual harassment by people with power over a woman's intimate life, such as ministers and psychiatrists, as well as street harassment (Langelan 1993). These efforts have been geared toward ensuring that women can enjoy both a public and private life free from sexual intimidation and coercion. Still, sexual harassment in employment has been the primary focus of the feminist frames (Saguy 2000a).

[2]   There is remarkably little evidence to support any of these allegations. It would be possible to consult the extensive scholarly literature on the kinds of behaviors that women label sexual harassment. If they had, they would find that women rarely use the label, and when they do, they confine the label to the kinds of intrusive behaviors that "originally" constituted sexual harassment.

4 The Meaning of Equality: Perceiving the Harm of Sexual Harassment

> I work with a guy who said to another worker what a hundred dollar bill in her breast would get him. She thought it was funny; she smiled. When he said it to me, I told him it would get him missing teeth. She said what he said was harmless, and she thought I over-reacted.
>
> – *Survey respondent*

The ongoing public debate about sexual harassment and its regulation is fueled by the fact that sex at work has not disappeared. In spite of dire warnings about humorless feminists, overzealous regulators, and paranoid plaintiffs squeezing every last vestige of sexuality out of the workplace, sexual banter and joking endures, along with more severe and intrusive behaviors. Thus, the experience the woman described in the quotation above is not unusual in the US workplace. Yet this comment also illustrates a pervasive concern among policy-makers and managers: people may have widely diverging interpretations of similar behaviors.

Differing interpretations are, at least in part, attributable to the controversial nature of the experience. There is no real societal consensus about what types of sexual behaviors are harmful at work, except perhaps at the extremes: rape on the job is unmistakably bad; an isolated sexual joke or comment is almost surely acceptable. But the debate about the harms of sexual harassment focuses on the range of behaviors between these two poles. And women participate in this debate, and therefore help construct the damage harassment does to their careers, when they encounter sex at work and decide whether they feel injured. In the case of sexual harassment, the injury is rarely automatic; rather it is revealed over time, the result of a highly variable, ongoing evaluative process subject to argument, counter-argument, and emotion.

Being able to analyze the perceptual process behind an injury is a unique advantage to studying the legal consciousness of injustice. In the politically controversial aspects of everyday life, people may not automatically acknowledge the unfairness of existing social conditions. Most take the status quo for granted until social movements begin to disrupt and challenge prevailing interpretations, substituting oppositional messages that re-shape tolerable conditions into unacceptable deprivations. When people start relying on those oppositional messages to interpret their everyday experiences, the movement's program for social change is under way. Law may be present in these re-interpretations but not exclusively so.

In this chapter, I examine the evaluative process behind women's perceptions of whether they were injured by their encounters with sexual behaviors at work. After outlining the theoretical factors that shape this process, I describe women's experiences with sex at work at the University. I then show that women did not automatically feel harmed by these experiences. Rather, their perception of harm reflected prevalent debates about appropriate behaviors in the workplace. They drew on frames circulated by feminists, employers, and others to evaluate the conduct and reach a decision about whether they felt injured.

The Origins of a Dispute: Generating the Injury of Sexual Harassment

Underlying all disputes is an experience, an event. Consumer disputes can begin when a product breaks, for example, and personal injury disputes can begin when limbs are broken. These experiences constitute the raw material for dispute transformation (Felstiner, Abel, and Sarat 1980–81, p. 634). In mapping the development of a dispute, Felstiner, Abel, and Sarat (1980–81, p. 633) note: "Trouble, problems, personal and social dislocation are everyday occurrences. Yet social scientists have rarely studied the capacity of people to tolerate substantial distress and injustice." They argued that the transformation begins when an "unperceived injurious experience" becomes a "perceived injurious experience; that is, any experience that is disvalued by the person to whom it occurs" (Felstiner, Abel, and Sarat 1980–81, p. 634).

Some experiences do not pose complicated interpretive quandaries because they are patently injurious – breaking a leg or getting fired from a job are obviously harmful events. However, some injuries may be latent; their full effect only develops over time, such as the harmful effects of exposure to asbestos. Other harms may be actively concealed from the injured parties, such as the efforts of Enron executives to cover up their fraudulent financial dealings that cost their shareholders and employees millions of dollars. Finally, people may simply differ in the meaning that they assign similar experiences. For example, to some, sexually explicit jokes can be very distressing, while to others, those jokes may be endlessly entertaining. This stage in the evolution of a dispute is critical because "the level and kind of disputing in a society may turn more on what is initially perceived as an injury than on any later decision" (Felstiner, Abel, and Sarat 1980–81, p. 635).

Finding an experience harmful is only the first perceptual step in the development of a dispute. After all, some injuries are simply one's own fault or the result of an accident. Harmful experiences only give rise to grievances when the injured party attributes responsibility for the injury to another individual or organization (Felstiner, Abel, and Sarat 1980–81, p. 635). Such attributions may be made when a norm governing behavior exists and when the other party's conduct violates that norm. "The definition takes the grievant's perspective: the injured person must feel wronged and believe that something might be done in response to the injury, however politically or sociologically improbable such a response might be" (Felstiner, Abel, and Sarat 1980–81, p. 635). Hence, one party must "blame" by attributing responsibility for the injury to another (Felstiner, Abel, and Sarat 1980–81).

In spite of their importance, the interpretive processes of "naming" and "blaming" are often overlooked in legal consciousness research. First, there are methodological difficulties associated with investigating the perception of harm. Merely asking about a possible injury may prompt a person to detect one (Felstiner, Abel, and Sarat 1980–81). Moreover, such research often occurs in a dispute-processing institution, such as courts (Merry 1990; Ewick and Silbey 1992, 1998), clerks' offices (Yngvesson 1993), court-ordered mediation services (Harrington and Merry 1988), and welfare offices (Sarat 1990). By the time disputants have reached these institutional arenas, not only do they know they have been harmed, they have assigned responsibility for the harm to another party and sought out assistance in resolving their complaints.

But while this stage of a dispute has remained relatively unexamined in legal consciousness research, the perception of harm is a driving question behind many studies of social movements and their struggles against domination. Social movements try to disrupt everyday understandings of the normal and the routine. They problematize acceptable social, political, economic, and cultural arrangements and render them unjust. Thus, social movements are in the business of generating discontent and grievances that ultimately lead to disputes. By situating a study of legal consciousness in the context of social problems and the ongoing construction of injustice, this crucial stage of the disputing process becomes available for analysis rather than relegated to an assumption.

Before it can generate grievances from previously tolerable living conditions, a social movement must develop collective identity among its adherents. The formation of collective identity is the process of constructing a sense of "we" among individuals who may not necessarily think of themselves as a group. Social movements engage in this process by emphasizing similarities and shared experiences among group members and also by distinguishing movement members from "the web of others in the contested world" – particularly the "others" in the dominant groups (Taylor and Whittier 1992, p. 111). Thus, social movements draw boundaries around their members that separate them from the rest of the world. These boundaries help movements nurture the collective identities that in turn support collective action.

Based on these collective identities, social movements offer new interpretations of experience. Contained in injustice frames (such as those discussed in Chapter 3), these alternative interpretive frameworks challenge the taken-for-granted features of daily life by punctuating the unfairness of everyday experiences and by blaming others for these conditions. By circulating these frames among members and potential members, movements seek to build oppositional consciousness (Taylor and Whittier 1992). Oppositional consciousness has been described as "that set of insurgent ideas and beliefs constructed and developed by an oppressed group for the purpose of guiding its struggle to undermine, reform, or overthrow a system of domination" (Morris 1992, p. 363). When members participate in the beliefs and practices that constitute oppositional consciousness, they may confront the conflicts that amount eventually to social change.

Oppositional consciousness, like legal consciousness, is not an ascriptive characteristic that is either switched on or off in a person. Instead, recent research has demonstrated that oppositional consciousness is a multivalent construct with many different dimensions (Mansbridge and Morris 2001). In elaborating the scope of oppositional consciousness, Mansbridge offered one basic definition: "any minimal definition of oppositional consciousness requires four factors – identifying with an unjustly subordinated group, recognizing the injustice in that group's position, opposing that injustice, and recognizing a group identity of interest in ending that injustice" (Mansbridge 2001, p. 240). On a deeper level, more "mature" oppositional consciousness might include recognizing that these injustices are not merely random acts but constitute systematic oppression. It may also include a broader commitment to collective action in order to challenge this oppression, a commitment actively cultivated by social movements seeking to promote their programs of reform or revolution.

Conceptualized then as a continuum, oppositional consciousness constitutes a set of beliefs and practices shared by the many different constituents of a social movement – not just its committed activists, but also its sympathizers and bystanders (McCarthy and Zald 1977; Snow, Zurcher, and Ekland-Olson 1980; Walsh and Warland 1983). Those among the latter groups may subscribe to a movement's ideologies and worldview, but may not be willing to sustain the sometimes high costs of collective action (Oliver 1984; Walsh and Warland 1983). Still, they may draw on a movement's frames to interpret their lives and to engage in everyday practices that resist domination and that create conflict. Indeed, a movement may suffer if individuals who identify with it still decline to participate in collective action (Snow and McAdam 2000; Friedman and McAdam 1992). Still, by articulating frames that generate new conflict and grievances among ordinary individuals, a movement may nevertheless promote its program of social change.

Consciousness is not created in a vacuum. Social networks are crucial in the circulation of oppositional interpretive frames. Social movements recruit members through interpersonal relationships in which activists can convey the beliefs and ideologies associated with the movement (Snow, Zurcher, and Ekland-Olson 1980; Snow et al. 1986). Friends, family, neighbors, and co-workers all assist individuals in making sense of confusing and ambiguous events. These audiences may supply and encourage insurgent interpretations of uninvited sexual behaviors in the workplace, for example, but they can also reinforce the dominant frames that make women responsible for their own injuries.

The perception of injury is a stage in the development of a dispute where oppositional consciousness and legal consciousness may intersect, but it is also a stage that has been overlooked in the legal consciousness literature. This chapter will demonstrate that the perception of injury cannot be taken for granted by analyzing women's varying interpretations of sex at work.

The Harms of Asking: Evidence on the Incidence and Injuries of Sexual Harassment

Existing research on sexual harassment has documented the fact that sexual conduct continues to occur in the workplace, in spite of 30 years of legal and organizational bans on such conduct. Studies of sexual harassment also show its detrimental effects on women's working lives, while recent ethnographic work has shown that sexuality has different meanings in different workplaces. Thus, existing sexual harassment research provides some insight into the origins of workplace disputes about sex at work.

According to many studies, women's experiences with unwanted sexual attention at work are commonplace. In the 1980s, several studies concluded that between 40 and 50 per cent of working women had at least one such experience. For example, the United States Merit Systems Protection Board (MSPB) has conducted the three largest surveys on the incidence of sexual harassment in 1980, 1987, and 1994 by sending questionnaires to all full-time federal employees (MSPB 1981, 1988, 1995). In the first two studies, 42 per cent of women responding reported at least one incident of unwanted sexual attention at work. In 1994, it was up to 44 per cent. In another study that used a random sample of working women in the Los Angeles area, Barbara Gutek found that 53 per cent had at least one experience that they considered sexual harassment during their careers (Gutek 1985). Finally, in a study of students, faculty, and staff conducted at a large university in the mid-1980s, Louise Fitzgerald and her colleagues found that roughly half reported some form of experience with unwanted sexual attention (Fitzgerald et al. 1988; Fitzgerald and Ormerod 1993).[1] While they relied on different data-gathering techniques, the consistent results across these studies strongly suggest that these experiences are prevalent for working women.

Sexual harassment comprises many different behaviors that vary in how intrusive they are and how frequently they occur. Working in the field of psychology, Louise Fitzgerald and her colleagues have developed a classification system, the Sexual Experiences Questionnaire, designed to capture the range of unwanted sexual conduct in the workplace. They have identified three dimensions of sexual harassment: gender harassment, unwanted sexual attention and sexual coercion (Gelfand, Fitzgerald and Drasgow 1995; Fitzgerald et al. 1988). Their measurement is behaviorally based, asking respondents to report behaviors rather than simply their perceptions of whether they had faced sexual harassment (Fitzgerald and Shullman 1993; Welsh 1999).

According to Fitzgerald and her colleagues, "gender harassment" consists of behaviors that convey insulting or hostile views of women but which are not necessarily "aimed at sexual cooperation" (Gelfand, Fitzgerald, and Drasgow 1995, p. 168). In other words, these behaviors do not consist of demands or invitations. These are the least intrusive forms of sexual harassment but also the most common. The second category of sexual harassment – unwanted sexual attention – consists of conduct that is more explicitly sexual than gender harassment (Gelfand, Fitzgerald, and Drasgow 1995). It takes the form of uninvited conversations about a target's sex life, pressure for dates, or unwanted physical contact with the target. If welcome, these behaviors might be considered relatively innocuous flirtatious behavior, but when unwelcome, such conduct is more intrusive and threatening to the target. The third type of unwanted sexual attention, "sexual coercion," includes demanding sexual favors backed by a threat or a promise of benefits (Gelfand, Fitzgerald, and Drasgow 1995). This conduct constitutes *quid pro quo* harassment – the form of sexual harassment that has been recognized as illegal since the mid-1970s.

Existing research has also documented the context in which sexual harassment is most likely to occur.[2] Some suggest, for example, that sexual harassment is the "product of culturally legitimated power and status differences between men and women" (Welsh 1999, p. 176, citing Farley 1978, MacKinnon 1979). Enshrined in potent stereotypes and gender socialization processes, male dominance over women extends into the workplace, making women vulnerable to sexual harassment (Tangri, Burt, and Johnson 1982; Gutek 1985). This is particularly true for young women who may be particularly vulnerable to male assertions of power (Kauppinen-Toropainen and Gruber 1993; Padavic and Orcutt 1997; Gruber and Bjorn 1982). On the other hand, there is evidence that this effect is mediated by the occupational context; youth may also be correlated with low job status (Gruber 1998).

Sexual harassment may also be related to the characteristics of the particular work setting and the organization. For example, informal power within organizations is also a powerful predictor of sexual harassment (Cleveland and Kerst 1993; Grauerholz 1996). Having less power in their workplaces, women are most likely to be harassed by their co-workers (Gutek 1985) and even by subordinates (McKinney 1994; Rospenda et al. 1998) than by supervisors. As one researcher noted: "[M]ale peers lack an institutional basis for dominating their female colleagues. For this group, sexual harassment may be one of the few means available for realizing this end" (LaFontaine and Tredeau 1986).

In addition, the incidence of sexual harassment is related to the proportion and number of women in a workplace (Gutek 1985; Gruber 1998). Barbara Gutek's sex-role spillover theory suggests that women are most likely to be harassed in workplaces where the proportion of workers is skewed – either more females or more males – because in such locations, women's "femaleness" is rendered more conspicuous (Stockdale 1996; Welsh 1999). More recent research has suggested that greater contact between men and women at work – particularly when men numerically dominate the workplace – is responsible for more sexual harassment (Gutek et al. 1990, Gruber 1998).

Women have different reactions to their experiences of unwanted sexual attention at work. For many women, such incidents can be devastating to a woman's career and well-being. Women report that as a result of sexual harassment, they suffer decreased morale on the job, increased absenteeism and other negative changes in both the quality and quantity of their work (MSPB 1988; Fitzgerald and Ormerod 1993). Women also lose their jobs in the aftermath of sexual harassment, either by resignation, transfer or even discharge (MSPB 1988; Coles 1986; Fitzgerald and Ormerod 1993). In addition to the work-related problems, targets suffer psychological damage because of sexual harassment. In clinical studies, victims report a series of symptoms – fear, anxiety, anger and depression, for example – similar to those suffered by victims of sexual assault (Koss 1990).

However, some have criticized existing research for emphasizing these harmful consequences by conflating all sexual expression in the workplace with sexual harassment (Williams, Giuffre, and Dellinger 1999). Ethnographic studies have demonstrated: "Workers themselves often conceive of sexual behaviors at work along a continuum, ranging from pleasurable, to tolerable, to harassing (Williams, Giuffre, and Dellinger 1999, 76; Giuffre and Williams 1994; Dellinger and Williams 2002; Williams 1997). For some workers, for example, sexual behavior and joking help to relieve stress. These critics emphasize the importance of context in evaluating the construction of sexuality in the workplace and assessing its harm (Williams 1997; Williams, Giuffre, and Dellinger 1999).

This extensive body of research shows that sex at work, wanted or not, has not withered away in the US workplace despite 30 years of regulation and widespread efforts by consultants and lawyers to wipe it out (Schultz 2003). However, the meanings that women attach to this conduct remain relatively unexamined. In the sections that follow, I analyze the way that women evaluate their encounters with uninvited sexual behaviors in the workplace; in particular, whether they found the experience harmful to their careers or their emotional state. Studying women's meaning-making practices in this context reveals the importance of frames other than law in legal consciousness and provides much-needed attention to the origins of a dispute.

The Event: The Incidence of Sexual Harassment at Work at the University

All disputes begin with an event. The events that eventually evolve into sexual harassment disputes are sexual behaviors in the workplace. Like many other studies, female employees in the University described experiences with such behaviors. In my survey of women working at the University, 26 per cent of those who responded to the questionnaire reported at least one experience with unwanted sexual attention at work.[3] Moreover, the women at the University reported the full range of sexual behaviors revealed in other studies.

Almost all the women I interviewed reported having had at least one experience with gender harassment – sexual comments or joking – at some point during their careers. For example, Nora reported that two faculty members traded off-color jokes near their mailboxes within her hearing, although the jokes were not directed at her. Abbie reported that during business meetings, her colleagues often used vulgar language referring to male and female genitalia. Nora and Abbie both also reported that these behaviors did not occur frequently – once or twice every month.

Gender harassment can become more intrusive, however, when frequently repeated. For example, Joanne reported that a senior officer often told crude and tasteless jokes to women around the office:

> My personal experience was that he told me a joke and the punch line was "nice hooters." But he'd been doing some things all along, I guess. I didn't get the worst of it. There was another woman who came forward to [Human Resources] and said something … One of the things that really bothered her was he would go by her desk, and he would be singing some sexually explicit song that he was making up with her name in it. He was really gross – a gross guy … [It happened] all the time. *All the time*. Every day. He was the type of personality that whenever you had to interact with him, you could expect to have some sort of sexual innuendo or a joke or something thrown in there. That was the kind of guy he is.

Although none of the women interviewed reported an experience with sexual coercion, eight of them described experiences with unwanted sexual attention, more intrusive conduct where harassers made sexual demands or engaged in physical contact. Megan reported having several such experiences during the course of her career. In her first job, a senior executive cornered her in a hallway and made his sexual interest in her clear. More recently, the doctor for whom she worked engaged her in explicit and personal sexual conversations every day: "He discusses my breasts, and he asks me if I'm getting any [sex]." Several women interviewed described various forms of physical imposition. Joanne reported within the first two months of accepting a job, her supervisor, a woman, grabbed her breast twice. Similarly, Dallas said that she worked for a doctor who had pinched her breast as part of a punch line to a joke.

Table 4.1 describes the survey respondents' experiences with sexual behaviors at the University within the two previous years of employment. Similar to other studies, gender harassment was the most common form of conduct, followed by unwanted sexual attention. Sexual coercion was clearly very rare in the University sample. Of the 26 per cent who reported having an experience with one or more of these behaviors, 57 per cent said the incident that made the greatest impression on them was gender harassment; 40 per cent said it was unwanted sexual attention; and 3 per cent reported that it was sexual coercion.

Table 4.1   Proportions of all survey respondents reporting experiences with unwanted sexual attention*   (N = 347)

	%
Gender Harassment	22
Sexist Remarks	14
Crude Sexual Remarks and Jokes	13
Displayed Sexual Materials	10
Unwanted Sexual Attention	17
Discussion of Sex Life	13
Unwanted Physical Contact	8
Repeated Requests for Dates	5
Sexual Coercion	2
Implied Faster Promotions	1
Threatened Revenge	1
Treated Badly	1

* *Survey respondents were able to report every behavior they had experienced in the past two years. For the purposes of this table, reporting the incidence of potentially harassing behaviors, the categories of conduct were not mutually exclusive. Therefore, the proportions in the table do not add up to 100 per cent.*

Compared to other sexual harassment research, women at the University experience less of each category of harassing conduct, but they experience each category in roughly the same proportion. In previous studies, the most common forms of unwanted sexual attention were those less intrusive sexist remarks and jokes that constitute gender harassment, followed by more sexually intrusive conduct, including sexual bribery and blackmail (Fitzgerald et al. 1988; MSPB 1981, 1988). Thus, the experiences of women at the University conform generally to patterns established in other research.

Experiences with sexual harassment vary not only in their intrusiveness but also in their frequency. Some harassers may engage in these behaviors in every interaction they have with their targets; others may only occasionally tell inappropriate jokes or use sexist or vulgar language in the course of their working days. Of the women responding to the questionnaire reporting experiences with unwanted sexual attention, 86 per cent said they occurred "once or twice" or "sometimes." The remaining 14 per cent reported that these experiences occurred either "often" or "many times." Table 4.2 shows that for the women whose most memorable experience was seductive behavior, 22 per cent said that it had occurred frequently. Because they consist of more serious and pervasive behaviors, they are most likely to constitute a hostile working environment within the legal definition of sexual harassment.

Table 4.2   **Frequency of respondents' most memorable experience (by severity of conduct)**

Frequency of Conduct	Gender Harassment (N = 53)	Seductive Behavior (N = 37)	Sexual Coercion (N = 3)
	%	%	%
Once or Twice	62	57	–
Sometimes	28	22	100
Often	4	11	–
Many Times	6	11	–

These encounters with sexual behaviors at the University resembled the sociocultural and organizational contexts found in other studies of sexual harassment. Young women were more likely to report being targeted for sexual pressure, while women of all ages reported encounters with gender harassment. Many women I interviewed reported being targeted for sexually intrusive behaviors when they were young – sometimes in their teenage years – just embarking on their careers. Preyed upon by much older men in more powerful positions, these women were often unsure of how to respond. For example, Jane was only 23 years old and a project assistant for a faculty member at the University. Her duties included interacting with faculty in other departments. She described her interactions with one of these faculty members:

And there's a certain professor here that I had to make copies for him and help him with his course set-up, so I actually basically only met this person once, and I've seen him for about five seconds. And ever since then, he's – at first it was a very nice email message – this is over email. It's a strange situation, like I said. And at first it was just a normal, "Where did you come from?" kind of thing, and "How are you doing today?" and stuff like that. And it developed into a lot of strange comments like him analyzing my new marriage, and telling me I shouldn't be marrying, and telling me that *we* should be together, for some reason, and, you know, telling me about his ex-wives, and their sex lives, and all sorts of strange things like that.

Young as she was, this was not Jane's first experience with unwanted sexual attention. She also reported that while she was still in high school, she worked as a production assistant in a television station. The station manager made prank phone calls to her "to make these rude comments to me; these were horrible things that I would not repeat." She said: "I was shocked, and I didn't know how to deal with that either." At Megan's first job, a much older senior executive made sexual advances toward her. She thought he was trying to intimidate her: "He just wanted to tell me what he thought of me, and treat me as a pawn like I could be at the young age of 22 or 23 when you're scared by that."

Many of the older women I interviewed, such as Nora and Rita, who were in their fifties, were not specifically targeted for sexual advances. Rather, their experiences reflected a working environment where jokes and comments were prevalent and where the harassers simply ignored the possibility that they were causing any offense. For example, two faculty members in Nora's department told off-color jokes within her hearing though she was not a participant in the conversations. Rita had one job where the executives – "all relatively young men" – told sexual jokes and used vulgar language when referring to women in the office. She attributed their conduct to youthful arrogance.

Among the women responding to the survey, those reporting experiences with unwanted sexual attention ranged in age from 22 to 66 years old, a clear sign that sexual harassment is a potential problem for women of all ages. Still, younger women were more likely to have experiences with sexual behaviors at work: women who reported such incidents were approximately 34 years old while those who had not faced unwanted sexual attention in the past two years had an average age of 40 ($F = 22.38$; $p < .01$).[4] In addition, women reporting the more sexually intrusive conduct of unwanted sexual attention were younger – about 33 years old – than women whose most memorable experiences were with gender harassment, who were an average age of 34 ($F = .63$; $p = .43$). These findings conform to other studies in which the average woman reporting harassment was under 35 years old, yet these studies also show that the range of ages of women reporting experiences was actually quite large (Gutek 1985; MSPB 1981, 1988).

Women's reports of sexual behaviors also reflected a variety of organizational contexts. About half of the women interviewed reported experiences in which their supervisor was the person responsible for the behavior or was a participant in the events. Some of these supervisors explicitly used their authority to make personnel decisions based on physical characteristics or personal grooming rather than competence, making sexuality a component of the job. Dallas's boss mistreated many of the employees in the office. For example, he frequently commented on his employees' personal appearances, their clothing, and he even ordered one woman to change her perfume. Turnover in the office was very high, and Dallas was sometimes in charge of finding replacements for the women who left or who were fired:

> I lost one secretary because she was overweight; he doesn't like overweight women. And she was great – great typist, great receptionist; all around, she was just great as a secretary … He was too afraid to come up front to me and tell me what to do, so he told his assistant to tell me that I needed to fire her – to come up with some creative way of saying we don't need you. You're too fat. So I had to get rid of her.

Thus, in addition to performing their job duties, women working for Dallas' supervisor had to tolerate his verbal abuse, stay slim and smell nice.

But sexual harassment by co-workers – implicitly or explicitly condoned by supervisors – also created an intimidating working environment for some of the women at the University. For example, Siena worked with a man who was not her supervisor but who supervised other employees in her immediate work area. Siena felt uncomfortable when he began to hang around her desk, making comments about her appearance and complimenting perfume that she was not wearing. When her own supervisor was unsympathetic to her complaints, Siena attributed it to the friendship between her supervisor and the harasser: "[H]e was close to her, and I felt that she took his side, and so… I felt like, not that my job was threatened; I don't think I would have *lost* my job, but I felt threatened." In written comments, one survey respondent described her experiences with frequent physical confrontations with one of her co-workers: "The 'gentleman' grabbed me and tried to force himself upon me. I promptly slugged him and almost threw him on [a] conveyor belt … Needless to say he apologized and only then were we able to talk like consenting adults." As a co-worker, the harasser had no formal authority over this survey respondent's job. Yet up until she physically confronted him, his conduct created a menacing working environment that interfered with the way the respondent performed her job.

In the course of their jobs, two of the women I interviewed confronted harassing behaviors from men who were neither supervisors nor strictly speaking co-workers. These men did not have direct authority over the employees, nor did the employees come in daily contact with the harassers, perhaps making it easier to ignore unpleasant behavior. However, these infrequent and casual contacts nevertheless created opportunities for sexual advances. As a high-level program coordinator, Lily interacted with faculty and personnel throughout the University who had no direct control over her job. When one of these colleagues made his sexual interest in her clear, she entertained the notion that he might harm her career, although she admitted that such fears were not "realistic:"

> I think they're fears about he'll tell my boss, and my boss will believe him because he'll never defend me, so my value to my boss will decrease ... Or maybe my boss would think that I was leading him on, or whatever, and that it was inappropriate to go for a professional lunch with him – you never do that, or whatever. But I think realistically I don't really believe he would do that.

While they may not directly control the employee's fate, women often perceive these outsiders to have sufficient informal power in the organization to endanger their careers.

Occasionally, women may also receive unwanted sexual attention from those who might be considered subordinates. In these interactions, gender can diminish the power women might otherwise enjoy due to their enhanced organizational status. Several of the survey respondents reported in written comments that they worked with student athletes and had frequent encounters with many forms of sexual harassment: comments, jokes, uninvited intimate sexual discussions, and unwanted physical contact.

The harassers in the survey represented a wide spectrum of power in the organization. Like other findings in sexual harassment research, the typical harasser among the survey respondents was a co-worker. A majority – 57 per cent – said that co-workers were solely responsible for the conduct that made the greatest impression on them. On the other hand, supervisors were involved in roughly a third of the respondents' most memorable incidents: 23 per cent identified supervisors as being responsible, while another 9 per cent said that both supervisors and co-workers participated in the behaviors they identified in the survey. Finally, 11 per cent reported that someone other than a supervisor or a co-worker was involved in the relevant incident. The same general pattern was true for women across personal income, family income, and occupational categories.

Although the evidence suggests that unwanted sexual attention may have decreased over time, such conduct persists. Women continue to be subject to sexual joking, teasing and demands. The structure of the workplace contributes to the persistence of this conduct. Organizational hierarchies give supervisors the power to shape the tone of a working environment. Because so many supervisors are men, these organizational hierarchies often reinforce male dominance and protect male interests. As a result, a working environment can be the site of a great many sexual interactions among employees, especially when supervisors condone such behavior or even engage in it themselves.

The Meaning of Hostile Environments

As just described, the women in this study confronted a variety of different experiences with harassing behaviors. Their stories of sexual advances and invitations, sexual joking and banter, and displays of graphic sexual materials in the workplace may not have been sufficiently severe or pervasive to satisfy the requirements of a legal claim, but they fell in the general category of conduct that might constitute a hostile environment.[5] But what did women make of these sexual interactions? Were they an acceptable form of conversation among employees? Or did the conduct create obstacles to women's career advancement? In the sections that follow, I show that women assigned different meanings to their experiences with sexual behaviors at work. Indeed, the more intrusive behaviors were more likely to seem harmful. However, women's accounts of their injuries were also tied to political debates about women in the workplace and sexual freedom, as well as management concerns about productivity and efficiency.

Seeing the Harm of Sexual Behaviour at Work: Injustice, Sexual Freedom, and Productivity

The women in the study did not take offense at every sexual behavior they encountered at work. Rather, their reactions were linked to the conduct, particularly the frequency of the behavior and the severity of the intrusion. For example, when women reported experiences with occasional sexist remarks or sexual jokes, they did not generally feel harmed. Nora was not bothered by off-color jokes she overheard two faculty members trading:

> I can't remember whether I thought the jokes were funny. You know, there are off-color jokes that are really funny and some that aren't … I felt a little uncomfortable. I suppose I'm a little old-fashioned, but I thought this is the kind of joke that my mommy told me we don't tell in mixed company.

Although the jokes made Nora feel "a little uncomfortable," she did not feel that they interfered with her working relationships with the faculty members.

On the other hand, women found more intrusive behaviors, such as unwanted physical contact, much more upsetting. Several women I interviewed reported unwanted physical contact from a supervisor. For example, Joanne was almost finished with her interview, and I asked her if she had anything to add. At that moment, she remembered two separate occasions when her female supervisor grabbed her breast. Having remembered these incidents, her distress was apparent as she described her reaction: "I was really shocked! Because it was horrible, and it sort of discombobulated me in a way. And it made me really uncomfortable around her." Similarly, Dallas described an occasion when a supervisor told a joke that crossed the boundary of acceptable behavior:

And he's telling me this joke – and even my nephews do this now; I've seen it several times – where they pinch your nipple? And he did it to me. *That* was it. Now, at this point, now you're touching me. So then, I had a very good friend who was an administrator. I told her – I was livid.

Most sexual conduct at work, however, falls between the two extremes of infrequent off-color jokes and physical contact. And a great deal of that conduct is subject to competing interpretations. In deciding whether or not they were harmed by their encounters with unwanted sexual attention, the women in the study offered interpretations that were grounded in the public debate surrounding sexual harassment. On the one hand, many women articulated the injustice frame by identifying their experiences as a manifestation of the barriers women face in trying to achieve equality at work. However, not all women adopted this discrimination frame. Rather some women attributed harassing behaviors to the ignorance of individual men, rather than a systematic problem with the way the workplace was structured. In using this frame, women aligned their interests with those of their employers, and were prepared to tolerate conduct that bothered them to further their careers. Other women found sexual behaviors in the workplace to be a friendly form of interaction that in certain circumstances could be empowering. Rarely did women deploy any single frame for understanding their experiences (Ewick and Silbey 1998). Instead, women balanced several of these frames, trying to reconcile competing explanations for what was happening to them.

These differences in perception of injury were related to varieties of oppositional consciousness. As suggested in Chapter 3, in the discussion of the public debate surrounding sexual harassment, feminists have hardly agreed on a single prescription for eradicating the practice from the workplace. Thus, many women may endorse the general principle of women's equality at work, yet have widely different perspectives on whether sexual behaviors on the job interfere with women actually achieving equality. I will show that women's choice of a frame for understanding sex at work is linked, at least in part, to their participation in the oppositional consciousness surrounding gender.

This analysis draws on both in-depth interviews and survey data. The interviews reveal the rich combinations of meanings that women use to talk about sex at work and the complex interplay between meaning and experience. On the other hand, while survey responses sacrifice these subtleties, the analysis confirms some general patterns detected in the interviews. Specifically, the surveys show that by participating in woman-centered oppositional consciousness, women have access to frames that render sexual harassment a troubling abuse of power in the workplace.

Injustice Frames: Discrimination and Inequality

Injustice frames identifying sexual harassment as a form of discrimination appeared in many women's accounts of their experiences with unwanted sexual attention. These women emphasized the way that harassing conduct imposed burdens on their working lives and created obstacles to advancement. In explaining why these incidents occurred, they adopted a power analysis that framed sexual harassment as a product of male dominance in the workplace where women are rendered vulnerable because of their marginalization in the workplace. Many of the women who deployed this frame were self-identified feminists (and comfortable with that label) who thought women were systematically disadvantaged at work and in society and who believed women were most likely to achieve equality if they worked together.

For example, Rose worked as a secretary in a coaching office, where all the coaches were men, but all the clerical workers were women. The receptionist in the office frequently engaged the coaches in sexual conversations:

> Innuendoes flew left and right. She would dress somewhat provocatively: low-cut – not overtly, but – if she wore blouses, which she did often, they were very low, low buttons, she'd unbutton it quite some distance ... She would get up and she would move it to where she would stand, literally, in front of my desk with a coach, and have a conversation for fifteen, twenty minutes, of this patter of sexual innuendo, within the distance you and I are from each other right now. So it was weird. It was just *weird*, and awkward.

Rose's objections to the receptionist's behavior were not based on the offensiveness of the conversations. In fact she prided herself on her composure under pressure: "[A]ctually, more people who know me say that I'm very solid; I don't ruffle easily." Rather, she complained of the way that the working environment added to her responsibilities: "It affected the work flow of the office too. I mean, she was never there to answer the phones. *I* answered the phones. She would get into a conversation with a coach, and the phone would be ringing, and she wouldn't pick it up, so I'd pick it up." But more seriously, Rose also felt that this sexual banter created expectations that she adopt a "more hostess-like demeanor:"

> It was a situation where people who were superior to me, who had authority over me in one form or another, were expecting a certain level of behavior that was sexual in nature, that I was uncomfortable with ... If this had no impact on the way I was being treated by that staff, and the expectations that were being put upon me, within the context of the office, I could have cared less. But it clearly became that there was an expectation of a certain flirtatiousness of the female staff within the context of the office environment. And I simply wasn't going to accept that.

The level of sexuality expected by Rose's supervisors imposed too high a cost on her working life.

To Rose, these practices emerged not simply from men's numerical dominance in the workplace but from a broader form of inequality, where qualities identified as "male" were valued while "female" characteristics were discounted:

> I think that [men] still hold the preponderance of business and financial power in the world. They still have molded the social constructs and models of what is of value, and that value is largely based on possessions and finance, and physical behavior, physical force, physical strength. And the notion that there is a greater value to the traditional female strengths of compassion or listening, nurturing, flexibility, you know – those kinds of traits that are traditionally feminine in nature – I think as a society, we value less. And so, from that perspective, and in broad brush strokes, men generally have a higher hand in society.

Some women recognized that sexual harassment could also be a tool that men used to intimidate and demean them, reminding them of their low status on the job. Emma, for example, was an administrative assistant in a science department. She had been having problems with one of the faculty members, who was unhappy with the way she had processed some paperwork. Emma claimed that men in the department had a hard time dealing with women on a professional basis, since there were so few women in the department. She described an incident that particularly bothered her:

> I had been walking in the hallway, and I passed several senior faculty members, one of whom was the chair, and in passing them, one of the faculty members asked if I minded if he would pinch my rear end. What could I say? …And I said to him, basically, "Don't say things like that." I was really pissed off. You can imagine! I mean, he didn't attempt it, but he said it, and he said it in front of these other senior faculty members, so it was kind of a – a pretty embarrassing situation for me.

According to Emma, he was using his more powerful position in the departmental hierarchy to embarrass her. She viewed this incident, like most sexual harassment, as an abuse of power that resulted from women's inequality: "[P]articularly in the university, as it's traditionally been, it's men who are faculty members and women who are staff members. And so there's immediately an unequal relationship there."

In keeping with the use of injustice frames, these women blamed employers and harassers for the injuries stemming from sexual harassment. In their accounts, men enjoyed economic power over women, and that power gave them the right to dictate working conditions, which often included sexual harassment. Rita found that the executives at one job were indifferent to the needs of the women who worked for them. The sexist comments and remarks that pervaded her day were simply a by-product of rich and powerful men enjoying the perquisites of being rich and powerful.

> And there would be a lot of bantering on their side, you know, innuendoes, off-color jokes, that I just ignored … Women for them were playthings. They were of that mentality … Their attitude was that women were possessions, sexual objects, not particularly … respectable.

This set of practices unsettled women and made them feel like outsiders, thus undermining their confidence on the job. At one of Joanne's previous workplaces, the chief financial officer was "really gross – a gross guy." He told sexual jokes and made sexist comments on a daily, sometimes hourly basis. He would walk by one secretary's desk singing vulgar song lyrics with the secretary's name in it. He told Joanne a joke with the punch line "Nice hooters." Given this pattern of behavior, Joanne found it difficult to work with him:

> It probably affected my ability to get things out of him that I needed to do my job. I would interact with him; we were doing a lot of grant writing and we needed his cooperation to create the budget and that sort of thing, and I definitely felt like … I couldn't get the cooperation from him that I felt I needed in order to do my job, and I did have to go to my supervisor.

Characterizing this man as a "big power guy" in the organization, Joanne argued that he told sexual jokes and used vulgar language to assert his authority over his female co-workers:

> It would certainly stop conversation … and it would be embarrassing. And there was a certain power aspect to it that he would have over not just you but all the women that were present … I was thinking that maybe he didn't want, didn't like being pushed around by women or feel that he was being pushed around by women, and this was a way for him to counter it and say "You can't push me around! Ha! You're a woman."

Joanne's view of sexual harassment as a by-product of male power in the workplace did not necessarily change when the harasser was female. In her most recent experience with harassing behavior, Joanne was working for a woman who grabbed her breast on two separate occasions. Characterizing her supervisor as "a really interesting, exciting woman who's done some unbelievable things," Joanne believed that this conduct was a reminder to subordinate employees that the supervisor was in charge.

> It's a power thing, and I suspect that she's done it to other people in the office, although I haven't asked anybody. I also hired – it's sort of, you know how when you first get into a job, you get excited and there's a certain enthusiasm that you have, and that sort of thing. It was probably some sort of a put down on her part … It could be that she doesn't want anybody stealing her parade, in a way. She wants to be the head – she's a good leader, but she also doesn't want anybody stealing the spotlight. And if you are really enthusiastic and showing some enthusiasm, she wants to take that from you and to put you down.

Similarly, Abbie had a female co-worker who often used crude and explicitly sexual language during business meetings. Abbie speculated that her colleague purposely used such language to shock the men in the office with whom she worked:

> That's how she identifies her feminism; she thinks she's advancing the cause of women by breaking down all sorts of barriers … She's trying to model the old girls' network after the old boys' network, but she makes it worse because the old boys' network isn't that bad anymore.

Thus, the power arrangements that men created in the workplace do not simply disappear because of a change in the sex of the people who occupy them. Yet Abbie offered a critique of such behavior: "I think women bring, by their nature and experience, a different set of skills to the work force, and we should celebrate and value those skills. I don't think we should become more like men."

Injustice frames were most readily available to women working in low-status occupations such as clerical work settings where there was little hope of career advancement. For example, Rose described the coaching office: "The power structure was definitely on the male side, and [support staff] was below that." Similarly, Rita was an office manager working in a small office of wealthy executives. She described her employers:

> They were all relatively young men. The president of the company and the chairman of the board, they were all under 45. And when you make four million dollars a year, that's young – you know, as salary. So anyway, I always felt that it gave them the sense that they could do no wrong and everybody was theirs to have however they wanted.

In such positions, where women's working lives are at the mercy of more powerful people, particularly men, sexual harassment is another set of practices that re-enforce obstacles to women's equality.

Women drawing on injustice frames recognized that male dominance in the workplace was connected to their broader power in most arenas of social, political, and economic life. They also believed that men used this power to shape arrangements in ways that preserved and extended their control over everyday working conditions. In this view, sexual harassment is an important tool in the patriarchal effort to maintain male supremacy in the workplace.

Sexual Freedom

The women discussed thus far may or may not have felt injured by their experiences with unwanted sexual behaviors, but they all took a dim view of the conduct. By contrast, several women in the study were active participants in sexual conversations and behaviors at work, and some even initiated such interactions. In their narratives, women reported feeling comfortable with and enjoying sexual interactions in the workplace. To these women, sexual expression at work could not only be a source of relaxation and bonding among employees, but also an assertion of their power.

For some of the women in the study, the workplace was the focal point of their social lives. They spent a great deal of free time with co-workers and supervisors, attending the same parties, meeting for dinner, going to movies. In this context, dating co-workers was a possibility, and flirtatious behavior, even when unwanted, was not necessarily threatening. For example, Ann's accounts of uninvited sexual comments were interwoven with stories about dates she had with men she met at work. A co-worker asked her out repeatedly until she finally agreed to a date. A few days later, she thought better of it and told him she did not want to have a relationship with someone with whom she worked so closely. She found his behavior "annoying," but did not take offense, attributing his "immaturity" to his youth: "He was pretty young, he's like mid-twenties, so… I think that's normal behavior." In addition, she saw his requests for dates as a logical outgrowth of their previous social contacts: "We did have a relationship outside the workplace. We had gone out as friends a number of times. He had been over to my place; he was friends with my roommates. So it was an understandable leap to have romantic feelings, to my mind."

Sexual joking and comments can also be part of the interactions that help co-workers establish bonds and friendships that make the workplace more pleasant. For example, Dallas reported that she often engaged in sexual banter and joking at most of her jobs. She felt that such conversation contributed to camaraderie in her working environments. She was amused, for example, when a faculty member analogized her conduct to that of Clarence Thomas rather than Anita Hill:

> He said "No, no, no – it's more like Dallas telling you a dirty joke or telling you the latest porno movie." And then [the other] said "Oh, you're right. You're right; that's how she is." It's sort of like we don't mean anything because, you know, that's how we are. That's how we get pressure off.

It was important to Dallas that she be able to draw the line to discourage some forms of this conduct – such as verbal abuse and physical contact. Still, by engaging in sexual joking, Dallas felt that she was dismantling some of the barriers between faculty and staff. Similarly, a survey respondent described her workplace: "Pictures, jokes, e-mails of a crude nature are only passed through a close circle of friends/co-workers. Everyone is a willing participant – we only send material to people who have sent us similar stuff. Overall, it's a friendly atmosphere, and there are no negative feelings associated with it." In this woman's workplace, sexual materials were apparently a channel for friendly communications among colleagues.

Women also identified sexual expression as a way for women to exercise power in the workplace. For example, Abbie claimed to use a male colleague's obsession about sex to her own benefit. She and her colleagues were "very amused" when they noticed that a supervisor stared at her breasts whenever he spoke to them. Abbie claimed not to be bothered by his behavior. Rather, she considered it a "weakness in him that I could take advantage of."

The women who framed sex at work as a pleasurable experience or as an instrument of female power were no less likely to offer a feminist critique of male dominance in the workplace. Nevertheless, they believed that women needed male cooperation in order to achieve equality in the workplace. Dallas believed, for example, that women needed to be more assertive and to stand up against bullying men, but she also rejected the "man-hating" that she associated with feminist ideology:

> I look out for females. I think … you ask any of the faculty, the males especially, I seem to bash them quite a bit – all the males. And it's not because I hate men; it's because I'm protective of females, especially the weaker ones. I try to instill that they should have a streetwise type of exterior; that if anyone's trying to do anything to them, that they should pull themselves out of the situation – pretend they're out on the street and say that this person is doing something to you, what would you do? You wouldn't say "Oh, you're a faculty member. Oh, I should lie down." No, you slap the crap out of him. That's what you should do. Don't let anyone push you around. So in a way, I'm a sort of in-the-middle feminist. I'm not like over there, I'm more moderate. I don't hate you guys – all you men. I just want us to be on an equal basis here. That's how I carry out my life – in a way like that. I want to do what I preach.

Thus, Dallas insisted that she did not have to hate men – a quality she associated with radical feminists – to make assertive demands for equality at work. Similarly, Abbie thought that sexist practices harmed men as much as women. She claimed that her male supervisor was also troubled by the vulgar tone of workplace conversations, but that he was reluctant to complain about it. Based on these experiences, Abbie argued: "Making it a problem specific to women is a mistake. Sexual harassment is a problem that can affect everyone."

When women tolerate such working conditions, however, they appear to consent, and for women, consent once given is hard to revoke. Co-workers and supervisors may make increasingly intrusive sexual demands on women working in these environments. In addition, some women reported that aggressive sexual banter transformed into abusive behavior that seriously intruded on their mental and physical well-being. For example, at her previous job, Dallas engaged in this kind of banter with her former supervisor and always felt that she could hold her own in their interactions. Given their already combative relationship, however, her former supervisor often exceeded the limits of permissible workplace behavior by verbally abusing Dallas. Dallas tried to tolerate this behavior, but she found that it was affecting not just her work but also her worldview. She compared her situation to that of other women she knew who had similar complaints about their supervisors:

But it's almost like they're in a situation where they're abused – say a marriage, or a relationship where the husband is constantly verbally abusing you or hitting you. There's no way out … When I came here [to a new job], I waited for them to start swearing at me. And then I realized – see I never realized until I came from there how often he would swear at me. And I don't think of myself as a very weak woman, but all of a sudden I found myself in a situation where who was the first one who was going to tell me to go f— myself, or say something. I mean, you become accustomed to being abused …

Finally, while some women may welcome opportunities for sexual expression at work, other employees, both male and female, may find such conduct troubling. Rose, for example, found the sexual conversations between the receptionist and the coaching staff annoying, distracting her from her work. One survey respondent echoed others by observing that her office colleague was the target of frequent sexualized comments about her appearance, but the survey respondent admitted: "It bothers me more than it does her." Thus, the exercise of sexual freedom in the workplace can impair the working environment where it is not tempered by respect for those who do not choose such arenas for sexual expression (Cornell 1995, p. 172; Bernstein 1997).

Management Frames: Internalizing Employers' Interests

Several employees' accounts of their experiences reflected frames that emerged from management concerns about sexual harassment. As managers themselves or as employees concerned about advancing their careers, they internalized their employer's interests in preventing problems with sexual harassment before they ripened into litigation, but they did so by trivializing the harm and by blaming themselves for any discomfort they felt. While they were familiar with their rights, they declined to conceptualize the problem as discrimination. Sexual harassment emerged not from sexist arrangements of power in the workplace but from a crude yet natural tendency of men to be sexually aggressive, particularly in groups. These women's views of the best remedy was to ignore these behaviors and to perform their jobs as though nothing were happening. Indeed, these women may have been simply deflecting the psychological consequences associated with being a "victim" (Bumiller 1988). But notably, they did so by articulating their interests in ways that overlapped with those of the employer.

When drawing on management frames, the women interviewed did not consider explicit sexual conversation and jokes at work harmful in and of themselves. For example, throughout her career, Megan had frequent experiences with unwanted sexual attention. At her first job, an executive cornered her in a hallway and explicitly expressed his sexual interest in her. At later jobs in sales, her clients frequently exchanged sexual jokes and commented on her physical appearance. Her supervisor at the time of our interview asked her questions about her sex life and made vulgar comments about her body. Megan claimed not to be bothered by such incidents because "my job doesn't depend on it. I am not threatened. And I just know that he probably is a little sick, and I just kind of laugh at him for it." Describing the sexual conversations she has had with her supervisor as "our banter," Megan admitted that she was occasionally irritated by his conduct, but she did not blame him for this reaction.

> There have been a few times where I said "enough." I have, and that's been more my mood than his. It's been more like "you know what? I don't feel like being messed with today. I'm upset, or I'm tired" or whatever it is. Every now and then, you have a day where he really rubs me the wrong way.

Megan retained complete responsibility for any emotional distress she might have felt in the face of the supervisor's comments.

To these women, sexual harassment was not a systematic problem but, at most, a lapse of professionalism or a personality conflict. For example, one survey respondent observed that her supervisor and colleagues engaged in fairly frequent sexual joking and banter, but she did not attribute their behavior to discrimination. She stated:

> It is my opinion that a good number of people are simply unaware of what behaviors are appropriate for work and what behaviors aren't. I have not felt that co-workers were purposefully causing me discomfort, but they seemed ignorant to the fact that certain topics are inappropriate for a discussion at work … I think that it is a lack of professionalism and no sense of what makes others uncomfortable which often leads to harassing conversations or comments.

To maintain their professional dignity, women drew on a number of strategies. For example, they endorsed employment policies and procedures designed to educate employees, but they also developed their own repertoires of strategies for dealing with such behaviors (Quinn 2000). For example, Megan observed:

> You kind of figure out how to deal with this and grow confidence, and I would change the subject or laugh it off and not give them the satisfaction of letting them see that maybe it affects you or shakes you up at all. And of course, at that point, it really doesn't shake you up because you think "Pig" and then you just change the topic. And this is a customer – someone I'm going to have to deal with – so you have to approach it a little more tactfully.

Megan also assumed that such working conditions will eventually be abandoned when men finally yield to the presence of increasing numbers of women in the workplace. Arguing that "most men have a bit of pig in them," Megan also believed that women who know this and are prepared to deal with it are in the best position to advance their careers:

You can't blame the system because that's the way it was, so I think that if men reap the benefits of the system, every year they reap a little less benefits because we're out there working that much harder to say, "Hey, what about me?" because we're just now getting to that.

The women who adopted these frames tended to be managers and supervisors themselves. For example, Megan described herself as "ambitious" and as having "male goals" because she was extremely concerned with career advancement. In fact, she was willing to tolerate sexual attention as the price of fitting in to male organizational culture. Moreover, as managers, these women often participated in organizational practices and routines that protected management interests. It is not entirely surprising then, that they should rely on a management perspective and aim to adapt to the system rather than restructure it when they confronted unwanted sexual behaviors. In doing so, they de-emphasized any injury they might have felt in the interests of being better employees.

For many of these women, their understanding of equal treatment is guided by a frame that distances sexual harassment from broader structures of inequality in the workplace. By personalizing such conduct or attributing it to men's innate characteristics, they place the conduct beyond the realm of meaningful regulation. Moreover, they absolve their employers of any significant responsibility for resolving the problem. Women relying on such frames may try to adapt to their surroundings in an effort to prove their mettle, but they run the risk of appearing to consent to behaviors that can, in the long run, create enormous distress.

Balancing Competing Frames

The women in this study rarely chose a single frame for understanding what happened to them. Instead, they tried to balance many competing interpretations of unwanted sexual attention. On the one hand, they were familiar with the injustice frames that characterized such experiences as discrimination and detrimental to their working lives. Yet they also entertained alternative perspectives on such behaviors – perspectives suggesting that they should not take it so seriously or that they themselves were responsible for male sexual conduct. Thus, some women could not decide whether they had even been injured.

Lily, for example, was having a hard time reconciling these competing interpretations when she thought about her own experiences. Lily came by her political beliefs about women's role in society through her own personal experience. While her ex-husband had never physically abused her, her difficult divorce raised her consciousness about the relationship between power and gender in families. One political issue important to her was controlling domestic violence, and she had volunteered her time in shelters for targets of domestic violence, doing everything from leading support groups to helping with housework. Thus, in some areas of her life, Lily had already identified the personal as political.

Lily also applied these insights to her experiences with her colleague. She recognized that by making sexual advances, he was trying to establish control over her job performance:

> It became about my competence. He told me that maybe he'd recommend me for a job. [He said] "You're doing a good job. I always come to you for information." Did he say that because it's true and he believes it, or did you say that because that would be what works? And now, because that question can't be answered, and if it becomes of value to me, then he's in control.

In this view, her colleague was responsible for making her uncomfortable and for making her question her ability to perform her job.

Yet Lily also believed that she herself was responsible for his sexual attentions, and her explanations for these events were based mostly on her own personality traits. For example, she blamed herself for being unable to tell her colleague she was not interested in a clear and direct manner: "I finally realized that it was because I am unable to address those things, to set those boundaries, and I thought, 'He doesn't even know what's going on with me'." In addition, she believed that her colleague was simply responding to what she described as her "hero-worship" of intelligent and successful men:

> While I may not be saying to them "I'm attracted to you; I want more from you," I am saying on some level I think he's admirable or better. And I think that in some part plays into what they might be responding to. And unfortunately, the particular people who will respond are those who are perhaps looking for that.

In this view, Lily brought her colleague's attention on herself. Lily's beliefs were bolstered by her previous experiences: "It had happened to me before, so it couldn't entirely be coincidence, so there must be some part I play, and what might my part be because I'm feeling so guilty."

There are many different ways to characterize unwanted sexual attention at work. Although the women's movement has had great success in placing sexual harassment on the public agenda, it has hardly been the exclusive source of frames on the issue. Employers protecting themselves from liability have also shaped the understanding. In addition, critics have questioned the impact of law on sexual freedoms. All these frames are reflected in women's accounts of their own experiences.

Social Networks

Although the development of grievances and disputes is an interpretative process, these interpretations are not simply the product of individuals' cognitions and mental states (Felstiner, Abel, and Sarat 1980–81). Instead, meaning is shaped by the many audiences to the dispute. In fact, people create audiences through narrative practices – telling stories that aim to make sense of their experiences (Engel and Munger 2003; Fleury-Steiner 2002; Ewick and Silbey 1998). As they reshape the story to win the sympathy of particular audiences, they may come to change their understanding of events. Moreover, the audiences themselves can exert an influence by offering support for particular interpretations and challenging others. Thus, in examining the perception of harm at the bottom of disputes, it is important to evaluate the social influences on meaning (Mather and Yngvesson 1980–81).

For many women, sexual harassment is a profoundly isolating experience. Harassers often target individual women and engage in these behaviors in private, out of view of other employees. Women's feelings of shame and guilt also make it difficult for them to disclose the events to others. Yet recurring public scandals and the ensuing conversation about sexual harassment have made sexual harassment less embarrassing for some. This public debate has created an audience for stories about sexual harassment in many workplaces, and as a result, many women come forward and share their stories about their experiences. In the process of talking about these experiences, women find that they are not alone – that other women confront the same behaviors, often by the same harasser.

Most of the women in the study told someone about their experience with sexual behaviors at work. Among the women I interviewed, the only ones who did not talk to anyone about the incident were those who were completely unaffected by the experience.[6] In telling their stories to others, women sought emotional support and validation of their feelings, particularly from family members and friends outside the workplace. Co-workers' stories also provided women with an early warning system, identifying harassers and the kinds of behavior that women can expect from them. These stories, therefore, constituted the foundation of a collective experience in the workplace. But even as it confirms events and eases women's emotional distress, the audience for these stories may encourage women to tolerate offensive behaviors, thus deflecting responsibility for the problem away from employers and harassers.

Women in the study often told family members and friends about their encounters with unwanted sexual attention at work. When they felt confused or angry, they turned to those they trusted to help them manage their emotions. When Joanne's supervisor grabbed her breast, she was stunned and felt too embarrassed to discuss the incident with her co-workers, but she told a friend and her partner:

> And I told a couple people about it afterwards because I thought it was important to tell somebody. My partner I told, and also one of my former graduate school student friends, and ... because I didn't know where it was going to lead; I didn't know what was going to happen.

By condemning the harasser's actions or making jokes at his expense, friends can help the target relieve the stress associated with the incident and direct blame to the harasser and away from herself.

In addition to offering each other emotional support, co-workers' stories about sexual harassment can create a subculture in the workplace that circulates information which women can use to protect themselves. Almost every woman interviewed described conversations she had with co-workers complaining about harassers. In these conversations, women identify the harassers for new employees. For example, Kay began her job at a restaurant having been warned about the owner's conduct:

> I was not unprepared. I'd heard he was a masher and I knew that going in. I heard that from other women who worked there. One of my fellow classmates had been singing out there, and she just said, "Watch out for Ricardo." And actually, even from one of the bartenders who was a friend of mine. He had told me to be careful. It was pretty well-known.

But these warnings are rarely sufficient to forestall an incident, and when harassing behaviors do occur, co-workers' stories can help make sense of the sometimes ambiguous conduct. For example, when the sexual conversations among the coaching staff became annoying, Rose was unsure whether she had a right to feel that way. She approached another woman in the office for her views:

> She was a manager in name only. She really wasn't in a true sense, and she didn't feel like she had the support or power to deal with that anyway. However, at least she validated my feelings in some respect because that was kind of one of those things – am I just being prudish here? Am I just seeing something from my own view that isn't there, but she validated my feelings – "no, you're right on this one; this is ridiculous."

Another woman, Lily, reported that in a previous job, a co-worker cornered her, put his arms around her, and asked for a kiss before she managed to push him off her. When she told her co-workers about the incident, the women all had similar stories about the same man.

> And it later turned out that he had hit on every woman in the company at some point ... It was a very gossipy kind of place, so everyone knew. It turned out he had hit on my friend before; then he hit on the secretary. At some point, he went through every woman, making an attempt in the office. And the owners of the company treated it kind of like a joke – like "oh, it's Tom again, hitting on people," you know ...Yeah, like my friend Elizabeth was like "Oh, he hit on you? The last time we were out, he was pinching my thigh under the table."

In their stories about their experiences, women often reported being confused about the meaning of ambiguous behaviors or the intention of the harasser.

But the stories that employees told each other about the harasser helped confirm that the events happened; similar events had occurred to other women in the past. Moreover, in revealing others who had been targeted for harassing conduct, these stories provide the basis for a shared experience that creates bonds among women in the workplace. Joanne reported that women in her previous job bonded with each other because of the behavior of an executive: "It ... changed from sort of cowering and being scared to sort of rolling my eyes, like okay. And then all the women would all look at each other. We would all [say] 'Okay, here he goes again. Jack is doing it again ... .'" By transforming isolating incidents into collective experience, these stories can defeat the shame and guilt that many women feel and lead women to blame harassers rather than themselves for their discomfort.

Still, at the same time that co-workers create a collective experience, they can also de-mobilize efforts to redress the problem. Even as co-workers confirm events, they offer each other interpretations of these incidents that locate all responsibility for the conduct in the personality of the harasser. They make excuses for harassers – they grew up in a different generation; they have a bad sense of humor; they "don't get it." Thus, co-workers encourage each other to tolerate offensive behavior for the sake of preserving the ongoing relationships in the workplace. These interpretations discourage grievances at the outset so that employers are never held accountable for problems. After telling her friend about the harasser's conduct, Lily found that her friend encouraged tolerance: "And she's just like 'Oh, he's a dirty old man. Let's leave it at that.' And then I heard from others that you know, he hit on the secretaries and others. So it was just part of his pattern, and you didn't take him seriously." Although his supervisors and colleagues laughed at him, the harasser in Lily's story was nevertheless included in company outings and social events. More importantly, his behavior continued, in spite of any subtle social pressure their ridicule might have suggested. Lily learned from her colleagues – and particularly her supervisors – not to take the harasser too seriously, that his conduct was not particularly troubling. In describing him as a "dirty old man," they gave him free rein to behave in a sexually aggressive manner, thus protecting a form of male sexual authority.

Patterns of Injury: Survey Responses

The survey results confirm the general patterns detected in the in-depth interviews regarding the extent of women's injuries in the face of sexual behaviors at work: women have varying reactions to these behaviors, ranging from complete indifference to serious emotional distress. These variations in the perception of harm are related to a number of factors, particularly the nature of the conduct, but there are other significant relationships. Based on the in-depth interviews, I expected women who adopted a woman-centered collective identity to be more likely to see the harm in sexual behaviors at work. The interviews, however, provided less insight into how an audience would affect women's perceptions of injury, given that co-workers provided the women interviewed with conflicting messages about sexual harassment. In the analysis that follows, I first describe the variables used to model women's perception of injury after an encounter with sexual behaviors at work. I then present an ordered probit model and predicted probabilities of women's perception of harm.

Perception of Harm

Survey respondents were asked to identify all their encounters with a list of potentially harassing behaviors over the previous 24 months. After identifying all the incidents, respondents were then asked to choose the experience that "made the greatest impression" on them and to answer more detailed questions about that experience. One of the questions was: "How much did this behavior bother you?"[7] Their responses to this question constitute the dependent variable in the analysis that follows.

The survey respondents reported a range of reactions to their experiences with sexual behaviors at work, as shown in Table 4.3. Twenty-nine per cent were deeply troubled by the experience that left the greatest impression on them, claiming that they were either very bothered or extremely bothered by the incident. On the other hand, about 40 per cent of the respondents said that they were not particularly bothered by that experience. The largest group of respondents – 31 per cent – reflected ambivalence about the conduct by reporting they were somewhat bothered by the experience.

Table 4.3   Extent to which respondent was bothered by sexual attention

How Bothered Was Respondent by the Experience?	(N = 93) %
Not at All	13
Slightly	27
Somewhat	31
Very Much	16
Extremely	13

Nature of the Conduct

The model includes a measure of the severity and frequency of the conduct based on the obvious assumption that women would feel most injured by the most severe and pervasive behaviors. The survey instrument provided respondents a list of behaviors and asked them to report how frequently each occurred within the past two years. Respondents were then asked to identify the experience that had "made the greatest impression" on them. The variables for the severity and frequency of the conduct were based on this choice. "Severity" reflected the three categories of harassing behavior identified by Fitzgerald and her colleagues – gender harassment, unwanted sexual attention and sexual coercion (Gelfand, Fitzgerald, and Drasgow 1995; Fitzgerald et al. 1988). "Frequency" was measured by the respondent's report of how often the behavior occurred. I multiplied these two variables to create an interaction term reflecting that even less intrusive behaviors, like sexual jokes and comments, can be disturbing if they are sufficiently pervasive. The resulting variable had a range of 1 to 8, with a mean of 2.46.

Women-Centered Collective Identity

Women's access to feminist frames was measured by their responses to several questions developed to capture gender consciousness (Gurin et al. 1980; Miller et al. 1981; Gurin 1985). In this research, gender consciousness has several different dimensions, including identification with other women, dissatisfaction with women's relative position in society; preference for women over members of other groups; and attribution for women's problems to society (Gurin et al. 1980; Miller et al. 1981; Gurin 1985). In addition, gender consciousness reflects a commitment to collective solutions to women's problems (Miller et al. 1981). The measures for these items are contained in Appendix C.

The women in this study reflect the successes of the women's movement in raising consciousness about the barriers to women's success at work and in society in general. As shown in Tables 4.4 and 4.5, women who reported experiences with sexual behaviors at work demonstrated high levels of gender consciousness on most dimensions of the construct.[8] These women identified with other women as a group, and they believed that women suffer because of discrimination rather than personal failings. However, they preferred individual rather than collective strategies to improve women's position in society. Well over 50 per cent of the women reporting experiences with unwanted sexual attention agreed strongly with the statement: "The best way for women to improve their position is for each woman to become better trained and more qualified and do the best she can as an individual." Correspondingly, they showed less enthusiasm for collective strategies on behalf of women. Fifty-seven per cent of the women reporting sexual behaviors agreed only slightly with the statement: "While individual effort is important, the best way for women to improve their position is if they work together."

Based on women's responses to these items, I created a scale for their gender consciousness. Because the variables were measured differently, I standardized the values and generated a mean of the standardized values for each respondent. The Cronbach's alpha of the scale is .72.

Table 4.4 Respondents' gender consciousness

	%
Identification with Women	(N = 90)
Not Identified	9
Identified	39
Closest to Group	52
Polar Power – Women's Influence in Society	(N = 86)
Too Much	0
Just Right	9
Too Little	91
Polar Effect – Anger about Women's Treatment	(N = 93)
Almost Never	9
Occasionally	26
Sometimes	40
Very Often	26
System Blame – Society Discriminates Against Women	(N = 93)
Agree Strongly	32
Agree Slightly	52
Disagree Slightly	11
Disagree Strongly	5

Table 4.5 Respondents' collective orientation

The Best Way to Improve Women's Position in Society	%
Individual Strategies	(N = 91)
Agree Strongly	53
Agree Slightly	37
Disagree Slightly	9
Disagree Strongly	1
Group Strategies	(N = 92)
Agree Strongly	37
Agree Slightly	51
Disagree Slightly	11
Disagree Strongly	1

Social Influences

Finally, the model includes a dichotomous variable reflecting whether or not the respondent told a co-worker about the incident.

To conduct this analysis, I rely on an ordered probit model. Ordered probit allows for a more precise estimate of the effects of each variable on women's reactions to their experiences with potentially harassing behaviors at work. The following is the specification of this model:

Perceived Injury = α + β * Nature of Conduct + β * Gender Consciousness + β * Told Co-Workers

Table 4.6 reports the coefficients for the variables in the model, all of which are significant. Moreover, the nature of the conduct and women's gender consciousness operate in the expected direction. That is, the more persistent and intrusive the conduct, the more likely a woman will be bothered by it. In addition, women who have higher levels of gender consciousness are also more likely to be bothered by harassing behaviors, even when controlling for the severity and frequency of the conduct.

Table 4.6   Ordered probit model of women's reactions to sexual behaviors at work (N = 82)

	B	S.E.	p-value
Nature of Conduct	.20	.07	.003
Gender Consciousness	.59	.21	.005
Told Co-Workers	.79	.25	.002

Psuedo R^2=.1002, Psuedo R^2 is a measure of the strength of association in the model; β is the unstandardized effect coefficient in the logit model; S.E. is he standard error for the coefficient the p-value is a measure of the significance of the coefficient.

The model also suggests that telling co-workers is positively related to perceiving an encounter with unwanted sexual attention as harmful. This relationship probably reflects women's sharing more disturbing experiences with co-workers while not commenting on more innocuous conduct. It may also reflect a woman's social networks affirming, and perhaps inflating, her sense of injury.

Using these coefficients, I predicted probabilities of women's perceptions of injury in the face of sexual behaviors at work, presented in Tables 4.7 and 4.8. In the first set of predicted probabilities, I examined how the nature of the conduct influenced the probability that a woman would be disturbed by the incident. After holding gender consciousness at its mean value, and assuming that women told co-workers, I generated probabilities of women being bothered by conduct of varying levels of severity and pervasiveness.

Table 4.7   Predicted probabilities of women's being bothered by sexual behaviors at work (by nature of the conduct)

Nature of Conduct	Not at All	Slightly	Somewhat	Very Much	Extremely
Infrequent / Less Severe Incident	.05	.24	.39	.21	.10
Mean Incident	.02	.18	.38	.28	.16
Frequent / Severe Incident Intrusion	.00	.03	.16	.27	.55

Table 4.8   Predicted probabilities of women's being bothered by sexual behaviors at work (by gender consciousness)

Gender Consciousness	Not at All	Slightly	Somewhat	Very Much	Extremely
Low	.19	.40	.30	.08	.02
Mean	.02	.17	.38	.26	.17
High	.13	.27	.31	.16	.13

Women confronting the most severe and pervasive behaviors are most likely to be bothered by these incidents. But even for the most intrusive behaviors, the probability of being "extremely bothered" is merely .55. On the other hand, the most likely reaction to the less intrusive incidents is to be "somewhat bothered."

I also examined the effects of differences in gender consciousness on women's perceptions of harm for women who confronted an incident at the mean level of intrusion and who told co-workers. As shown in Table 4.8, women with mean levels of gender consciousness were more bothered by their experiences with sexual behaviors at work. On the other hand, women with higher levels of gender consciousness were less likely to take serious offense at an average incident. There are two possible reasons for this finding. First, it is possible that women with more feminist attitudes are resigned to sexual behaviors at work and are therefore less disturbed when they occur. On the other hand, this finding also suggests that women with higher levels of gender consciousness are comfortable with a certain level of sexual conversation and behavior at work. The latter interpretation is supported by the interview data.

While there is some evidence of a relationship, the survey responses do not overwhelmingly establish that feminists are more bothered by their experiences with unwanted sexual attention. In this sample, ideological attitudes are relatively poor predictors of the relationship between the political and the personal. According to these findings, in keeping with a reputation for humorlessness, a self-identified feminist who believes women are targets of discrimination might be far more offended by a sexual overture than the average woman. Yet these attitudes could just as easily lead the women in the sample to enjoy their sexual interactions at work. Thus, the measurement of attitudes does not necessarily capture the multiple voices of the women's movement.

Frame analysis, however, accounts for this variety of messages. Those messages are available to anyone who hears them, regardless of political attitudes or preferences. Admittedly, those who subscribe to the movement's goals and strategies may be more conversant with these frames and therefore more likely to use them. But one measure of a frame's success is the extent to which outsiders use it to interpret their experiences. Thus, women need not be feminists to recognize the damage sexual harassment does to their careers or to hold men responsible for abusing their power.

Summary

This snapshot of the University's female employees shows that sex at work persists in at least one US workplace. The critics of sexual harassment law can take heart – flirtation and sexual banter have not yet been stamped out. But after years of legal regulation and organizational policy-making, women continue to report encounters with unwanted sexual attention, some of which are extremely intrusive and seriously disturbing.

Moreover, women at the University assigned many different meanings to their experiences with sex at work. While some were deeply disturbed and confused by the harasser's conduct, others took it in their stride. Still others actively sought out opportunities to participate in sexual banter and joking, thinking that it promoted camaraderie and equality. These interpretations reflect ongoing political debates about the meaning of women's equality at work and in society at large. Does equality mean that women should act more like men? Does acting like men require accepting sexual behavior? Should women challenge the structural inequalities in the arrangements of work or simply wait patiently until they disappear with the introduction of more women to positions of power? These abstract political questions are the filters though which women evaluate their experiences with sexual harassment.

More generally, however, this chapter has shown that the perception of harm is an evaluative process that should be included in studies of legal consciousness. Many women conduct an interior dialogue with themselves on the very basic question of whether their experiences with unwanted sexual attention are harmful or not. In these dialogues, they weigh different perspectives and arguments about the behavior. While they draw on their personal feelings in making this evaluation, they draw on general frames obtained in the political and cultural debates on equality and sexual freedom for women that problematize everyday life. Thus, the perception of harm should not be taken for granted in analyzing the legal consciousness of injustice.

Notes

[1]   Fitzgerald's study is most comparable to my own. Fitzgerald and her colleagues used a mail-back questionnaire to survey all women at the university – students, faculty, and staff. The response rate was 48 per cent among all faculty and staff, and the sample size in this subpopulation was 231. The questionnaire provided the respondents with a list of specific behaviors constituting unwanted sexual attention at work and asked how frequently each had occurred. Those behaviors were then collapsed into three different categories representing different dimensions of sexual harassment (Fitzgerald et al. 1988).

[2]   Sexual harassment researchers have noted that while there are many studies establishing the covariates of sexual harassment, few studies have established theoretical explanations for the causes of sexual harassment (Tangri and Hayes 1997; Welsh 1999). Such theories would include variables reflecting the many complex influences on harassing practices, including organizational, sociocultural and individual factors (Tangri and Hayes 1997; Fitzgerald and Shullman 1993).

[3]   This proportion is lower than several other major studies of the incidence of sexual harassment in the workplace. There are several possible explanations for this difference. For example, women working in universities may not be subjected to sexually harassing behaviors at the same rate as employees in other settings. On the other hand, according to Fitzgerald's research, almost half of female employees at a large university reported having an experience with some form of sexual harassment. Thus, there is some evidence that universities are comparable to other employers in rates of sexual harassment. The passage of time may account for this study's low incidence rate compared to other similar research. Many of the studies were conducted in the 1980s when the major scandals associated with sexual harassment had not yet happened – Anita Hill had not testified, and Paula Jones had not sued Bill Clinton. These highly publicized news events and others may have performed an educative function about the harms of sexual harassment and may therefore have deterred some of these behaviors.

[4]   The mean age for the entire sample was 38.5 years old. The F-statistic assesses the goodness of fit of a model. The p-value is a measure of the significance of the model.

[5]   No one in the qualitative study reported an experience with *quid pro quo* harassment.

[6]   The women in the survey were similar. Fifty-four per cent of the women responding to the survey who had had an experience with unwanted sexual attention told someone else about the experience, either a family member or co-worker. Of those who did not tell anyone else about the incident, 58 per cent had an experience with gender harassment.

[7]   There were 5 available responses to this question: "Not at all," "Slightly," "Somewhat," "Very Much," and "Extremely."

[8]   Women reporting experiences with sexual behaviors at work were not significantly different from women in the rest of the sample with respect to any of the variables measuring gender consciousness with one exception. Women reporting such experiences were slightly less likely to agree with the statement that "Men have more of the top jobs because our society discriminates against women."

5 'I Guess That Was Sexual Harassment': Naming Sexual Harassment

Some women, if you blink at them cross-eyed, they consider that harassment. You know, what are the standards? And other women, you'd have to just about fling them on the floor and jump on them, before they would consider it anything … and there's everything in between.

– Blanche, interview subject

Blanche has identified an aspect of sexual harassment that keeps human resource managers and defense lawyers up at night. The legal definitions of sexual harassment are confusing, obscure, and often based, it seems, on the emotional state of the victims, not to mention the harassers, rather than on any factor under the employer's control. While the rules may be unclear to everyone affected, they are nevertheless powerful forces shaping interactions in the workplace. As shown in Chapter 2, employers have adopted elaborate policies and procedures in response to judicial opinions and EEOC regulations; they have designed training programs to implement those policies. But the crucial question is: what do these rules mean to their intended beneficiaries? Does the right to be protected from sexual harassment on the job mean anything to women who encounter harassing behaviors in their daily lives?

The labeling of behaviors as sexual harassment is obviously shaped by many different factors. The level of distress produced by the incident is one factor that affects the use of the label and, as described in the previous chapter, the level of distress that women feel is related to their views about women's status in the workplace. But women do not automatically label every distressing behavior sexual harassment. Rather, women's assessments reflect legalistic judgments about the conduct and whether it rises to the level of sexual harassment. Thus, the perception of harm and the use of the label are separate stages of the disputing process and reflect different concerns. Politics is more important in assessing harm, while law is more influential in assigning the label of sexual harassment.

In this aspect of the legal consciousness of injustice, legal rules are important. They actually provide definitions of behavior that matter to women, that women try to use to describe their own experiences. Moreover, women's use or failure to use these rules has significant consequences for the meaning of sexual harassment in particular workplaces. When women consistently decline to call behaviors sexual harassment, then the legal category of sexual harassment loses its power to define social situations.

Studying What's Legal in Legal Consciousness

The "legal" in legal consciousness transcends the technicalities of specific statutes and regulations. The broad conceptualization of "legality" used in most legal consciousness research emphasizes "the meanings, sources of authority, and cultural practices that are commonly recognized as legal, regardless of who employs them or for what ends" (Ewick and Silbey 1998). In this view, law is not simply the sum total of laws "on the books." Sarat and Kearns have observed: "Even where people are not familiar in detail with legal rules and doctrines, their habits of mind and social practices will tend to be highly legal in character" (Sarat and Kearns 1993, p. 28). Among these "habits of the mind" is legal reasoning. People may rely on "sources of authority" such as legal norms to evaluate experience, events and make judgments about whether the harm they have suffered is legal in nature.

Indeed, this grassroots legal reasoning may be very different from what we expect of a lawyer. In particular, ordinary people may get the rules wrong. They may have an inaccurate picture of the existing state of the law; or they may invoke the law in inappropriate circumstances. But even when they are wrong, law is nevertheless meaningful to them, shaping the meaning of their injuries and problems. Thus, the flexible definition of the "legal" in legal consciousness permits analysis of legal claims without getting bogged down in questions about whether people's legal interpretations are "right" or "wrong." This process is important because it precedes formal demands on the legal system.

Still, this flexibility does not mean that official legal doctrines are irrelevant to the analysis of legal consciousness (Mezey 2001; McCann 1999). Instead, legal regimes represent very specific social norms that may be considerably more salient than other norms in shaping behavior. In particular, legal norms are relatively specific in describing proscribed and permitted behaviors. They therefore offer at least the possibility of constructing settled categories of acceptable conduct. Of course, legal experts know that most legal categories are open to debate and re-construction, but ordinary people think of legal norms as fixed and determinative, even when they are wrong about the substantive rules.

In addition, legal norms delineate particular outcomes associated with legal violations and opportunities. Crimes carry specific sentences. Tax laws delineate the requirements for claiming tax deductions. Tort laws determine who bears the costs of automobile accidents or a doctor's malpractice. Moreover, these outcomes are enforceable with the considerable power of the state which can seize assets, put people in prison, and even take their lives. Finally, legal institutions and actors emerge to enforce and enact the laws. Police, prosecutors, and other lawyers act as gatekeepers to official legal arenas; their interpretations and practices implementing legal rules shape the kinds of justice that ordinary people enjoy. In addition, in trying to fulfill their legal obligations, organizations generate practices and routines that comply with legal standards yet protect their own interests (Edelman, Erlanger, and Lande 1993). And ordinary people interact with these legal actors and institutions. Through these interactions, people learn about the way that law shapes their experiences.

These aspects of the "legal" should be reflected in our analyses of the legal consciousness of injustice. Social movements deploying legal strategies often seek the development of new rights – the right to vote for African-Americans, the right to equal employment opportunity for the disabled, the right to marriage for same-sex couples (Scheingold 1974; McCann 1994). When successful, movements often see their demands enshrined in new statutes and regulations. But those rights are meaningless if they are not understood and invoked, if they do not reach their intended beneficiaries and shape the way they understand their lives.

This attention to specific legal rules was prominent in the legal mobilization literature, which largely adopted an instrumentalist perspective on the laws, depicting legal rules as a set of resources that people drew on to resolve problems or to advance their interests (Zemans 1983; Sarat and Kearns 1993; Jacob 1969). Particular types of problems were intimately connected to legal rules, and when a household was having that problem, they almost inevitably mobilized the law (Miller and Sarat 1980–81; Curran 1977). People seeking divorces almost always had a lawyer and went to court. People who thought they were targets of race or sex discrimination almost never did (Miller and Sarat 1980–81; Bumiller 1987, 1988). These differences hinted at but never fully uncovered the underlying process where people evaluate their problems and ask whether those problems have legal solutions or consequences – the process in which people assign legal meanings to their experiences.

In the disputing process, naming consists of identifying oneself as being harmed; blaming is attributing responsibility for that harm to another party. Yet, as I show in this chapter, characterizing that injury as legal can be a separate analysis dependent on legal rules and institutions. Bumiller (1987, 1988) illustrated this gap between injury and naming in her study of victims of employment discrimination. In her study, people who had suffered negative treatment on the job were reluctant to describe those experiences as discrimination because the legal category required them to assume the role of victim – an identity that only made the problem worse.

Sexual harassment researchers have also identified a gap between the objective conduct and women's subjective perceptions of sexual harassment (Welsh 1999, pp. 173–76; Fitzgerald, Swan and Magley 1997). Some studies have suggested that both men and women with traditional views of sex roles are more likely to perceive some behaviors as sexual harassment (Tangri and Hayes 1997). While this research has never entirely incorporated variables capturing the legal rules, studies have shown that the context of the conduct – the severity, the frequency, the status of the harasser – influences the labeling of sexual harassment (Stockdale, Vaux, and Cashin 1995; Giuffre and Williams 1994). These are factors relevant to the legal determination of whether conduct constituted a hostile working environment.

In the analysis that follows, I show that women did not automatically describe their encounters with sex at work as sexual harassment. Rather, legal rules shaped their use of that label. Women engaged in a form of legal reasoning in which they compared their experiences to their understanding of the legal definitions of sexual harassment. These definitions were rarely accurate. Indeed, most women too narrowly construed the limits of harassing conduct. In spite of their inaccuracy, these understandings of the rules were still potent in their power to shape women's assessment of whether they had been sexually harassed.

Sources of Information About Sexual Harassment Law

As explained in Chapter 2, sexual harassment in the United States is conceptualized as a form of sex discrimination (MacKinnon 1979; Schultz 1998; Saguy 2000a, 2000b).[1] The Equal Employment Opportunity Commission (EEOC) and the courts have identified two basic types of sexual harassment. The first type, *quid pro quo* harassment, occurs when supervisors make compliance with sexual demands a requirement of the job (MacKinnon 1979; *Williams v. Saxbe* 1976; *Barnes v. Costle* 1977). The second form of sexual harassment is the hostile working environment (Schultz 1998; Francke 1997; Saguy 2000a). A hostile working environment is one where sexual behaviors interfere with an employee's ability to perform his or her job in a discriminatory way (Saguy 2000a; *Oncale v. Sundowner Offshore Services* 1998).

The standard for determining whether a working environment is hostile has two components. First, the behaviors must be "sufficiently severe or pervasive to alter the conditions of the victim's employment and create an abusive working environment" (*Meritor Savings Bank v. Vinson* 1986, p. 67; *Harris v. Forklift Systems, Inc.* 1993).[2] On the other hand, to constitute a hostile working environment, the behaviors must also interfere with the employee's performance of her job duties. The Supreme Court in *Harris* observed: "If the victim does not subjectively perceive the environment to be abusive, the conduct has not actually altered the conditions of the victim's employment, and there is no Title VII violation. But Title VII comes into play before the harassing conduct leads to a nervous breakdown" (*Harris v. Forklift Systems, Inc.* 1993).

The legal definition of sexual harassment continues to be a subject of debate in the courts, and in the EEOC, as well as among activists, human resource professionals, and academics. For example, critics have argued that the current law places too much emphasis on sexual behavior and consequently leaves unregulated the most problematic aspects of sexual harassment at work. Schultz (1998) argues that the requirement of sexual behaviors ignores many forms of gender harassment that denigrate women's competence on the job and thus push them away from male-dominated occupations and relegate them to low-status employment. She urges the inclusion of non-sexual gender harassment in the legal prohibition (Schultz 1998). Others have argued that the standard for sexual harassment should be grounded in concepts like respect and workers' dignity rather than sexual practices (Bernstein 1994, 1997; Cornell 1995).

Most women participating in this study were generally familiar with the legal regime surrounding sexual harassment. They had a rough understanding of the legal definitions of harassing behaviors, and most knew that their employer, the University, had a grievance procedure, even if they were not necessarily conversant with the details of the provisions. Interestingly, most women in the study learned what they knew about sexual harassment from their employers, although many also learned about the law from coverage in the mass media of public scandals. Through these sources of information, employees learned that there was more to the law than just the protection of their rights as female workers.

A few of women had read about sexual harassment law by doing research or attending talks in college or graduate school. For example, Abbie's familiarity with the legal rules came from "law-related courses I took in college and talks at [the University's] Women's Center in my student days." Similarly, Joanne was taking a legal issues class for her master's degree in public administration: "I did a research project on sexual harassment in the state of Illinois and the laws. We had to go to the law library and do that kind of stuff." Both Abbie and Joanne were confident that they knew the legal rules surrounding sexual harassment.

Most other women, however, got their information filtered through other sources. Notably, most of the women interviewed reported receiving pamphlets and brochures from the University. They drew on these materials for their definitions of sexual harassment. For example, Erna stated: "I got a lot of information when I was [working] in human resources. I mean, I had to read a lot of stuff. And then here they do send sexual harassment pamphlets around, and I don't know, I think I just read it because I was just interested." Rose reported that when the coaches and receptionist in her office were exchanging sexual banter: "It was about this time that I think the University came out with their sexual harassment policy. Or at least there was a point in that period when they redistributed the policy with pamphlets, and I can remember reading through it." This pamphlet prompted her to think about the definition of sexual harassment as a form of prohibited conduct.

Like other employers, the University also offered training programs, particularly to employees in management who were among those designated to handle complaints. Some women reported that in the course of these programs, they learned a great deal about protecting themselves and not just other employees. For example, Abbie said that she attended a management training seminar at the University where she "learned about sexual harassment and what goes into personnel files." Megan claimed that she learned most about sexual harassment at an annual sales meeting sponsored by her previous employer. She described the session:

> They had attorneys come in for the corporation and speak to the entire sales force – female attorneys – speak to the entire sales force about sexual harassment, the seriousness of sexual harassment, and what exactly it means because it had been such a problem within the company. And there had been so many complaints and lawsuits there that they addressed the entire sales force on the issue – probably two or three hours on it in one day. It was significant. And that was my first exposure to "here's what it is, here's how it's defined, here's what's going to happen to you if you do it."

Women also got a great deal of information about sexual harassment law from the mass media. Many women were attentive to news stories about prominent lawsuits, such as the EEOC's case against Mitsubishi. The dramatic allegations in that case – of physical assault on the shopfloor and company parties staffed by strippers – were much different than the kinds of harassing conduct that they encountered in their working lives. The women were also familiar with allegations of sexual harassment against politicians and other public figures. Many mentioned Tailhook, Bob Packwood, and Paula Jones' allegations against Bill Clinton which were just starting to be made public. And all of the women interviewed mentioned Anita Hill and her testimony against Clarence Thomas at his confirmation hearings before the Senate.

The women interviewed drew similar lessons from Anita Hill's experience. All the women believed her story about Thomas' conduct. To Lily, Thomas' conduct was an example of the most blatant forms of sexual harassment: "He was talking about pubic hair on his coke. I mean, that was clearly not right … I was like, this is ridiculous. The woman was harassed. There's no doubt in my mind." Joanne remembered also believed Hill's story about Thomas and remembered discussing it with her more skeptical colleagues at work at the time:

> The discussion about the Anita Hill … thing was always "she must have done something," and they didn't believe her …. and I wouldn't really participate all that much because there really wasn't anything to be gained. But I remember wearing – I've got a button – I still have it somewhere – it was a pink button that said "I Believe Anita." I would wear it to the office.

Although they believed Hill's allegations against Thomas, some women questioned her motives in waiting so long to come forward. To others, Hill's relationship with Thomas was an example of the ambiguity inherent in many cases of sexual harassment. For example, Megan said:

> I believed the truth was somewhere in the middle between her testimony and his testimony ... Again, I think there's probably an element of truth in both because it's one person's word against another. I think you can have two people in the same situation and have them see it completely different, and I think that is what can cause confusion in sexual harassment.

Yet whether or not they believed her story, all the women I interviewed empathized with Hill because of the way that she was treated in the press and the Senate after she made her allegations. Many claimed that this treatment reinforced something that they already knew – women who complain about sexual harassment are rarely believed. Dallas admitted that she herself was suspicious of Hill's claims:

> No one believes you. No one believes that it actually could happen; that it happened to you, especially when they said "why now are you coming forward?" Because I even doubted her – why are you coming after two years, or something like that, to fight against this man? ... I felt like they're not going to believe you, sweetheart; they never do, and especially when you're coming too late. Now, they're never going to believe what you're saying to them. They're going to grill you until there's nothing left of you. And sure enough ...

Thus, women learned from watching the spectacle surrounding Hill's allegations against Thomas that complaining about harassment presented serious risks.

Finally, at least one woman learned about relevant laws and regulations through a friend who had consulted a lawyer about a possible sex discrimination suit. Kay claimed that she had gotten most of her information about sexual harassment from the mass media and from talking to friends. She said:

> I had a very good friend who had a very strong gender discrimination case, and decided – actually consulted with a lawyer, and decided not to pursue it, because she was basically told, "Well, whether you win or lose, you will never work again; you'd better be sure you get a big settlement." At that point, she walked away from it. So that was a good source of information, to really hear – of course, secondhand – but to really hear from the legal profession, what really constitutes a case.

Based on these varied sources of information, women receive mixed messages about the value of sexual harassment regulations. Some women think of it as part of the legal regime designed to promote women's equality.

Yet women also recognize risks associated with invoking those rights – damage to her reputation and credibility and possible damage to their careers.

Legal Consciousness in Action: Applying Legal Rules to Experience

The women in the study brought this information about sexual harassment to bear on their own encounters with sexual behaviors at work. They understood that not every behavior amounted to sexual harassment. Instead, most women recognized that there were rules governing the definition of sexual harassment – prohibited behaviors and effects on the job – and they asked whether those rules governed their experiences. The women may not have gotten the rules right – in fact, most offered relatively narrow readings of the laws and even made up some legal requirements that did not exist. But they adopted legalistic "habits of mind" – reasoning by analogy, fitting experience into categories and drawing conclusions about whether the law (or employment policy) had been violated. In doing so, they acted as their own lawyers, using a legal definition to decide whether or not they have a complaint. In doing so, women enacted legality by drawing on a definition of sexual harassment that offered them narrower protection than they were entitled to by law.

When asked whether they had been sexually harassed, most of the women interviewed treated it as though it were a legal question. Many of them claimed to be unsure of the legal definition, and some asked me if they were getting it right. For example, when I asked her if she felt she had been sexually harassed, Emma responded "How do you define that?" Joan said "I'm not really sure because I don't know." After listing a series of factors that led her to conclude she had not been sexually harassed, Rita observed: "I'm not sure if I'm defining sexual harassment correctly." Yet their uncertainty about the specifics of the legal rule nevertheless demonstrated their awareness that the rules existed and governed the question of whether they had been sexually harassed. Generally, women's definitions of sexual harassment reflected three factors closely related to the legal rules: the nature of the conduct, the frequency of the conduct, and the job consequences.

Nature of the Conduct

Even though they were unsure of the details, many women knew that it required some form of sexual conduct. Kay, for example, distinguished sexual harassment from other forms of sex discrimination:

> I always distinguish between sexual harassment and gender harassment. Sexual harassment, to me, is unwanted sexual attention, whether it is explicitly "If you want to work here, you will put out," or whatever, or the more sort of off-the-cuff "Oh, you're here, you're available, so I'm going to get away with everything I can." To me, the difference in gender harassment, because I think

it works for both men *and* women, is the more glass-ceiling, the more "Well, you're a woman, so you can't be taken seriously." Or, in some cases, "You're a white male, you may be the most qualified, but we've got to fill a quota." To me, that's, to a certain extent, gender discrimination as well. And that's why I like "gender discrimination" rather than sexual discrimination, because I think "sexual" makes it sound like there is the sexual part rather than the gender part. And I think women on the whole are much – I think that gender harassment/gender discrimination works both ways. I think women are much more the recipients of sexual harassment.

For Kay, sex discrimination was a phenomenon that could affect both men and women, while sexual harassment, which included sexualized practices, was much more likely to be directed at women.

Most women also recognized that the legal standard for sexual harassment did not completely overlap with their personal feelings about unwanted sexual attention at work. For example, one survey respondent distinguished between offensive workplace conduct and sexual harassment: "Tasteless postcards, sexual in nature, were circulated in department. Tasteless, sexually explicit images were displayed on terminals via the Internet. However, no individuals were targeted. I don't consider this harassment although it is inappropriate work place behavior." Abbie noted that she had a personal definition of sexual harassment that included more behaviors than the legal standard. Indeed, Abbie's personal definition revolved around her level of comfort in the workplace: "Is it a situation making me ... uncomfortable? My personal definition of sexual harassment is in work situation where I don't think about sex, when in a work situation and have to think about sex." However, Abbie distinguished her perspective from the legal definition which she argued required "behavior that interfered with the job, somehow negatively affects the job."

Some women argued that men and women might have different views of sexual harassment. Matilda's supervisor had the personal habit of putting his hand down the front of his pants when he talked to both men and women. Matilda herself did not believe that this conduct was sexual harassment because he behaved this way in front of everyone, yet she recognized that women might have a different reaction to this conduct than men:

> For the women, I think it *was* sexual harassment. Or it could have been viewed as. But it's hard to determine, because he did do it in front of everybody else. But I could see the men just saying, "Huh, yeah ...", passing it off as gross behavior, and women being more touchy about it and more, you know, "They should behave."

Indeed, some women who were bothered by their experiences applied a fairly broad definition of the kinds of conduct that were prohibited – definitions that included their situations. One survey respondent felt unsure of the definition of sexual harassment, but still felt that it probably applied to her:

> Very fuzzy – with my particular experiences – jokes. My experiences have not
> been bad – just a few (not always excessive) sexual jokes not aimed at me but
> things I feel are in poor taste in an office setting. I guess I feel it's harassment
> because it made me feel uncomfortable and it's not appropriate for an office
> setting.

Her definition accounted for her discomfort, but it also evaluated the conduct,
although with a very broad standard. Similarly, Siena's definition of sexual
harassment included a wide range of behaviors, but emphasized the level of
discomfort the target felt: "Oh, it's a variety of things. Anything from
touching somebody, to making lewd remarks, um … to just making anybody
uncomfortable, you know, about what they're wearing, how they wear their
hair, um … obviously holding it over their head, if they're in a supervisory
position and … you feel threatened with your job." Using this definition,
Siena concluded that her co-worker's attention to her personal appearance
constituted sexual harassment "because I was uncomfortable."

For some women interviewed, their broader definitions of harassing
conduct were linked to their perspective that sexual harassment was an abuse
of power targeted at women. These women tended to believe that harassing
behaviors could be subtle practices that made the working environment
uncomfortable for women. They articulated the ill effects of harassment in
terms of environmental considerations rather than specific sexual demands
directed at individuals. Categorizing as sexual harassment the incident where
the faculty member asked if he could pinch her butt, Emma said she had a
"very loose" definition of sexual harassment:

> So this, I think, would come under it. I guess I would think of it as being more
> repetitive, but – which this was not, obviously – but I guess I still would think
> of it as that. I tend to think of climate … more. You know, whether it's
> comfortable for you to be female in that climate. Whether you can live in it
> without people making comments about your skirts or your legs or whatever.
> And whether you're respected for the job that you do, and treated equally.
> That's climate. And that's – And I guess if there are things that make it
> unpleasant, that don't make it the kind of climate I just described to you, I guess
> I might very broadly describe that as harassment … We tend to think of it as
> being – or at least I do – kind of dark, startling incidents, and I think of it as
> broader and more pervasive.

Emma recognized that because it was an isolated incident, the remark might
not meet the definition of sexual harassment but, as one of a set of related
practices that devalued women in the department, she believed it deserved
that label.

Similarly, Rose's daily exposure to sexual banter from the receptionists
and the coaches was confusing to her until she started thinking about the
definition of sexual harassment she found in the University's policy. After
reading through that policy, she said: "But it wasn't until maybe a month later,

where I started reflecting on the definitions of sexual harassment, and said, 'Hey, this is sexual harassment. I don't have to put up with this in my workplace'." It was a difficult conclusion for her to reach, particularly since the situation involved another woman. She said:

> As I say, it took a while to accept that. It took a while to kind of internalize that and figure that out. But I did. I felt that, while it wasn't a traditional situation, it was a situation in which people who were superior to me, namely the coaches, who had authority over me in one form or another, were expecting a certain level of behavior that was sexual in nature, that I was uncomfortable.

Rose's definition, therefore, included her discomfort in the working environment, but also accounted for the sexualized nature of that environment.

Most other women had much narrower definitions of sexual harassment that included more intrusive sexual behaviors. For some of the women in the study, sexual harassment was limited to unwanted physical contact. One survey respondent complained of a colleague's attention that bothered her a great deal. Yet she declined to describe it as sexual harassment: "And the man didn't touch me sexually – he just invaded my intimate/personal space and followed me around all the time. So because it wasn't a sexual contact, I didn't regard it as sexual harassment ..." To Dallas, the steady stream of sexual innuendo, joking and verbal abuse from her supervisor were not harassing behaviors. She distinguished his joking about chasing her around a hotel room from other incidents involving physical contact:

> To me, sexual harassment means you're just about to touch me, or you're going to be asking things that are no longer funny. That's sexual harassment to me. If the example of running around the bed ... we'll keep that on the humor side because it's just stupid. We're going to treat you as an ignorant butt.

For other women, sexual harassment did not require physical contact, but it did require extremely intrusive behaviors, like demands for sexual favors. For example, the executives in Rita's office frequently made sexual jokes, used vulgar language to refer to women's anatomy and made comments about her personal appearance. Yet Rita did not think she had been sexually harassed because they did not press sexual demands on her. She said:

> I didn't feel that it was harassing me because I didn't feel, really, that my job was on the [line] ... They never came and asked me to do anything ... I think it was more a feeling of belittling. So I don't know if I'm not defining sexual harassment correctly ... To me, [sexual harassment] would be if a person of the opposite sex would approach a person, do something physical – touch – or make propositions, whether or not the job depended on it. I was never propositioned.

Like Rita, other women declined to label behaviors sexual harassment when they were not the ones explicitly targeted by the behaviors. One survey respondent reported: "Sexual/'sexist' comments were not addressed to one person in particular or just to women. They were said in passing or in reference to something else, so I really didn't consider them a form of sexual harassment." Another said:

> Currently I work with another female and although I don't get the kinds of comments she does, I feel bothered by what is said to her even though she laughs along with the males who tell her those things. She seems to enjoy the situation so I don't consider it to be harassment but I do think it's very inappropriate. However, I'm not approached the same way she is.

For women like Dallas, Rita and these survey respondents, practices that simply bother them or that create an uncomfortable working environment do not amount to sexual harassment. Rather, sexual harassment consists of intrusive sexual behaviors targeting them as individuals. Yet this definition constitutes a significant restriction on the breadth of legal protection.

Some women have also incorporated the idea of intent into their definition of sexual harassment. They consult the intent of the harasser in evaluating the conduct and deciding whether or not they have been harassed. Generally, however, when they rely on this criteria, they generate arguments that excuse the harasser for his behavior, even when the behavior is disturbing. For example, at the time of our interview, Megan's supervisor repeatedly made sexual comments and jokes at her expense, discussing her physical appearance, such as the size of her breasts, and asking her about her sex life. Yet Megan was willing to condone his behavior in part because of his age and his background. She observed:

> Therefore, keeping in mind that this individual is again, 65 years old, from the South, from the old school, someone who I care for dearly, and I know he means no harm towards me, would never in a million years think about touching me inappropriately, I don't think anything of it. And if he says things like that to me, I always laugh at him and call him a dirty old man, and he'll laugh right back. And that's about it. It's our banter … I think my definition of sexual harassment has become a little bit, okay, a lot more lenient. But I think in that situation I would never ever accept that kind of behavior from someone I didn't know well in this office or from somebody that I – you know, if I was in a meeting and someone talked to me in that way, I would just let them know how it is, but again, it's the dynamics of this office, and it's the intent of the individual. Sexual harassment is so personal. It's almost intangible in some ways to really put words to paper about what it is because it's so much about how that person feels about what is being said or presented to him or her.

To Megan, the doctor did not mean her harm and had no intention of physically assaulting her, and therefore his behavior was annoying but tolerable, and certainly not worth complaining about. Survey respondents had similar reactions to some of their experiences. One said:

> The issue I'm using as a reference involved a male co-worker suggesting that our office have a stricter dress code since some of the women (part-time staff) wore clothing that made this person "aroused." (He didn't say that but it was implied.) My feelings were mostly disgust that someone would bring something like that up in discussion at work. It wasn't meant as harassment I'm sure, but it was offensive to myself and other female co-workers present.

Another referred to the harassers in her working environment: "Annoying but not intended to be malicious. They just like to tease. The two concerned are all talk; no action." Rather than broadening responsibility for harassing conduct, the women's incorporation of intent into the definition of sexual harassment more often excused the harasser.

Frequency of the conduct

Another factor in women's assessment of whether their experience was sexual harassment was the frequency of the behavior. Conduct that was a daily affront to a person's sensibilities is more likely to be labeled sexual harassment. Rose complained that the receptionist in the coaching office complained: "There wasn't a day that went by that there wasn't a time period that was spent in flirtation with the coaches." Similarly, Joanne claimed that the chief financial officer made sexual jokes and comments: "Oh god, all the time. *All the time*. Every day. He was the type of personality that whenever you had to interact with him, you could expect to have some sort of sexual innuendo or a joke or something thrown in there." Kay fought off the physical advances of the owner of a restaurant where she worked every night. He would approach her: "Whenever he had a chance. It would be passing in the hallway. I would be walking out to go sing and he would rub up against me or something. So really, any chance he had."

On the other hand, when the behavior was less frequent – and easier to ignore – women declined to call it sexual harassment. The joke-telling professors in Nora's department were not bothersome because "over the course of the year, maybe it happened a half-dozen times." For Ann, her co-worker's invitation for a date happened only once and was never repeated. One survey respondent reported:

> A male co-worker made a joke that was a "double entendre." It made me feel slightly uncomfortable, and I didn't acknowledge the remark. I also avoided the person except when it was necessary for work purposes. The behavior did not re-occur, and I did not feel that the co-worker persisted or harassed me.

Thus, these women were willing to overlook less disruptive behaviors and did not categorize them as sexual harassment.

Negative Effects on the Job

Finally, the women in this study also considered the job consequences before using the label sexual harassment. While some women, as described above, thought the job consequences could simply be the hostile climate created by sexual behaviors, others thought that sexual harassment required more material harm. In particular, many women believed that a behavior had to pose a threat to a woman's job. For example, Erna observed:

> Well, there's different levels of sexual harassment. Some sexual harassment is outright words and actions. Some of them are subtle. Um … I mean, you can be touched; you can be propositioned, with the idea that you're not going to continue in your present position until you do what they ask you to do. And some of them are very subtle.

Subtle behaviors could nevertheless create meaningful threats for women's working lives.

But when they were not threatened with dismissal or when their job performance did not suffer, women were more reluctant to call the behavior sexual harassment. To Nora, the sexual jokes made by faculty members were not sexual harassment because they caused her mild discomfort and did not affect her interactions with the faculty. But even when the unwanted sexual attention made women feel uncomfortable, they would not use the label "sexual harassment" because their jobs were not vulnerable to adverse job decisions by the harasser. When Abbie's co-workers used vulgar and sexually explicit language during business meetings, she knew that she was not being sexually harassed, even though she found the behavior offensive, because it was not "behavior that interfered with the job, somehow negatively affects the job."

For some women, the requirement that there be negative job consequences led them to limit their definition of sexual harassment to the conduct of supervisors. Ann's definition revolved around supervisors using sexual harassment to abuse their power over female employees:

> I feel most strongly that it has to involve a power dynamic. I mean, I kind of feel like it has to involve some level of threat, that can be as slight as making the workplace uncomfortable for you. But it has to be – I feel like it has to be somebody who is in a higher position, or is in some way threatening. I mean, I've never really thought about the issue of whether someone beneath is you in the hiring hierarchy – if they are big and kind of scary, that counts as harassment. But I think it definitely has to have that power dynamic involved. I mean, I wouldn't want to see things like an employee asking another employee out as being considered sexual harassment. Especially if it's not pushy. If it's a one-time shot.

Ann had a series of encounters with unwanted sexual behaviors in the course of her working life that she declined to characterize as sexual harassment based on this definition. Indeed, when her co-worker asked her out a single time, the isolation of the incident made it relatively innocuous, but when asked whether she considered this example sexual harassment, she focused on his equal status at work:

> Well, for one, he's not, he wasn't in a position above me. We did have a relationship outside the workplace. We had gone out as friends a number of times. He had been over to my place, he was friends with my roommates. So it was an understandable leap to have romantic feelings, to my mind. And it wasn't any exploitation of a power position, so it wasn't objectionable on that level.

In another incident, while interviewing her for a job, a professor she had never met before gave her a long, close hug and made several sexual remarks. When asked whether this conduct was sexual harassment, she said:

> Um … more so than the event I've already described. Again, I wouldn't think of it as anything I could consider actionable, because I hadn't taken employment. To the extent that, had I really needed the employment, it would have been problematic. If I had really needed that job, I think there would have been an issue there. I didn't need it that badly, so it wasn't an issue. I'd say, considering that it was supposed to be a work situation, I would consider it – I'd say, if we can think of a continuum, rather than a yes or no – more so, sexual harassment.

Although these behaviors were closer to sexual harassment than the request for a date, Ann still did not think they amounted to sexual harassment, largely because the professor was not yet her supervisor, and so, in her mind, there were no negative job consequences.

Many women also understood sexual harassment to be a form of sex discrimination where women were treated worse than men, although some recognized that men might also be subjected to harassing behaviors. Rita couched her definition of sexual harassment in gender-neutral language: "To me, it would be if a person of the opposite sex would approach a person, do something physical – touch – or make propositions, whether or not the job depended on it." Matilda also argued: "I suppose a male could be sexually harassed too, if the boss is a woman." Notably, these women – like many others – thought of sexual harassment as something that occurred between members of the opposite sex. When a woman was responsible for the harassing behaviors, the women I interviewed were reluctant to characterize the conduct as sexual harassment. Because a woman was involved in creating the sexualized atmosphere of her office, it took Rose a while to accept that it was a form of sexual harassment. Similarly, Abbie thought that her female co-worker's crude language was offensive but not sexual harassment. Thus, most women had a definition that associated sexual harassment with heterosexual expression.

Ambiguity in the Standards

The women in this study clearly did not simply adopt the label "sexual harassment" to every form of conduct that bothered them. Instead, they relied on several different standards that resembled the legal test for hostile working environments. Yet these standards are not always easy to apply and may lead to greater confusion among the employees they are designed to help. The conduct in question may be ambiguous; the target may be unsure of the harasser's intentions, what the incident meant, whether the target, in fact, invited the behavior, whether the behavior was even sexual or not. In view of the ambiguity inherent in some sexual conduct at work, the standards are not particularly helpful in clarifying whether an incident meets the definition of sexual harassment.

When a doctor she worked with began asking her out and pressing sexual demands on her, Lily was confused by his attention. When asked whether his attention was sexual harassment, she observed that she was of two minds on this question: "I have two answers. On a logical, reasonable, mental level? Yes, probably it would meet the definition. On an emotional level, no." She explained her confusion beginning with her assessment that it was sexual harassment:

> Because it's unwanted attention that is brought to someone without their inviting it. On an emotional level, though, I still have this component of yes, but I play a part in it. It's part of my pattern of behavior that this is how I react with men of success or authority. And I see that. And I guess part of it too is because it reminds me so much of my marriage, which was very much about power and control. It was very much about my husband being the superior, more important one, and being sort of insulted a lot and being told that I wasn't very bright, or stupid, or whatever. And I always felt very lucky to have him because that was sort of like the best that I could do. And I still have trouble letting that go.

Thus, the legal definition could not disrupt her confusion about the doctor's conduct and her own sense of guilt over the incident.

Women also become confused when the behavior in question meets some parts of the definition but not others. Jane was unsure of whether a faculty member's e-mails amounted to sexual harassment. On one hand, she thought the content of the e-mail messages was sexually intrusive:

> The part that I think is harassment is when he starts telling me what to do with my marriage, and telling me that I should go out to lunch with him, and the sexual comments. Like, he'll use words like "titillate" and things like that in what he's saying, and it's obvious to me what he's trying to get across. And he actually does mention his sex life, and tells me that he's not "getting any", and all sorts of things, and I just ignore him. I don't ever say anything like that. I think that's out of line and inappropriate.

But she also recognized that there were other factors that made the label "sexual harassment" less appropriate, particularly the ambiguity of the conduct and the fact that her job was not at risk:

> Because it is over e-mail, I think it's harder for me to tell. Because it's easy to misinterpret things. Although, I mean, it would be hard to misinterpret what he said. But it just seems strange. Because it's a strange situation, to have it over e-mail instead of being face-to-face. And like I told you earlier, he's not really my supervisor or anything, so he's not, you know, threatening me with anything.

Women also claimed that their definitions of sexual harassment had changed over the course of their careers. Women incorporated their own experiences – and the experiences of others – into their understandings of sexual harassment. This updating of the definition could lead women in different directions. Encounters with sexual conduct at work radicalized some women, leading them to expand their definitions of sexual harassment to include subtle behaviors that made women feel uncomfortable. Rose cited her experience in the coaching office as the basis for her definition of sexual harassment:

> What I came out of this experience with is that sexual harassment in the workplace is all about the work. If you're in an environment where sexual innuendo, tension, undertone, behaviors between people, are taken in a sexual way, they impact your ability to work or your ability to feel comfortable in doing your work, then to me, that's sexual harassment. But it's an environmental kind of situation, it's not necessarily a specific incident, or a specific element of anything, but if you feel that you've got to justify or give value to your sexuality in one way or another, in order to be able to work in that office, then that's, to me, sexual harassment.

For other women, however, the persistence of unwanted sexual attention throughout their careers convinced them that sexual conduct was unavoidable at work and that only the worst behaviors deserved the label "sexual harassment." When asked to define sexual harassment, Megan said:

> It's really hard. I think it can take a lot of forms. I think that I've become a little bit callous to it where I'm probably a lot more lenient with it than I used to be just because it happens a lot that I have a tendency to probably blow it off or laugh it off more than I would have had I been younger … And I would probably say that for me now, at this point, it's got to be pretty overt, like a comment about, perhaps my body or something.

After being groped by a prior boss, propositioned by salesmen, and sexually teased by her existing supervisor, Megan concluded that the definition of sexual harassment covered only the most intrusive forms of sexual intrusion at work.

Patterns of Naming: Survey Responses

Like the women interviewed, the survey respondents in this study were selective in the experiences that they described as sexual harassment. Only 42 per cent thought that the incident was sexual harassment; a majority declined to use that label. The analysis of the interviews suggests that women's decisions to name their experiences sexual harassment were based on standards reflected in the legal rules; specifically, the nature of the conduct and the women's subjective reaction to the incident. Women's gender consciousness seemed far less salient. For some women, their feminist identity made them less tolerant of sexual conduct in the workplace and therefore made them more willing to describe an experience as sexual harassment. But for most women interviewed, the evaluation of whether an incident amounted to sexual harassment reflected the legal limits on political outrage. In the analysis that follows, I outline the variables used to model women's use of the label "sexual harassment." I then present a probit model and the marginal effects on women's decision to call an experience sexual harassment.

Naming Sexual Harassment

After choosing an incident from a list of behaviors that "made the greatest impression" on them, survey respondents were asked a series of more detailed questions about that incident. At the end of those questions, women were asked: "Did you consider this experience to be sexual harassment?" Respondents could only answer "yes" or "no." Although that choice that may not accurately reflect women's ambivalence or the complex reasoning process involved in answering the question, the question produced 89 analyzable responses that reflect the respondent's final assessment of the conduct.

Independent variables   The model includes variables reflecting the legal criteria for sexual harassment. Described in Chapter 4, these variables include women's perception of harm and the seriousness of the intrusion of the incident. The model also includes the variables for women's gender consciousness and whether or not they had told co-workers.
I used a probit model to analyze the dichotomous variable that captured whether women considered themselves to have been sexually harassed. The following is a specification of the model:

Sexually Harassed = α + β *Bothered by Incident + β *Nature of the Conduct + β *Gender Consciousness + β *Told Co-Workers

In Table 5.1, I present the marginal effects for this model. Only the nature of the conduct and being bothered by it are significant in this model. Although they both make women more likely to describe an experience as sexual harassment, women's gender consciousness and discussions with co-workers do not rise to the level of significance.

Table 5.1   Marginal effects on women's use of the label "sexual harassment" (N = 76)

	Marginal Effects dF/dx	Standard Error	P
Bothered	.231	.075	.002
Nature of the Conduct	.082	.039	.034
Gender Consciousness	.241	.134	.075
Told Co-Workers	.254	.133	.062

Pseudo R2 = .3312

The marginal effects in the model show that very small increases in a woman's level of distress raises the probability of labeling it sexual harassment by about .23. Similarly, slightly more intrusive experiences raise the probability by about .08. Thus, while women's negative reactions have a greater effect on their decisions to label the experience sexual harassment, the nature of the conduct nevertheless exerts an independent influence on this naming process.

Summary

Sexual harassment is a concept where law and politics are thoroughly intertwined. Apart from its political significance, sexual harassment is a legal category of behavior, complete with official definitions, balancing tests, and sanctions. Simply because it is a legal category, however, does not mean that lawyers and judges exercise sole dominion over its meaning. Instead, information about the law of sexual harassment – mediated by journalists, pundits, experts, employers and even lawyers – has been circulating through the general public for years, often in the midst of some political crisis. Not simply enshrined in legal texts, the definition of sexual harassment has an active life in women's work experiences.

Moreover, the definitions associated with the legal concept of sexual harassment are not mere abstractions. In some form, women's understanding of the legal rules helps to shape the way they understand their experiences, particularly their interactions with their supervisors and their colleagues. When they hear sexual jokes, when they see pornography on a computer screen, when they repeatedly turn down requests for dates, they rely on "legal" rules and "legal" reasoning to evaluate the conduct and to decide whether it is harassment or not. In this way, women are enacting legal rules and creating the legality of sexual harassment in the workplace.

Notes

[1]   Sexual harassment is also a discriminatory educational practice under Title IX. In addition, courts have found that sexual harassment violates the Fair Housing Act (Saguy 2000a). But in the US, sexual harassment is most often associated with workplace behaviors.

[2]   The Supreme Court has stated: "Conduct that is not severe or pervasive enough to create an objectively hostile or abusive work environment – an environment that a reasonable person would find hostile or abusive – is beyond Title VII's purview" (*Harris v. Forklift Systems, Inc.* 1993). To determine whether the conduct was offensive, some courts rely on a "reasonable woman" standard, which acknowledges that men and women assign different meanings to sexual harassment at work (*Ellison v. Brady,* 1991).

6   Idle Rights: Employee Complaints and Management Responses

I think that the pain and suffering that women who report sexual harassment have to go through really sucks and it's just not worth it to me to go through that.
– Survey respondent

The law of sexual harassment was supposed to protect women from the obstacles that unwanted sexual attention poses to women's equality in the workplace. However, the courts have entrusted the protection of these rights to employers, requiring them to implement sexual harassment policies and procedures to process women's complaints, and now, women must use those procedures to enforce their rights. Thus, women's protests against sexual harassment have been effectively channeled into institutional domains that may be adverse to their interests.

But as the survey respondent observes at the beginning of this chapter, complaining about sexual harassment can be worse than the experience itself. Women fear retaliation or worry that complaining will generate ill-will among co-workers. So rather than challenge sexual harassment, women engage in self-help either on their own or with others, or they simply learn to tolerate troublesome working conditions. Thus, after 30 years of efforts to regulate sexual harassment in the US, many women are essentially on their own when confronting sexual harassment at work.

In exploring this gap between the law on the books and the law in action, a logical starting point is the grievance procedures that seem to be inadequate to the task of protecting women. We already know from institutional analyses of organizations that employment policies are symbols of an organization's commitment to societal values, such as equality and due process (Edelman, Erlanger, and Lande 1993; Edelman 1990). But those symbols may come to mean very different things to the employees supposedly being protected. Rather than enforcing equality, the policies may seem to enforce existing power relations in the workplace. Thus, they may no longer appear to be satisfactory solutions to employee problems.

142   *Confronting Sexual Harassment*

Studying the legal consciousness of inequality requires consideration of the way that legal reforms actually operate in the organizational and institutional arenas they were designed to modify. Such reforms often give rise to institutions that are designed to implement the law, but those institutions may adapt the law in unexpected ways. The question is whether the beneficiaries of the laws are aware of these possible distortions. The answer to that question may shape the ways that people invoke the law on their own behalf and the meanings that they assign to new rights and obligations.

Studying Sexual Harassment and Grievance Procedures

In clarifying the standards of an employer's liability for sexual harassment, the Supreme Court made grievance procedures almost mandatory. Employers can defend themselves from sexual harassment claims if they can show that they had a functioning anti-harassment policy and complaint procedure and that employees knew about it. Moreover, the Supreme Court also held that employees had to use the grievance procedure or lose their legal claim (*Faragher v. Boca Raton* 1998; *Burlington Industries v. Ellerth* 1998). Thus, the Supreme Court imposed an obligation on sexual harassment targets to do something they almost never do – complain.

One of the most prevalent findings in sexual harassment research is that women only very rarely report their experiences with unwanted sexual attention to third parties (Gutek 1985; Fitzgerald, Swan and Fischer 1995; Gruber and Smith 1995; MSPB 1995; Welsh 1999). For example, in a 1994 survey of federal employees, the Merit Systems Protection Board found that only 12 per cent reported the incident to a supervisor, and only 6 per cent filed formal complaints (MSPB 1995).[1] Thirty-five per cent of the respondents engaged in self-help by asking or telling the harasser to stop the behavior. Yet the survey reveals that many federal employees engaged in less confrontational strategies of ignoring the harasser (44 per cent), avoiding the harasser (28 per cent), making a joke of the behavior (15 per cent), or going along with the behavior (7 per cent) (MSPB 1995, p. 30).[2]

Researchers have explored the reasons for this reluctance to complain by asking survey respondents why they did not take formal action. In many studies, their answers reflect ambivalence about the grievance procedures and the personnel who administered them (Welsh 1999; Cochran et al. 1997; Fitzgerald, Swan and Fischer 1995). First, employees often feel that such procedures are reserved for only the most intrusive harassing behaviors. In the 1994 MSPB survey, 50 per cent of the respondents who did not complain reported that the incident was not "serious" enough to report. Some of these employees faced infrequent behaviors that were not particularly troubling or disruptive. For these employees, this explanation reflects a commonsense judgment that mildly offensive acts should be redressed through informal means.[3]

Second, employees perceive grievance procedures to be adversarial and hostile processes. In the MSPB survey, employees worried that they would be blamed for the incident or that they would not be believed. Employees were also worried that the situation would not be kept confidential (MSPB 1995). The MSPB survey respondents were also concerned that management's reaction to the complaint would be at best ineffectual and at worst threatening.[4]

Survey-based research, then, suggests that women are reluctant to complain about sexual harassment because workplace policies do not address their problems or because they fear further victimization in an adversarial grievance procedure. Unfortunately, this type of research does not provide much insight into the organizational and institutional practices that generate and sustain women's sense of powerlessness (Williams 1997). Qualitative studies of groups such as temporary workers and women firefighters, however, have contextualized the study of resistance to sexual harassment in specific organizational settings characterized by particular power arrangements (Rogers and Henson 1997; Yoder and Aniakudo 1995). But such studies have not yet focused on the operation of grievance procedures.

Employment grievance procedures are a popular mechanism for protecting a range of employee rights against a range of employer abuses, including discrimination and health and safety risks (Edelman 1990; Edelman, Uggen, and Erlanger 1999; Sutton et al. 1994). Advocates of such procedures argue that they provide much-needed dispute resolution resources to the less powerful members of an organization. Such procedures are more accessible than the formal legal system (Kihnley 2000). Employees need not – and often cannot – involve lawyers in the complaint process; all grievances are directed to supervisors or other managers. In addition, grievance procedures are more flexible than the formal legal process, and thus better able to respond to employee needs that might go unaddressed in a formal legal arena (Menkel-Meadow 1985; Hill 1990). Without strict rules of evidence, standing and procedure, internal dispute resolution mechanisms are both less costly (Hunter and Leonard 1997; Kihnley 2000) and less adversarial (Goldberg, Green, and Sander 1986; Hill 1990). Moreover, because they have been officially sanctioned by regulatory agencies and the courts, internal dispute resolution mechanisms can insulate employers from liability if a conflict does ripen into litigation (Edelman, Uggen, and Erlanger 1999). Thus, in the world of human resource professionals, grievance procedures are an efficient, mutually beneficial service that employers can provide employees to ensure a safe, productive workplace (Edelman, Uggen, and Erlanger 1999; Edelman, Erlanger, and Lande 1993).

On the other hand, critics argue that grievance procedures are inadequate to protect employee rights. By resolving conflict privately within single organizations, these procedures limit the development of jurisprudence in employment law and privatize public rights (Harkavy 1999). Moreover, the confidentiality of these proceedings diminishes public awareness of discriminatory practices, such as those that constitute sexual harassment and the remedies for redressing those practices. Thus, employees are left unaware that others have problems or that pervasive problems are being redressed (Kihnley 2000). Critics also argue that grievance procedures are susceptible to the prejudices and power disparities that exist in their organizational contexts (Delgado et al. 1985; Bobo 1992; Edelman, Erlanger, and Lande 1993; Gutek 1992; Kihnley 2000).

Institutional studies of organizations, like those conducted by Lauren Edelman and her colleagues, have shown that grievance procedures are as likely to protect organizational interests as employee rights. Organizations adopt such policies for symbolic purposes to demonstrate organizational commitment to prevailing norms and values – like due process and equality (Edelman, Erlanger, and Lande 1993; Edelman 1990; see also Dobbin and Sutton 1998; Sutton et al. 1994). But in their implementation of the grievance procedure, managers face competing obligations to redress employee grievances even as they try to shield the employer from liability (Kihnley 2000; Edelman, Erlanger, and Lande 1993). To resolve this tension between conflicting goals, human resource professionals re-frame workplace disputes as management lapses or personality conflicts and deny that there are discrimination problems in the workplace. Thus, they interpret employee rights in terms of management interests rather than civil rights. And while managers often try to settle disputes among employees, they rarely do so to vindicate the principle of equal opportunity, leading Edelman and her colleagues to observe: "The legal right to a nondiscriminatory workplace in effect becomes a 'right' to complaint resolution" (Edelman, Erlanger, and Lande 1993, p. 529).

Human resource professionals may also adopt a proactive approach to protecting an employer. In the wake of Supreme Court decisions and other major legal developments, human resources professionals and defense lawyers offer extensive advice about adopting grievance procedures and instituting training programs to protect employers (Edelman, Uggen, and Erlanger 1999; Edelman, Abraham, and Erlanger 1992; Bisom-Rapp 1999). In a recent study of a university's sexual harassment policy, Kihnley (2000) found that supervisors were more likely to take the side of the alleged harasser than the employee making the complaint. As one official reported: "When a complaint is made, often times [the] complainant becomes an outsider, a troublemaker, and the harasser becomes the institution" (Kihnley 2000, p. 80).

These institutional analyses of organizational practices raise serious questions about the ability of grievance procedures to meet employee needs when those needs conflict with organizational interests. These studies, however, focus on the ways that organizational representatives interpret the policies rather than what officials and supervisors do when processing employee complaints. Yet employees are no less responsible for re-constructing the law than supervisors. Employees are not simply passive objects, acted upon by managers. Instead, as previous chapters have shown, employees have experiences, interpret them as grievances – sometimes using legal schema – and make decisions about whether or not to lodge a complaint. Thus, employees are active participants in the construction of an organization's legal environment, and their practices in the shadow of the grievance procedure ought to be included in an analysis of how that procedure works.

This attention to ordinary employees is situated in the study of legal consciousness which recognizes that to maintain its vitality, legality "must also be continually produced and worked on – invoked and deployed – by individual and group actors" (Ewick and Silbey 1998, p. 43; Sewell 1992). It is in the enactment of legal consciousness that the meaning of law is repeatedly transformed and re-shaped as individuals deploy legal meanings in new settings. According to Ewick and Silbey, "Every time a person interprets some event in terms of legal concepts or terminology – whether to applaud or criticize, whether to appropriate or resist – legality is produced. The production may include innovations as well as faithful replication. Either way, repeated invocation of the law sustains its capacity to comprise social relations" (Ewick and Silbey 1998, p. 45). Yet law may also lose its power "to comprise social relations" if it falls into disuse. When a person ignores or rejects some right or benefit authorized by law, those rights remain idle. Law's ability to shape meanings and opportunities in those situations is therefore diminished (Quinn 2000; Bumiller 1988).

By focusing on specific social problems and the legal regimes that grow up around them, the framework for studying the legal consciousness of inequality offers an opportunity for the theoretical development of legal consciousness. First, it demonstrates that laws such as those protecting equal employment opportunity can become an arena for struggles against inequality, or they can ratify existing conditions of domination and subordination (McCann 1994; Merry 1995; Quinn 2000; Bumiller 1988).[5] By examining both employees who did not complain and those who did, I can conduct a more complex analysis of the sometimes contradictory consciousness of law: law provides oppositional meanings and opportunities for resistance, but mechanisms for enforcing the law – in this case, the sexual harassment policy – can undermine this resistance.

Second, focusing on workplace grievance procedures places legal consciousness in an organizational setting. Although they concentrate on the development of disputes in everyday life, many studies of legal consciousness are nevertheless conducted outside of the neighborhoods, schools and workplaces where everyday problems develop (Ewick and Silbey 1998). As a result, accounts of legal consciousness fail to consider ways that organizational practices can re-shape legal rules. Everyday disputes often develop in the context of organizations and institutions that have their own routines and practices that shape the meaning of the experience (Heimer 1999). Organizations themselves are an important source of messages about law, translating legal rules in ways that serve organizational interests (Edelman, Fuller, and Mara-Drita 2001; Edelman, Uggen, and Erlanger 1999; Edelman, Erlanger, and Lande 1993; Edelman 1990). Thus, accounts of legal consciousness should consider not just the legal domain but also particular organizational practices in the context of specific problems.

In this chapter, I analyze a particular set of organizational practices: interactions between supervisors and women deciding how to respond to sexual harassment at work. These interactions confirm the findings of institutional theorists that supervisors prioritize management interests over employee rights. By taking the perspective of employees, however, I can show that supervisors' practices influence what employees say and think and do when responding to sexual harassment. Employees' understanding of their rights at work are powerfully shaped by management practices. These employee responses, in turn, shape the effectiveness of law in the workplace.

Navigating the Grievance Procedure: Social Practices and Legal Consciousness

The University had an anti-harassment policy (the "Written Policy") that met all the requirements for protecting it from liability.[6] The Written Policy had an expansive definition of sexual harassment dedicated to protecting University employees from the indignities of discrimination. It provided a flexible grievance procedure with a mix of formal and informal process for investigating and resolving complaints and a wide range of officials designated to take those complaints, so an employee could bypass the supervisor if the supervisor was the harasser. The policy was widely circulated to all its employees and was permanently available on its website. Thus, on paper, the University offered its employees a model sexual harassment policy. But did employees turn to this policy when they encountered unwanted sexual attention at work? Was the policy a resource they could deploy to resolve such problems, or did it become a problem in and of itself?

In this section, I provide an account of the University's sexual harassment policy from the perspective of its intended beneficiaries – the employees, rather than human resources professionals (Edelman. Erlanger, and Lande 1993; Edelman, Uggen, and Erlanger 1999; Bisom-Rapp 1999). Through the eyes of employees, the University's grievance procedures appeared to be an adversarial process that at worst, attacked their credibility and at best, was completely irrelevant to solving their problems. As a result, women usually did not complain, but when they did, they adapted to the policy by finding ways to bolster their cases. In the course of their interactions with supervisors and human resources officials, women assigned a new meaning to the Written Policy. Where the Written Policy's symbolic purpose was to protect employee rights and dignity, women understood it as a mechanism designed to protect the most powerful actors in the organization. Moreover, in some cases, the operation of the complaint process led women to narrow their very definitions of sexual harassment.

Management Practices

According to the women in the study, supervisors rarely observed the Written Policy's promise of informality and broad protection. Rather, many women reported that their supervisors responded with comments and practices that enacted an adversarial process and turned women away from filing formal grievances. In one management strategy, supervisors assumed the role of the harasser's representative (Kihnley 2000). Several women reported that after hearing complaints of offensive conduct, their supervisors automatically took the harasser's side by making excuses and condoning their behavior. One survey respondent reported that a harasser was a "total jerk who can't refrain from insulting or bullying anyone, period," yet his fellow supervisors, whom the respondent characterized as "male chauvinists," trivialized his conduct:

> His actions are constantly excused, and you are told simply, that "you are too sensitive." "That's the way he is" is also a popular comment, although it's obviously not okay that I am a certain "way" as well – bothered by what he says.

In the wake of a series of disagreements with a faculty member for whom she did clerical work, Emma passed him and several of his colleagues in the hall. The faculty member "asked if I minded if he would pinch my rear end. What could I say?" After thinking about this incident in the context of other problems she was having with the faculty member, she complained to the chair of the department who told her: ... [H]e's just going through a stage. You need to be very – you need to handle him with kid gloves, and you need to be very tolerant. This was, of course, not what I wanted to hear."

Some women felt that supervisors and human resource managers were much less sympathetic when the harasser was a friend of theirs. In such cases, those receiving the complaints did not treat the problem with the seriousness the complainants thought it deserved. For example, a project leader told one survey respondent that she would not work on the project unless she slept with him: "I was sexually harassed by a co-worker and my complaints to my female supervisor were not only laughed at but I was removed from the project for complaining ... He was a friend of my married, female supervisor." When Joanne went to the human resources director to complain about the chief financial officer at a previous job who was continually making crude jokes and comments, she found the two of them together sharing raunchy jokes. Their friendliness with each other made her suspect that her complaints were not being taken seriously.

Apart from "representing" the harasser, supervisors also exercised their discretion by, in effect, dismissing many of the complaints that they heard on the grounds that the incident did not violate the Written Policy. In dismissing these complaints, these University officials relied on narrow interpretations that restricted the policy's broad promise to protect worker dignity. Supervisors enacted these narrow interpretations in a number of ways. First, supervisors informed employees that the harassing conduct was not offensive enough to constitute a violation of the Written Policy. For example, Siena had a co-worker who lingered near her desk, making subtly sexual comments. She said:

> He started making comments about what I was wearing … He said something about [my] perfume, and I explained to him that I didn't wear perfume … It wasn't what he said; it was the way it was said. It was like a double entendre. It could be taken one way or another. He always did it while we were alone, and there was never anything that was blatantly physical.

After listening to Siena's account of her co-worker's behavior, her supervisor told her that the comments were too ambiguous to merit a complaint. The supervisor's reaction persuaded Siena that there was no point in pursuing a formal complaint. Siena observed:

> After I had talked to my boss, I felt really let down and betrayed. And I didn't feel like I had any other place to go. I thought I'd gone to somebody that would help me, and it was somebody who had known me for three years. And I thought if she acted this way, that I wouldn't have a leg to stand on anywhere else … I did the first step and got nowhere, so I stopped because I figured I needed her backing in order to go any further.

The supervisor's skepticism about the seriousness of the incidents strongly suggested to Siena that the conduct was subject to multiple interpretations and therefore would not be construed as sexual harassment by other decision-makers further up the chain of command in the complaint process.

In addition to supervisors, the human resources department also offered preliminary assessments of complainants' cases and concluded that the behaviors were too trivial to violate the Written Policy. For example, another survey respondent's supervisor frequently made crude sexual remarks – remarks that bothered her a great deal. Yet she was discouraged from pursuing a complaint: "I discussed it with the EEOC rep – she didn't feel the case was strong enough to bring a formal complaint." For all these women, the conduct in question consisted of "sexual advances, requests for sexual favors, and other verbal … conduct of a sexual nature" and "created … an offensive employment environment," that could be construed as violating the terms of the Written Policy. Yet supervisors and human resource managers refused to pursue their complaints.

The second way that supervisors enacted narrow interpretations of the Written Policy was by creating exemptions for certain categories of harassment and harassers – exemptions not mentioned in the Written Policy. Rose's problem involved a female receptionist who engaged in frequent sexually explicit conversations with the male coaches in the office where she worked. When she complained to her supervisors, they told her that because a woman was involved and because the behavior consisted only of conversations, the conduct was not sexual harassment and therefore did not violate the Written Policy. Rose was dissatisfied with what she characterized as "formal conversations":

> There was kind of this, "We hear what you're saying, and we'll do what we can do, but you know, our hands are kind of tied without there being a major incident." Without her, like, grabbing me and throwing me against the wall, or ... Who knows what that could have been? You know, without finding her and a coach, naked, on top of the coffee table – who knows what would have been legitimate?

The supervisors also argued that such a violation was a prerequisite to taking any steps to resolve the problem. Thus, they did not offer Rose their services in resolving the dispute informally, as suggested in the Written Policy.

Other women reported that faculty conduct seemed exempt from the Written Policy. When she got nowhere with the chair of the department where she worked, Emma decided to approach the human resources department. She remembered:

> But I was unhappy enough about it that I went and I wrote up the circumstance ... and had taken it to Human Resources, and complained about it. And they were very, uh, not tremendously sympathetic about it. They said, "Really, if the person is a faculty member, you know, there's nothing we can do about it." Only in very egregious circumstances, when there's very obvious, overt abuse, if you will, or harassment, would they do something. So they basically said, you know, "Tell him to lay off, and hope that he does."

The human resource representative here did not just abandon responsibility for anything other than "obvious, overt abuse," but also claimed that the conduct of faculty was beyond reach.

Finally, as gatekeepers, supervisors can complicate the complaint process itself by erecting hurdles not specifically included in the grievance procedure. With their extensive discretion about how to handle investigations of complaints, supervisors can add steps that make complaints a less attractive option for aggrieved employees. For example, like most such procedures, the Written Policy did not require employees to confront their harassers. However, as an office manager, Megan imposed this requirement on a group of women who wanted to complain about a co-worker whose behavior was bothering them. Megan herself had been a target of his harassing conduct; she admitted that he had been "very sexually inappropriate throughout the entire year that he was here." Yet when a group of other women wanted to file formal charges, she sent them away:

> I put the kibosh on that because I said: "Have these people addressed him personally on these issues? Have they approached him?" Well, some did but mostly no. And I thought I'm going to interject here and say that's not fair. This person – much as I do not care for him – we owe him ... the opportunity to change his behavior ... Before you start pushing paper through those channels, let him know he's a jerk, and [you] don't like what [he's] doing. Otherwise it's not fair ...

Although Megan admitted that the women may not have felt comfortable coming forward, she dismissed their concerns because the harasser had no formal authority or influence over their jobs. Thus, Megan's authority to administer the grievance procedure also gave her the authority to interpret its provisions in a manner in keeping with her conceptions of fairness, which created new obstacles for the women who sought to complain about the harasser.

Women's Complaints: Adapting to Management Practices

Women's use of the grievance procedure depended first of all on the seriousness of the intrusion that they encountered. Among the women interviewed for the study who complained about their encounter with sex at work, all of them were convinced that the experience amounted to sexual harassment. These incidents tended to involve extremely explicit sexual overtures or physical contact, and thus probably met the behavioral tests for sexual harassment. In addition, when they complained, the women all reported being upset by the attention. Thus, identifying the behavior as sexual harassment was an important preliminary step.

Once that threshold was crossed, however, not every women braved the grievance procedure. Instead, their decisions about whether or not to endure the management practices depended on the support they found in the organization. It also depended on their efforts to substantiate their claims, usually by observing evidentiary routines and practices. These strategies bolstered their cases in the face of aggressive management gatekeeping.

For example, some women reported that they found the University's staff were very helpful in addressing sexual harassment when it occurred. Several survey respondents reported incidents with student athletes, but their prompt intervention – with the help of human resources personnel – solved the problems. One reported:

> I specifically spoke to the students about the comments and how I felt about it. It was a teachable moment for them. They seemed remorseful and apologized. They seemed to understand the error of the display. It has not happened again. I think [the university] does a good job about informing its employees about the issue ...

The respondent then went on to identify a member of the human resources department who was particularly helpful.

Women also found it easier to complain when they enjoyed the support of their direct supervisors. If they had good relationships with their supervisors, the supervisors were much more likely to believe the complaint and to take it seriously. For example, Dallas was working as a clerical staff member in a doctor's office at the University. Although she often exchanged off-color jokes with her co-workers, she drew the line at physical contact. One doctor she worked for crossed the line by telling a joke where the punch line included pinching her nipple:

> *That* was it. Now, at this point, now you're touching me. So then, I had a very good friend who was an administrator. I told her – I was livid. And I told her what happened. She just went at him. She said: "I want you to get him now." I heard so much screaming in there.

In this case, Dallas was able to use her friendship ties with a manager to resolve a workplace dispute informally. This informal access to organizational power is often missing from the lives of ordinary working women.

Many women also enjoyed the support of their co-workers who could corroborate their stories about harassing incidents. When everyone in a working environment objects to some form of conduct, supervisors and managers take the situation much more seriously. But co-workers also provide social support through the complaint process. They act as sounding boards for the complainant, offering sympathy and advice about how to pursue the complaint. Thus, when an individual has the backing of her co-workers, she is more likely to be able to withstand the adversarial nature of the process.

For example, Matilda was a departmental assistant where the chair had a foul temper and offensive personal habits: "He's come to talk to you and he'd have his hands down his pants, and he'd be playing with himself in the front, or he'd have it down the back and be scratching himself." Although Matilda had complained about his various behaviors, her complaints had not been taken seriously by the dean or by human resources. Then one day, in a rage because a document had not been photocopied, he screamed at the staff using racist and sexist epithets, directed particularly at a Chinese woman:

> And then he knocked everything off of her desk, and he went over to the other lady, the Program Assistant, and threw his letter at her, and then knocked everything off the desk, yelling and screaming, "You're all stupid!" And I came out of my office, and I was standing in the main office, and I was trying to get him, either to come into my office, or go out in the hall, or go in his office, or *anything* – to just – to break this up. And I said, "Could we talk about this?" At

which case, he turned – he turned *beet* red. He came up to me and took his fist, and [gesture] came that close. One inch. From hitting me.

In Matilda's case, all four staff members left and went to the human resources department. With all four women standing in the office seeking transfers out of the department, a human resources representative contacted an assistant dean at the college who was sympathetic: "They sent one of the assistant deans back to the department, with us, to confront the [chair]. And they ended up fighting. And he was in there – they were yelling and screaming an hour or more." The unanimity and urgency of the complaint provided University officials with a compelling justification for intervention.

Women who had complained to supervisors often prepared themselves by generating evidence that would support their claims and that would bolster their credibility. For example, some preserved incriminating evidence in case they ever needed to substantiate their allegations. Jane worked with a professor from another unit in the University. On an almost daily basis, he sent her e-mails that critiqued her marriage, complained about his sex life, and asked her out on dates. When asked whether she had thought about filing a complaint, she said: "Yeah, I have, but ... I kept the messages, and I, you know, made sure I had a backlog of things just in case I had to, but I didn't think that I would do it unless I really had to." She showed the e-mails to her supervisor who was sympathetic but advised her not to mention the incident to anyone else. Although she agreed not to tell anyone else, she kept hard copies of the messages in case she finally decided to file a complaint.

When there was no incriminating evidence, women tried to create it by documenting the harassing incidents. For example, Siena had told a friend working in the office that her co-worker's lingering near her desk making suggestive comments was making her feel uncomfortable. Her friend suggested that she record each event. She said: "I'm pretty thorough at documentation. I wrote down word for word what happened and what I said in response to it as well." She would later produce this document when she went to her supervisor to complain about her co-worker's behavior. Notably, every other woman I interviewed – even the ones who did not complain – had committed the incident to writing.

Most of the women in the study who had complained were dissatisfied with the results. They claimed that harassers did not modify their conduct, leaving the women to believe that their supervisors had not made a serious effort to exercise control over the problem. In fact, many women themselves bore the burdens of complaining about the harassment. If they were not singled out for retaliatory treatment, their workplaces became unfriendly, leading them to seek transfers away from their harassers and their supervisors. Because of these outcomes, women questioned the value of complaining about harassing behaviors.

Several women reported that their complaints seemed to attract little attention from their supervisors, and even when they did, nothing ever seemed to happen to the harasser. Often, the conduct continued just as it had before the complaint. When Matilda and her colleagues complained to human resources and to the dean's office, they got an initial response: an associate dean came to the department and yelled at the chair about his threat of violence against Matilda. But in the end, nothing happened to the chair, and he returned to his obnoxious personal habits and verbal abuse. She said:

> That assistant dean, who I think was sympathetic to our problem, he left the University shortly after that. Nothing really was done … [W]hat made us go back was them coming after us, and us believing that there would be some sort of a solution to the problem. And then there never was. There was never any mention of it after that.

Similarly, Rose's complaints about the receptionist's sexual conversations with the coaches never resulted in any supervisory response. She said: "Basically, I don't think anything happened. If there was a conversation with the woman, it was certainly not handled in such a way that had any impact on her whatsoever. Nothing happened."

Worse than inaction, women also found themselves to be targets of retaliatory action. This retaliation took a number of different forms. Some women reported receiving negative performance evaluations when they complained about their experiences. One survey respondent whose supervisors and co-workers engaged in daily efforts to engage her in conversation about her sex life reported: "The men aware of the situation intimidated me every time I brought it up. I was led to believe there would be repercussions if I continued to bring it up – and there were – I received two consecutive performance evaluations indicating that I had an inability to get along with co-workers."

Another form of retaliation was removing the complainant from job duties or projects. In another of Dallas' experiences with sexual harassment, she was a senior departmental assistant to a faculty member who was directing a profitable enterprise for the University. This official was frequently verbally abusive to Dallas and the rest of his staff. In addition, he frequently made sexual jokes and observations about his employees' physical appearances and sex lives. Dallas withstood much of this attention by playing along or fighting back, but one day, he screamed at her using profanity when she asked him for some information. In the aftermath of this incident, Dallas began to complain about his general conduct: she complained to the office manager, to human resources, and the dean of the college where the project resided. None of these complaints had any effect. In fact, the only thing that happened was that Dallas was demoted to a lower clerical position and moved to a location out of the director's presence. She said: "He moved me from my office to the secretarial pool. He didn't want me close to him. He then gave my job to this other woman there who was prettier than me."

Even when women did not face direct, negative job consequences, they nevertheless found that their daily working lives suffered when they complained about harassment. One survey respondent had a male boss who complained about the high level of sexual materials displayed in the workplace. She reported: "When my (male) boss reported it to our supervisor, I was asked if I was offended. Despite that, action *was* taken by this supervisor. My boss and I have received a lot of comments (only half-joking) about our sensitivity to sexual materials." Another survey respondent reported: "The comments about me and behavior towards me were symptoms of a very large problem on the part of my ex-supervisor. When I involved HR, the problem worsened because I had called attention to my supervisor's bad behavior. It was two months after involving HR that I quit."

Thus, there was – perhaps not surprisingly – a gap between the theory and practice in the implementation of the Written Policy that placed alternative dispute resolution (ADR) mechanisms in an unexpectedly adversarial light. In the interactions where employees lodge complaints and managers receive them, grievance procedures recreate the formalism of the legal system, antithetical to the purposes of ADR. Women sought advocates and representatives to support their allegations. They also developed evidentiary records to repel challenges to their credibility and the validity of their complaints. Thus, even in the informal complaint process, managers and employees reproduce the characteristics that make the legal system so costly. Moreover, they found that when they did complain, their jobs became more unpleasant.

Other Strategies: Self-Help and Lumping It

Self-Help: Confronting the Harasser

Other women combined complaints and direct confrontations with harassers as part of a multi-strategy effort to get the harassment to stop. Women reported "educating" their harassers about the limits of appropriate behavior in the workplace. Supervisors sometimes re-enforced these lessons by having informal discussions with the harassers about their conduct. One survey respondent reported: "There were a few faculty members who made inappropriate, sexually harassing comments. One left. The other has been educated – partly by me, partly by a firmer dean. This person thought jokes and cartoons of a sexual nature were appropriate for work but now knows they are not and has been 'rehabilitated'." Thus, both employees and University supervisors used the Written Policy as a basis to encourage harassers to adapt to their working environments.

Directly confronting the harasser was sometimes a last resort when the grievance procedure failed. When managers declined to invoke the policy to protect employees, those employees directly invoked their rights by telling the harasser that the behavior had to stop. After Rose was turned away by every University official in the grievance procedure, she decided to take matters into her own hands:

> So basically I finally said, "Screw the system." Because I went through the system. And I said, "I'm going to confront her on my own." And all four of us, all four of the secretary staff got together, and I just said it right to her face. I said, "I'm completely uncomfortable with the way you behave around the office. I think you're inappropriate in your behavior with the coaches. I don't need to be told that I'm a prude, or that I'm being irrational, but I've talked to some of the staff about it; they see it as well. If nothing else, you need to do your job. And you're not doing your job. I'm doing your job for you. I've had enough of it, and I'm not going to do it anymore."

Some women's personality traits made confrontation a more appealing option than the cumbersome grievance procedure. For example, some women felt responsible for enforcing their own boundaries, particularly if they felt they were unusually sensitive to some kinds of behaviors. One survey respondent said:

> I am very particular about my personal space, and I am mindful of the fact that it is not professional for a co-worker to be physical. I have had to clearly say "Don't touch me; I'm not comfortable with that" even if the other person might think that they are just trying to be friendly. It might seem innocent to someone for them to put their hand on my back – but I am quite verbal if someone crosses that boundary.

On the other hand, many women felt confident of their interpersonal skills and insisted that they did not need third parties to intervene in their problems. For example, one survey respondent stated:

> I have experienced many sexual harassment type comments/situations, etc. However, none of them were situations that I felt threatened to the point of needing assistance to handle it. I would not hesitate if needed. However, my self-esteem, comfort with others, and ability to be direct have enabled me to handle them effectively on my own.

Another stated:

> If the unwanted attention is not coming from someone with power over me; does not in any way threaten my job promotion, salary increases, etc.; is not a constant barrage of crude, explicit or insulting remarks of the sort that would constitute a hostile environment and make me feel constantly threatened; then I don't regard the attention as harassment. The occasional sexual remark, mildly inappropriate touching or invitation to go out for drinks are all attentions I feel I can handle without formal complaints to anyone.

In addition, some women responded with aggressive humor of their own: "I work with a guy who [asked] another worker what a hundred dollar bill in her breast would get him. She thought it was funny; she smiled. When he said it to me, I told him it would get him missing teeth" (Quinn 2000). These women knew that the grievance procedure was available, but did not feel the need to get third-party intervention to solve their problems.

Lumping It: Rejecting the Complaint Process

Most women in the study did not complain to supervisors about their experiences with unwanted sexual attention at work. This decision was sometimes based on a judgment that the conduct was not sufficiently serious to merit a complaint. Other women, however, experienced the incidents as disruptive and distracting to their work performance and would have liked some assistance in resolving the problem. When considering whether to make a complaint, however, they anticipated their supervisors' response. Many believed that this response would be adversarial and hostile to their complaints; some believed that their supervisors would be ineffectual in solving the problem; others were concerned about retaliation, and so they decided not to complain. Thus, they acted as their own gatekeepers, incorporating the anticipated negative response into their own evaluation of the situation.

When the harassing conduct was neither severe nor harmful, women were not inclined to complain about the behavior. Infrequent jokes, occasional physical contact, sexist comments were mostly shrugged off or ignored. For example, Nora concluded that occasional sexual jokes told within her hearing by some faculty members were not sexual harassment; the faculty members did not make a habit of telling such jokes, nor was Nora a target of such attention on a regular basis. Another employee, Ann, was asked out several times by a co-worker, but he stopped bothering her when she explained that she was not interested in a personal relationship. One of her faculty supervisors even hugged her once. Because these incidents did not constitute part of their everyday working environments, had no effect on their job performance, and were easily resolved informally, neither Ann nor Nora considered behaviors serious enough to warrant a complaint.

Other women in the study, however, might have invoked the grievance procedure but were apprehensive about the reception they might get if they did. These women expected supervisors to tell them to handle the situation themselves or to accuse them of leading on the harasser. For example, Erna worked in an office with a middle-aged man whose relentless sexual comments and innuendo were a constant annoyance in an office made up mostly of women. Erna described him as:

> ... always making sexual innuendos; and with every word you said, he found
> something to make an innuendo about it ... To me, it is almost worse than having
> somebody come up and *grab* you. Because it's a constant barrage of innuendo.

And it just gets really annoying. And then you don't know how to handle it. And if you would say, "Look, you're always making this innuendo," then he would start to say, "Are you one of those dykes too?" or whatever the case was. That sort of thing. He just didn't understand that that was not appropriate.

Although her contact with the harasser was a daily irritant, Erna did not complain about his conduct to her supervisor. She anticipated that her supervisor would suggest that she was at fault for failing to handle the harasser in an appropriate manner. She said: "I think when you go to tell your supervisor, it always comes back: 'Well, what did you do?' You know, 'Just tell him no…,' 'Well, I haven't heard this from anybody else,' type of thing."

Similarly, Lily was concerned that her boss would use her complaint about a harasser to find fault with her conduct. She was employed in a unit that worked with personnel across the University, including the medical school. One of the doctors she worked with invited her out to lunch to discuss work-related issues, but after their lunch together, he began calling her to ask her out on dates, and eventually he suggested that they have sex. Although she admitted that her fears were not necessarily "realistic," she nevertheless identified a specific list of the negative conclusions her boss would reach about a possible complaint:

I think they're fears … my boss will believe him because he'll never defend me, so my value to my boss will decrease … Or maybe my boss would think that I was leading him on, or whatever, and that it was inappropriate to go for a professional lunch with him – you never do that.

Thus, women expected that if they made complaints, supervisors would adopt an adversarial posture and interrogate the complainant's behavior. Such challenges to their credibility were better avoided.

For other women, their reluctance to complain was based on their skepticism that their supervisors could solve problems. Like other women I interviewed, Erna was pessimistic about the University's ability to resolve any kind of personnel problem, let alone an issue as sensitive as an allegation of sexual harassment. She observed:

The procedures here don't work … If I had wanted to complain about [the harasser] I really had two choices. I could have gone to my boss. Or I could have gone to the office manager. And my boss … might have told me to go to the office manager, or he might have said to me "Why don't you just leave it?" And that was the whole chain of this process that was going on [with a different personnel problem], and people trying to take it up the chain of command, and it didn't work. In our particular case, our office manager just doesn't deal with this stuff. And I don't know if she doesn't deal with it, or if she just gets no reinforcement from her point of view … And then you have another choice: you could go to Human Resources. And that seems to have been a very negative thing because Human Resources … has never come through with any other problems that people have had. So people don't do that.

In the course of her employment, Erna had watched the supervisors and human resources professionals as they tried to settle employee conflict with very little success. Their ineffectual responses to employee problems undermined Erna's confidence that they would ever be able to get the harasser to stop his behavior.

Finally, although the University's sexual harassment policy specially promised to protect employees from retaliation, women still feared the effects of a complaint. While they acknowledged that their jobs might not have been in danger, they feared that by coming forward, their more powerful harassers would make subtle but consequential changes in the working environment. At a previous job, Joanne had noticed such changes when she complained about a high-ranking company official. When she entered a room, he would either stop talking or loudly comment on her humorlessness to colleagues. This experience made her reluctant to complain at the University when her female supervisor grabbed her breast: "If I didn't lose my job, it would make for a more hostile environment than it was working with her, being how she is."

These fears about the grievance procedures were sometimes magnified by co-workers and colleagues. Megan reported that, early in her career, a manager high above her in the corporate chain cornered her in a conference room, making suggestive remarks about her appearance. After that, he was made inappropriate comments every time he saw her. She turned to her fellow employees for advice:

> I remember talking to a few other women in the company that I trusted and told them what happened. And they had told me "You know what? It happened to me a million times from that exact same individual." And it was kind of like "You want to make it in this company? You learn to deal with it, and you suck it up because you're going to get blackballed if you fight this."

Thus, while they might offer emotional support to women planning to lodge complaints, social networks can also provide powerful reminders of the costs of complaint.

Because they feared antagonistic or skeptical treatment from supervisors, many women were discouraged from making complaints. Most of the University employees who declined to complain had grievances against their co-workers or employees without direct power over them. Most of them were also complaining about intrusive or persistent conduct that arguably created a hostile working environment. Thus, these were the kinds of experiences that research suggests are more likely to be subject of a complaint. But when women declined to participate in the routines and practices of the grievance procedure, some made that choice because they perceived the procedure to be ineffectual at best and, at worst, hostile to their needs. Their apprehension about using the grievance procedure rendered it irrelevant when they encountered sexual harassment, thus limiting its usefulness in protecting women's rights at work (Quinn 2000; Bumiller 1988).

Social Practice Shaping Legal Consciousness

Women in the study rarely trusted the grievance procedure to handle their complaints about sexual harassment, viewing the Written Policy as a management wolf in judicially designed sheep's clothing. Indeed, this widespread mistrust among employees raises questions about the Supreme Court's endorsement of a cure that appears worse than the disease. But grievance procedures also shape management and worker interactions. They are sets of social practices in which the meaning of the Written Policy and the law itself are enacted and re-enacted. So while the Written Policy was designed to offer employees expansive protection from the indignities of harassing behaviors, the management practices enforcing it significantly shrank that protection. And as a result, women's very definitions of sexual harassment narrowed in a way that reflected the adversarial nature of the complaint process.

Specifically, women incorporated their fear of the grievance procedure into their definitions of sexual harassment itself. To several women in the study, an incident could not be characterized as sexual harassment without evidence that it had occurred and that it was a serious affront to the woman's working life. If the incident could not be documented or if it did not meet some external standard of offensiveness, then women argued that it was not sexual harassment and would not meet the threshold of behavior required to file a complaint.

Lily, for example, distinguished between blatant forms of sexual harassment, which included unwanted physical contact and explicitly derogatory remarks, and

> … the subtle kind of thing, where you're not really sure … . Not being really sure, not having anything to grab onto – look, here's the definitive proof. I mean, all the doubting – it's gray; it's too gray. So I think that must happen on many occasions that you suspect motives, but you have no concrete evidence to support it, so then you doubt yourself.

Other employees also imported evidentiary requirements into their understanding of sexual harassment. One survey respondent who was repeatedly propositioned by other employees – both supervisors and co-workers – ignored and avoided her harassers. She did not complain largely out of confusion about what constituted harassment – a confusion that was tied to her anxiety about proving any allegations she might make: "Mainly, it is hard to define the boundaries of what is considered harassment and what is not. For example, is staring at my chest repeatedly harassment? If so, how can I prove he was doing it? Will I be believed? What if he is friends with the management?"

In the adversarial atmosphere created by the Written Policy's complaint process, women's definition of sexual harassment *narrowed* to include only those behaviors they could prove. This perceived evidentiary requirement further reduced employees' interest in complaining. For these women, supervisors did not need to dismiss complaints for failing to violate the policy. Women's own frames for sexual harassment accomplished this task by censoring complaints before they ever formed.

The women in the study also re-framed the meaning of the Written Policy itself. Rather than associating the policy with the protection of their rights, some women offered their own institutionalist critique of the grievance procedures and argued that the Written Policy was ineffective because the University's main priority was to protect itself from liability. When Rose complained about the receptionist's sexually explicit conversations with the coaches, she found herself bouncing back and forth among several different lines of authority – an office administrator who was not in Rose's office, the human resources department and the supervisors in the office itself. Yet no one took responsibility for the working conditions:

> If you get involved with employee relations, invariably everything is colored by the question of risk management. Everything is colored by the question of the University's liability, and "Will we ever come to suit on this?" And so all of the information that you want as a manager, in my experience at least, has been CYA – cover your ass – make sure you put it in writing, and not nearly enough of, and a much less clear emphasis on dealing with the practicality of the situation … I think if you get Employee Relations involved, it just seems like you instantaneously feel like you're in a court of law. You feel like you have to get all your ducks in a row, to be able to put together the prosecution for this case.

Having been both a clerical worker and a manager at the University gave Rose insight into the management concerns behind the policies and procedures. She detected that such policies placed managers in the position of having to act as lawyers for the University, charged with "putting together the prosecution for this case."

In addition, many women in the study believed that the Written Policy was actually a mechanism that protected the most powerful employees in the organization. When the harasser was a powerful person, women believed the University would take whatever action was necessary to safeguard the harasser's position. For example, when Siena was considering pursuing a complaint, she thought about her observations of the grievance procedures in a previous position. These observations supported her view that employee complaints would be resolved in favor of the University. She said: "I would say that I wouldn't have gotten very far, and that I think the University would have taken the University's side and not the employee's side." Similarly, Matilda argued that the chair of her department suffered no real consequences because the University would protect the faculty over the staff. She said:

> I think they normally don't stand up for the staff anyhow. If a faculty member wants something, they usually get it. So are you going to go to them with this problem? I don't think so. I don't think they're impartial. I don't at all. I think

there's too much interest in "Well, he makes a lot of money for the University, we have to appease him." I see it every day.

In these accounts, sexual harassment policies offer employees little protection from the excesses of powerful harassers. When Dallas could no longer tolerate her abusive supervisor, she asked for a transfer. In all her exit interviews – with the Human Resources Department and other administrators – she made it clear that she was making this request because of her supervisor's behavior, but she never filed a formal complaint because she thought it would be futile:

> Staff are peons. [The University] is not going to get much money out of us. He is generating money for the University so whatever he does [they] are going to overlook. Besides ... he was created out of a plan that the Provost had created and that the President loved, and so they're not going to lose money and get embarrassed by someone saying he's doing this and this, and he makes work intolerable, and he "f—'s" everybody, and he is prejudiced against everybody except himself ... He's bringing in revenue, and the University is not going to take the word of one female who is going to make him trouble.

Women felt that complaints in these situations were futile. When one of the assistant deans suggested that she might be preparing a case against the harasser, Dallas was skeptical that anything would ever come of it. Dallas reported:

> She said: "If I ever prepared something; if something were to happen, would you be willing to testify?" I said: "Yeah, I'd be willing to testify." But nothing's going to happen. I just said: "You're up against the system, and it's very nice that you're willing to in case something happens, but it's not going to happen."

In addition to constructing an adversarial complaint policy, the interactions between managers and employees also shaped the symbolic significance of the Written Policy. The Written Policy articulated a set of legal schemas that broadly defined sexual harassment and that prescribed a mechanism ostensibly protecting employee rights. Yet in the shadow of the practices implementing the Written Policy, women's definitions of sexual harassment narrowed considerably. And rather than a process for enforcing their rights, women interpreted the Written Policy as an instrument through which the University protected the powerful rather than a process for enforcing employee rights. Thus, the employees enacted a Written Policy whose meaning in practice was very different than its symbolic purpose.

Patterns of Complaint: Survey Responses

Like the University employees interviewed for this study, the women responding to the survey rarely complained about their experiences with unwanted sexual attention. No one among the 93 women who reported encounters with sex at work filed an EEOC complaint or a lawsuit. No one even filed a formal grievance with the University. Still some employees did confront the harasser and ask him to stop his behavior, while others reported the incidents to a supervisor or human resource manager. In this analysis, I examine some of the factors that might explain why women chose to register these complaints rather than remain silent about the incident.

Confrontational Strategies

The dependent variable in this analysis is whether or not women relied on a confrontational strategy to protest her experience. The survey asked women how they responded to the incident that "made the greatest impression" on them. It presented them with a list of possible responses and asked them to mark all that applied.

The list described a wide range of responses. First, it included avoidance strategies. Avoidance strategies can be both cognitive and behavioral. Cognitive strategies are internal coping mechanisms that women use to try to trivialize the harm, such as ignoring the behavior or going along with the conduct. Behavioral avoidance consists of more proactive efforts to deter the harasser and may include making a joke of the behavior or transferring out of the department. Another more passive response to sex at work is telling family, friends, and co-workers about the behavior (Fitzgerald, Swan, and Fischer 1995).

The more assertive strategies protesting sexual harassment can include confronting the harasser directly and either asking him to stop his behavior or threatening to tell a supervisor if he does not stop. Finally, the most assertive strategy that survey respondents used was reporting the behavior to a third-party supervisor who had authority to do something about it.

People were assigned to one of these four categories – avoidance, seeking social support, confrontation, and invoking third parties – based on the most assertive response that they reported. Table 6.1 shows that the least assertive strategies were by far the most common:

Table 6.1 Respondents' responses to sex at work

Strategy (N = 93)	%
Avoidance	29
Seeking Social Support	32
Confronting the Harasser	22
Invoking Third Party	17

Although some argue that this categorization of responses reflects increasing levels of assertiveness (Gruber and Smith 1995), there is little consensus about whether this variable can be treated as ordered for purposes of multivariate analysis. Thus, I collapsed these categories into a dichotomous variable reflecting only whether or not the respondent chose a confrontational strategy to protest about her encounter with sex at work, to either the harasser or a third party. Thirty-nine per cent of the women reporting an incident chose an assertive response.

Independent variables   First, I included measures for whether or not the employee believed that the incident constituted sexual harassment. On the one hand, critics of grievance procedures argue that they discourage women from complaining even when they have legitimate complaints. On the other hand, employers worry that the availability of grievance procedures makes employees more likely to complain about minor incidents. Including the respondents' assessment of whether they have been sexually harassed provides a means of seeing whether women are abusing the grievance procedure. (Because this measure is so highly correlated with the characteristics of the harassment and women's being bothered by the conduct, I omitted those variables from this model. I ran this model using those measures but omitting the evaluation of sexual harassment and obtained similar results.)

Second, I included the scale of feminist attitudes. Critics of sexual harassment regulation argue that feminists have engendered a culture of complaint. Women with more feminist attitudes would be most likely to enact that culture with frequent complaints.

Finally, I included a variable measuring women's familiarity with the University's sexual harassment policies and procedures. Respondents were asked if the University had a special procedure for dealing with sexual harassment complaints; they could respond either "yes," "no," or "don't know." Surprisingly few women responding to the survey were familiar with the University's sexual harassment policies; only 47 per cent were aware of the procedure. For the purposes of this analysis, I created a dichotomous variable by collapsing those answering "no" and "don't know" into a single group. Mere knowledge of the sexual harassment procedure does not capture the complexity of women's attitudes and practices with respect to the grievance procedure, but it is a useful starting point for analyzing the influence of policies on complaint behavior (Gruber and Smith 1995).

Table 6.2   Marginal effects on women's confrontation strategies against sex at work (N = 76)

	Marginal Effects (dF/dx)	Standard Error	P-value
Sexually Harassed?	.304	.113	.010
Gender Consciousness	.149	.098	.128
Sexual Harassment Policies?	− .001	.065	.986

Pseudo R2 = .077

I used a probit analysis to test this model of complaint behavior. Reporting the marginal effects, Table 6.2 shows that the only significant variable is whether or not the respondent felt herself to be sexually harassed. It was very significant, and the marginal effects of that variable on a woman's use of an assertive strategy were large: if a woman thought she had been sexually harassed, she was 30 per cent more likely to confront the harasser or complain about the incident to a supervisor.

The other variables – gender consciousness and familiarity with the grievance procedure – were not significant, although the direction of the signs is interesting. These findings suggest that gender consciousness and familiarity with the grievance procedures exert a slightly negative effect on women's decisions about whether or not to pursue an assertive strategy. But these coefficients are far from significant and so it is impossible to draw any conclusions from these results.

The respondents themselves provided reasons for not pursuing complaints against their harassers, reasons similar to those found in other studies of sexual harassment. Sixty-six per cent did not report the incident because they did not think it was important enough to warrant a complaint. Others were worried that the experience of reporting would be too embarrassing (12 per cent) while another 36 per cent were concerned that complaining would make their working environments unpleasant. Finally, many respondents showed little confidence in the working of the grievance procedure. Nineteen per cent thought that nothing could be done to redress the problem; 27 per cent were concerned that something bad would happen to the harasser; while 18 per cent feared reprisals.

Summary

This chapter has analyzed sexual harassment policies from an important but often missing perspective – that of their intended beneficiaries, employees. By adopting the Written Policy, the University fulfilled its legal obligations to protect its employees from sexual harassment. It broadly defined sexual harassment to include behaviors that had the effect of creating a hostile working environment and undermining a worker's dignity. It also authorized supervisors to seek out informal solutions to employee problems. Yet the policy provided far less protection in practice than it did on paper. Only the most serious forms of harassment got past management gatekeepers who declined to intervene unless the behavior "violated" the Written Policy. Moreover, employees perceived the complaint process as a forum that was adverse to their interests, where managers would take the harasser's side and demand proof of their allegations. Thus, women often abandoned their complaints or chose not to complain at all.

While these findings confirm that women are reluctant to complain about their experiences with sexual harassment, it also suggests that grievance procedures themselves can help to explain this reluctance. The same power imbalances that render women susceptible to sexual harassment in the first place govern the grievance procedures that are supposed to redress women's complaints. Sexual harassment researchers should therefore try to account for these organizational practices in their analyses of women's responses to sexual harassment.

Grounded in the problem of sexual harassment, this analysis also demonstrates the many meanings of the grievance procedures endorsed by the Supreme Court and the EEOC. In the realm of legal doctrine, these grievance procedures help employers demonstrate their compliance with the law. Moreover, these grievance procedures themselves evoke a variety of legal schemas – definitions of sexual harassment, evidence, burdens of proof, due process. Yet the meaning of these schemas is constantly reproduced and re-shaped by the practices of both employees making choices about how to respond to sexual harassment and managers implementing the grievance procedures. In this case, managers and employees enacted a narrow definition of the right against sexual harassment that protected women against only the most serious and intrusive conduct.

Moreover, this study establishes the theoretical advantages of studying the legal consciousness of injustice. The problem of sexual harassment implicates a specific legal domain with a complex web of laws that defines inappropriate behaviors, establishes conditions of holding employers liable and specifies remedies for rights violations. These rules provide women with the opportunity to resist unwanted sexual attention at work – interpretive frames through which women understand that conduct is wrong and should be resisted. Yet the organizational setting in which laws are constructed can re-shape the meaning of those rights. The schema embodying workers' rights, for example, is more likely to reflect management interests than aggressive protection for employees. And employees are witnesses and participants in these organizational practices where the institutional meanings can diverge from the law on the books. Thus, the legal consciousness of ordinary individuals should "bring institutions back in" and account for the influence of specific organizational practices in shaping legal consciousness.

Finally, this chapter emphasizes the importance of understanding legal consciousness as social and cultural practice. Judicial opinions and EEOC regulations articulate rights, but those rights depend heavily on the initiative of ordinary individuals to enforce them. This initiative, in turn, depends on the availability and the relevance of legal schema to people confronting problems in the workplace. Beyond these commonplace understandings, the meaning of rights also depends on what people do. They may invoke rights to make demands and to seek the intervention of third parties to resolve disputes, and as this study demonstrates, the context of those practices shapes the meaning of those rights. But in analyzing legal consciousness as a social practice, it is also worth noting the times when rights are ignored. When employees reject a grievance procedure, when they say that the policy is not relevant to their dispute, when they let their rights remain idle, they diminish the power of law to constitute their everyday relationships at work.

Notes

[1]   Ten per cent of the respondents reported that they either threatened to tell or told others, but the questionnaire did not define who the "others" were (MSPB 1995).
[2]   The categories sum to more than 100 per cent because respondents were asked to identify all the behaviors that they engaged in when responding to the unwanted sexual attention (MSPB 1995).
[3]   Other studies have shown that women are most likely to complain when the harassing acts are most severe or intrusive (Cochran et al. 1997; Gutek and Koss 1993; Welsh 1999).
[4]   Twenty per cent reported that they believed nothing would be done in response to their complaints while 29 per cent were worried that complaining would make their work situation unpleasant. Seventeen per cent claimed that a complaint would adversely affect their careers. Studies also show that women are more likely to complain when the harassers are co-workers (Gruber and Smith 1995). Complaints about co-workers do not create the same risk of retaliation as a complaint about a supervisor.
[5]   In one study of employees who rejected the label of sexual harassment to describe their experiences, Quinn (2000) found that employees did not complain about those experiences and instead relied on tactics such as deflection and "not taking it personal" to ward off the negative consequences of harassing behaviors. Thus, Quinn concluded that the law has limited instrumental or symbolic power in women's efforts to resist sexual harassment at work. Yet Quinn did not interview anyone who did complain about sexual harassment. Thus, she is unable to evaluate the significance of law for such individuals.
[6]   See Chapter 2 for a more detailed discussion of the University's anti-harassment policy and procedure.

7 Sexual Harassment, Law, and Social Change: A View from the Ground

Almost 30 years after it was "discovered," sexual harassment remains a controversial topic in US political debate. Feminists argue that sexual harassment remains a major structural impediment to women's equality in employment and education. Their opponents argue that the threat of sexual harassment is greatly exaggerated and that humorless feminists threaten to stamp out men and women's most basic instinct – flirtation and sexual conversation – in the places they spend most of their time. While this debate rages, human resources managers subsume sexual harassment within a broader range of personnel problems that plague corporate life.

As a political concept, sexual harassment is thoroughly steeped in law. It represents the translation of women's problems into a legal claim, a relatively new right that arguably furthers women's equality. Developed through the steady accretion of individual lawsuits (Marshall 1998), the legal definitions and rules are designed to protect women from sexually harassing behaviors, but those legal rules also gave rise to a set of policies and procedures that do not necessarily vindicate women's rights (Edelman, Uggen, and Erlanger 1999; Bisom-Rapp 1999; Grossman 2003).

And while sexual harassment is strenuously debated among elites and policy-makers, surprisingly little attention is paid to the intended beneficiaries of the laws – working women. What kinds of harassing behaviors interfere with their working lives? Do they invoke their rights when they confront such behaviors? What meaning do those rights hold for working women? In this book, I have tried to answer these questions in the context of a single workplace by analyzing the role of law and politics in women's everyday experiences with sexual behavior at work.

The findings in this study are similar to those in other sexual harassment research. For example, this study shows that sexual harassment continues to occur in US workplaces, even those that have well-designed policies and procedures that comply with formal legal requirements. In addition, this study demonstrates that women have varying reactions to sexual attention at work, and that those reactions vary with the severity of the intrusion and the frequency of the behavior. The women in this study did not label every behavior sexual harassment, reserving that description for the most serious intrusions. Finally, the women in this study almost never complained about their experiences. But while confirming these general findings, this study has also generated some insights because of its focus on the meanings and social practices that constitute sexual harassment and resistance to sexual harassment.

First, women's accounts of their experiences with sex at work resound with the prevailing political debates about sexual harassment. Some women describe their harassers as abusing the power they enjoy because they are men presiding over an already male-dominated working world. Other women see sex itself as a way to wield power over unsuspecting male colleagues. Still other women are resigned to being powerless for the time being; they seek only to fit in with their male bosses and co-workers, hoping that by being a little smarter and working a little harder, they will eventually succeed. These different themes come from the ongoing political struggle over not just sexual harassment but the broader meaning of women's equality in US society.

Second, women only sparingly use the label sexual harassment, in large part because of its legal meanings. Most of the women in this study believed that sexual harassment had meaning independent of the forms of conduct that bothered or annoyed them. Instead, they thought of sexual harassment as a standard of conduct against which experience is measured. Moreover, the standard of sexual harassment that women deployed closely resembled the legal factors that constitute a hostile working environment: the behavior had to be severe, pervasive, and it had to have a negative impact on the woman's job. But most often, if there was some ambiguity, women were likely to interpret this standard narrowly and conclude that they had not been harassed.

In addition, this study has provided a new perspective on sexual harassment policies and procedures. The Supreme Court has entrusted employers with the protection of employees' rights to a workplace free from sexual harassment. But the managers who administer the anti-harassment policies may be more concerned with defending the employer's interests than with vindicating employees' rights. Their vigorous gatekeeping can discourage women from lodging complaints or even from mentioning some troubling behavior to a supervisor. By creating an adversarial procedure and thus instilling fear in employees, employers further narrow the scope of legal protection against sexual harassment.

Thus, it appears that the law plays a limiting and limited role in women's encounters with sex at work. First, legal definitions limit the types of behavior that women are willing to describe as sexual harassment. As a result, women may tolerate a great deal of disruptive conduct simply because it does not, in their view, amount to sexual harassment and therefore cannot be challenged. Thus, people who engage in unwanted sexual behaviors at work are ironically less likely to be challenged than office mates who spend too much time on personal phone calls or who play their radios too loudly. Second, legal institutions, like the social practices that constitute a sexual harassment grievance procedure, have only limited power to disrupt entrenched structural inequalities.

So, some might argue, working women have not benefitted at all from years of sexual harassment regulation. They would be no worse off if sexual harassment laws and policies and procedures disappeared tomorrow. But clearly, that is wrong. In fact, if they were strengthened, sexual harassment laws could have a dramatic effect on employers' incentives to protect employees' rights. For example, the Supreme Court or Congress could eliminate the employers' affirmative defense and make them strictly liable for all sexual harassment that occurs in their workplaces (Grossman 2003). Strict liability would make employers truly proactive about seeking out and stopping sexual harassment before it seriously unsettled a workplace. Of course, in the current political climate, such a reversal is unlikely to occur.

But existing sexual harassment laws can be productively implemented by employers who are actually committed to making the working environment more hospitable to women. Some employers have adopted proactive policies that overcome some of the limitations of most anti-harassment grievance procedures. For example, instead of designating a few officials as complaint handlers, employers like DuPont train dozens of ordinary employees on what to do when someone tells them about an experience with sexual harassment. Spread widely through all levels of management in the organization, these employees interact with almost everyone in the company on a daily basis and are plugged into the social networks where the common knowledge about harassers circulates. Their training emphasizes informal solutions to sexual harassment, including low-key conversations with harassers asking them to stop their behaviors. Strategies such as these mobilize already existing gossip networks that disseminate valuable information. Moreover, they do not assume that every problem will end in litigation, and therefore are willing to seek out common sense solutions.

Finally, while the institutions that enforce it might be flawed, the law of sexual harassment represents a potent set of symbols for women who are plagued by sexual behaviors at work. Knowing that they have a right to a workplace free from sexual harassment helps women understand that at least some sexual behaviors in the workplace are wrong simply because they interfere with their job performance. Moreover, the existence of a potential legal claim against employers demonstrates that the woman is not at fault and that the employer itself is responsible when harassment is allowed to continue. Women may not always be able to translate this sense of injustice into a successful challenge to the harassing behavior through the complaint process. But this sense of injustice often fuels collective self-help in the workplace. Thus, even as it imposes constraints on women's options, the law has provided liberatory messages that support women in their everyday confrontations with sexual harassment.

Thus, this study has also provided a new look at the relationship between law and social change. I have argued that social change should not be solely assessed in macro-level variables measuring shifts in education or income or in the clash of elites in policy-making arenas. Instead, social change can often be seen in the conflicts of everyday life, where ordinary people, inspired by social movements and liberatory ideals like rights, make demands on family, friends, employers, teachers and others for better treatment. Moreover, law can shape these conflicts, these demands for better treatment. Thus, to study law and social change from the "bottom up" – what I've called the legal consciousness of injustice – we must examine the relationship in the context of everyday life.

The legal consciousness framework provides the basic building block for conducting such an inquiry. It takes seriously the notion that ordinary people can be legal actors, invoking the law to suit their purposes, avoiding the law when it threatens to thwart their plans. Moreover, legality shapes people's thoughts and actions, and in turn, those thoughts and actions re-create the rules themselves.

But to analyze everyday struggles over inequality and injustice, the legal consciousness framework itself requires the theoretical developments I have suggested in this book. First, legal consciousness should be situated in the context of the political struggles and debates surrounding social problems. Law is not the only source of frames that people use to make sense of their lives. In political struggles, there are many frames circulated by social movements that develop new interpretations of experience designed to persuade people to see the injustice in existing social conditions. But most injustice frames are contested by both counter-movements and other powerful established forces resisting social change. All are competing to win the hearts and minds of the general public. These frames function, along with legality, to shape meaning, and their inclusion in the analysis de-centers the law while enriching the account of conflict in daily life.

Second, legal consciousness should be situated in a particular legal regime. Indeed, many political struggles lead to the creation of new rights for ordinary individuals. It is certainly worth asking what meaning those rights hold for their beneficiaries. Indeed, we may ask whether they know their rights and whether they invoke them in appropriate circumstances. But we should also ask the constitutive questions about how legal rules shape the way they think about their problems and their opportunities.

Finally, legal consciousness should be situated in a particular institutional and organizational context. We know that through the practices of their actors, organizations adapt the law to their own instrumental and symbolic purposes (Edelman, Erlanger, and Lande 1993). In the interactions between employers and employees, students and teachers, parents and children, institutional and organizational actors engage in social practices that enact the law, but they do so in ways that protect the institutions. Thus, these organizational and institutional interests should also be accounted for in our analyses of legal consciousness.

In this elaborated framework for the legal consciousness of injustice, we have the opportunity to fulfill the promise of studying the role of law in everyday life. We can see how specific legal rights and obligations are transformed in the context of quotidian social practice at the same time that we de-center the law by including accounts of political struggle. These analyses will show that the relationship between law and social change does not originate with the Supreme Court but actually springs from everyday life.

Appendix A: Interview Schedule

INTRODUCTION

As I mentioned in my e-mail, I'm studying the ways that individuals respond to problems in the workplace, particularly with unwanted sexual attention.

I'll be asking you questions about these experiences and about some other things like your political views, your experiences with the legal system, and your personal background and social activities.

To protect your confidentiality, I'm going to ask you to pick a fake name. I'm going to use that fake name to identify all the tapes, transcripts and notes I have from this interview. I'm going to have only one list with your real name on my home computer, and a back-up in a safe place.

JOB

I'll start with some general questions about your job at the time of the events. Without telling me what division or department you're in, please describe what your job was.

How long had you been working there?

Were there other women working there?

What about the racial mix?

Are you a member of a union?

Roughly, what is its racial and sexual composition?

SEX AT WORK

Starting with your most recent experience with unwanted sexual attention at work:

Can you tell me what happened? (Please use only initials or false names to talk about the other people involved.)

Verbal comments, materials of a sexual nature, or physical contact?

Without revealing any real names, was the person giving you this attention a supervisor? Co-worker? Subordinate? Customer or client?

How often did it occur? Is it still going on?

Did it cost you anything? Medical expenses? Sick time?

Was there a threat to your job? If so, was the threat implicit or explicit?

How did you feel about this? About your harasser?

Did you do anything in response?

Did you take any formal action?

Did it make things better or worse?

Why did you decide to pursue this action?

How did you feel about the outcome?

Does your employer have a procedure against sexual harassment?

Do you know much about it? Who to go to? What happens when you complain?

Do you think it works?

[If the subject decided against doing anything in response] why did you decide against pursuing any course of action against the person paying this attention to you?

Did you talk to anyone (else) about your experiences?

Who? (Again, please use only initials or false names.)

Did they give you advice?

What was their advice?

Did you decide to follow that advice or did you decide against it?

Do you know anyone else this sort of thing has happened to?

How do you know that person? Do you talk to them often?

Did they decide to do anything about it?

Did what happened to them affect your decision in any way?

Did you consider yourself to be sexually harassed?

Why or why not?

What do you think sexual harassment is?

Where have you gotten your information about sexual harassment?

Any other experiences within the last two years? [Go through those too, if time allows].

ENVIRONMENT

Do you think sexual harassment is a problem for most women?

Have you paid much attention to news about sexual harassment? [Prompt with Anita Hill, Tailhook, Bob Packwood.]

Regarding [the news item most salient to the subject], what did you think about the outcome?

Did you discuss the issue with anyone?

Did you agree or disagree with the person you talked to?

Do you think that discussion changed anyone's mind?

Did you think [the most salient news item] had anything in common with your situation?

POLITICS

Do you consider yourself a Democrat, a Republican, or an Independent?

Would you characterize yourself as a liberal, a moderate or a conservative?

Group Identification
Are there any groups in society you feel close to, where the members are most
like you in your ideas, interests and feelings about things?

Some examples:

poor people	business people
Asian-Americans	young people
liberals	conservatives
the elderly	Hispanic-Americans
blacks	women
labor unions	working-class people
feminists	whites
gay men or lesbians	middle-class people
men	

Is there any other reason you feel close to that group?

Organizations
Do you belong to any organizations or take part in any activities with other
members of that group?

What organizations? What activities? How often?

Power
Let me ask you some questions about who gets what in society.
What groups do you think have more advantages and get more benefits in
society?

For women compared to men?

For whites compared to African-Americans?

For workers compared to managers?

Can you think of any examples in your own experience where you've seen
such power differences?

Attribution
Is that because society discriminates against the group or because members of the group don't have enough drive?

Feminism
Would you consider yourself a feminist?

Why or Why not?

LEGAL

Have you personally ever been involved in a legal dispute?

> Would you tell me about it?

> When did it occur?

> What was the substance of the dispute?

> Did you hire a lawyer?

> Did you go to court? Some other forum? (for example, arbitration, mediation, etc.)

> What was the outcome?

Do you think you were treated fairly by [the court] [the arbitrator/mediator] [your lawyer] [other officials?]

> What was positive about the experience?

> What was negative about the experience?

> Would you do it again?

What do you think about using the legal system to solve problems? Would you ever use it?

> Biased?

> Complicated?

> Expensive?

> How would you go about finding a lawyer?

Do you feel like you know much about your legal rights at work?

Have there been any recent laws or court decisions that have caught your attention?

  If yes, which one(s)?

  Why did that case catch your attention?

SOCIAL NETWORKS

I'd like to know something about the groups or organizations you belong to. Are you a member of any social or political organizations? [Probe: church groups, sports groups, nationality groups, service groups, fraternal organizations, professional societies, etc].

Does [group mentioned] do anything to try to solve individual or community problems?

Have you participated in any of the group's activities? [Probe: been a leader, served on committees, attended conferences, given money?]

While participating in [group's] activities, do you ever discuss legal issues with other members?

BACKGROUND

Finally, I'd like to ask you some questions about your background.

What was the last level of education you completed?

What is your marital status? Children? How many? Genders?

I'll give you some ranges of personal income, and you tell me which range you fit into:

- under $10,000
- $10,001 – 20,000
- $20,001 – 30,000
- $30,001 – 40,000
- $40,001 – 50,000
- more than $50,000

If applicable, repeat question for family income.

- under $10,000
- $10,001 – 20,000
- $20,001 – 30,000
- $30,001 – 40,000
- $40,001 – 50,000
- more than $50,000

Are there any lawyers among your family and friends?

Your age?

Those are the last of my questions. Are there any issues regarding your encounters with the legal system or your work experience that we haven't covered that you'd like to discuss?

Appendix B: Questionnaire

SECTION I – SEXUAL ATTENTION AT WORK

In this part of the questionnaire, we would like to know about your experiences at work. Please answer as frankly and completely as you can; remember that YOUR ANSWERS ARE COMPLETELY CONFIDENTIAL.

Q-1. During the PAST 24 MONTHS, have you been in a situation where anyone you work with: (Please circle the answer that most closely describes your own experience)

A) Made unwanted attempts to draw you into a discussion of personal or sexual matters (for example, attempted to discuss or comment on your sex life).	NEVER	ONCE/ TWICE	SOME- TIMES	OFTEN	MANY TIMES
B) Made crude or offensive remarks about your appearance, body or sexual activities.	NEVER	ONCE/ TWICE	SOME- TIMES	OFTEN	MANY TIMES
C) Implied faster promotions or better treatment if you were sexually cooperative.	NEVER	ONCE/ TWICE	SOME- TIMES	OFTEN	MANY TIMES
D) Continued to ask you for dates, drinks, dinner even though you have said no.	NEVER	ONCE/ TWICE	SOME- TIMES	OFTEN	MANY TIMES
E) Made crude or offensive sexual remarks either publicly or to you privately.	NEVER	ONCE/ TWICE	SOME- TIMES	OFTEN	MANY TIMES
F) Displayed, used or distributed sexist or suggestive materials (such as pictures, stories or pornography).	NEVER	ONCE/ TWICE	SOME- TIMES	OFTEN	MANY TIMES
G) Touched you in a way that made you feel uncomfortable.	NEVER	ONCE/ TWICE	SOME- TIMES	OFTEN	MANY TIMES
H) Made you afraid that you would be treated poorly if you didn't cooperate sexually.	NEVER	ONCE/ TWICE	SOME- TIMES	OFTEN	MANY TIMES
I) Treated you badly for refusing to have sex with a co-worker or supervisor.	NEVER	ONCE/ TWICE	SOME- TIMES	OFTEN	MANY TIMES

IF YOU RESPONDED "NEVER" TO ALL PARTS OF Q-1, PLEASE TURN TO Q-16 ON PAGE 6 TO COMPLETE THE QUESTIONNAIRE.

Q-2. If you have had one or more than one of the experiences listed in Q-1, please write the letter of the experience that made the greatest impression on you. _____

Please think about the experience identified in Q-2 when responding to the remaining questions in Section I.

Q-3. Was this experience the result of conduct by: (Please circle the number of your response)
1. ONE PERSON
2. A FEW PEOPLE
3. MANY PEOPLE

Q-4. Were the person or persons involved: (Please circle the number of your response)
1. MALE
2. FEMALE
3. BOTH

Q-5. Were the person or persons involved: (Please circle the number of your response)
1. YOUR SUPERVISOR
2. A CO-WORKER
3. BOTH
4. OTHER (Please specify)

Q-6. Who were the targets of this conduct? (Please circle the number of your response)
1. JUST YOURSELF
2. A FEW OTHER WOMEN AT WORK
3. MOST OTHER WOMEN AT WORK

Q-7. How much did this behavior bother you? (Please circle the number of your response)
1. NOT AT ALL
2. SLIGHTLY
3. SOMEWHAT
4. VERY MUCH
5. EXTREMELY

Q-8. Please read each item below and indicate, by placing an "X" next to ALL the statements that best describe the way you responded to the situation. Remember there is no *right* way to respond – each situation is different. We are interested in how *you* responded.

Q-9. What effect did your response have? (Please circle one *for each statement you check*)

_____	A) I ignored the behavior	MADE IT BETTER	NO EFFECT	MADE IT WORSE
_____	B) I avoided the person	MADE IT BETTER	NO EFFECT	MADE IT WORSE
_____	C) I asked the person to stop	MADE IT BETTER	NO EFFECT	MADE IT WORSE
_____	D) I made a joke about the behavior	MADE IT BETTER	NO EFFECT	MADE IT WORSE
_____	E) I threatened to tell others	MADE IT BETTER	NO EFFECT	MADE IT WORSE
_____	F) I told other people in the office	MADE IT BETTER	NO EFFECT	MADE IT WORSE
_____	G) I told family and/or friends	MADE IT BETTER	NO EFFECT	MADE IT WORSE
_____	H) I reported the behavior to a supervisor	MADE IT BETTER	NO EFFECT	MADE IT WORSE
_____	I) I went along with the behavior	MADE IT BETTER	NO EFFECT	MADE IT WORSE
_____	J) I transferred to another department	MADE IT BETTER	NO EFFECT	MADE IT WORSE
_____	K) I filed a formal complaint with my employer	MADE IT BETTER	NO EFFECT	MADE IT WORSE
_____	L) I filed a formal complaint with a government agency	MADE IT BETTER	NO EFFECT	MADE IT WORSE
_____	M) I pursued a legal action	MADE IT BETTER	NO EFFECT	MADE IT WORSE
_____	N) I did something other than the actions listed above (Please describe below)	MADE IT BETTER	NO EFFECT	MADE IT WORSE

_____

_____

_____

Q-10. If you chose NOT to file a formal complaint against the person with your employer or a government agency, please place an "X" next to ALL the statements which best describe your reasons for not doing so:

——   A) I did not feel it was important enough to report.
——   B) I thought it would make my work situation unpleasant.
——   C) I did not think anything could be done about the situation.
——   D) I did not want to hurt the person who bothered me.
——   E) I thought it would be held against me or that I would be blamed.
——   F) I was too embarrassed.
——   G) I did not know what actions to take.
——   H) Other (Please describe below)

_____

_____

Q-11. Did your employer have a procedure for handling employee complaints? (Please circle the number of your response)
1. YES
2. NO
3. DON'T KNOW

Q-12. Did your employer have a *special* procedure for handling employee complaints about sexual harassment? (Please circle the number of your response)
1. YES
2. NO
3. DON'T KNOW

Q-13. Did you consider this experience to be sexual harassment? (Please circle the number of your response)
1. YES
2. NO

Q-14. Where have you gotten *most* of your information about sexual harassment? (Please circle *one*)
1. NEWSPAPERS OR MAGAZINES
2. TELEVISION
3. FRIENDS OR RELATIVES
4. CO-WORKERS
5. YOUR EMPLOYER
6. OTHER (Please Specify)

Q-15. Please use the space below to add your thoughts or comments about your experiences with sexual attention at work.

_____

_____

_____

SECTION II – POLITICAL AND SOCIAL VIEWS

Another important purpose of this study is to learn more about the political and social views of women in the workplace. The following questions will ask you for some of these views.

Q-16. Here is a list of groups in American society. Please read over this list and circle the phrase which best describes how close you feel to the group – which are most like you in your ideas and interests and feelings about things.

A) Blacks	VERY CLOSE	FAIRLY CLOSE	NEUTRAL	NOT TOO CLOSE	NOT CLOSE AT ALL
B) Feminists	VERY CLOSE	FAIRLY CLOSE	NEUTRAL	NOT TOO CLOSE	NOT CLOSE AT ALL
C) Gay Men/Lesbians	VERY CLOSE	FAIRLY CLOSE	NEUTRAL	NOT TOO CLOSE	NOT CLOSE AT ALL
D) Men	VERY CLOSE	FAIRLY CLOSE	NEUTRAL	NOT TOO CLOSE	NOT CLOSE AT ALL
E) Business People	VERY CLOSE	FAIRLY CLOSE	NEUTRAL	NOT TOO CLOSE	NOT CLOSE AT ALL
F) Hispanics	VERY CLOSE	FAIRLY CLOSE	NEUTRAL	NOT TOO CLOSE	NOT CLOSE AT ALL
G) Women	VERY CLOSE	FAIRLY CLOSE	NEUTRAL	NOT TOO CLOSE	NOT CLOSE AT ALL
H) Working People	VERY CLOSE	FAIRLY CLOSE	NEUTRAL	NOT TOO CLOSE	NOT CLOSE AT ALL
I) Whites	VERY CLOSE	FAIRLY CLOSE	NEUTRAL	NOT TOO CLOSE	NOT CLOSE AT ALL
J) Asians	VERY CLOSE	FAIRLY CLOSE	NEUTRAL	NOT TOO CLOSE	NOT CLOSE AT ALL

Q-17. Which of the groups listed in Q-16 do you feel closest to? (Please write the letter of the group in the space provided)_____

Q-18. How often do you find yourself angry about the way that the group you identified above in Q-16 is treated in American society?
1. ALMOST NEVER
2. OCCASIONALLY
3. SOMETIMES
4. VERY OFTEN

Q-19. When reading or listening to the news, how much attention do you pay to issues that especially affect the group you identified above in Q-16?
1. ALMOST NEVER
2. OCCASIONALLY
3. SOMETIMES
4. VERY OFTEN

Q-20. Some people think that certain groups have too much influence in American life and politics, while other people feel certain groups don't have as much influence as they deserve. Please read the following list of groups and circle the phrase that best describes your view of how much influence the group has in American life and politics.

A) Blacks	TOO MUCH INFLUENCE	JUST RIGHT INFLUENCE	TOO LITTLE INFLUENCE
B) Whites	TOO MUCH INFLUENCE	JUST RIGHT INFLUENCE	TOO LITTLE INFLUENCE
C) Working People	TOO MUCH INFLUENCE	JUST RIGHT INFLUENCE	TOO LITTLE INFLUENCE
D) Business people	TOO MUCH INFLUENCE	JUST RIGHT INFLUENCE	TOO LITTLE INFLUENCE
E) Women	TOO MUCH INFLUENCE	JUST RIGHT INFLUENCE	TOO LITTLE INFLUENCE
F) Men	TOO MUCH INFLUENCE	JUST RIGHT INFLUENCE	TOO LITTLE INFLUENCE
G) Gay Men/Lesbians	TOO MUCH INFLUENCE	JUST RIGHT INFLUENCE	TOO LITTLE INFLUENCE
H) Hispanics	TOO MUCH INFLUENCE	JUST RIGHT INFLUENCE	TOO LITTLE INFLUENCE
I) Asians	TOO MUCH INFLUENCE	JUST RIGHT INFLUENCE	TOO LITTLE INFLUENCE

Q-21. When reading or listening to the news, how much attention do you pay to issues that especially affect women? (Please circle the number of your response)

1. ALMOST NEVER
2. OCCASIONALLY
3. SOMETIMES
4. VERY OFTEN

Q-22. How often do you find yourself angry about the way women are treated in American society? (Please circle the number of your response)

1. ALMOST NEVER
2. OCCASIONALLY
3. SOMETIMES
4. VERY OFTEN

Q-23. Please read over the following statements and circle the phrase that best describes whether you agree or disagree with the statements:

A) The best way for women to improve their position is for each woman to become better trained and more qualified and do the best she can as an individual.	AGREE STRONGLY	AGREE SLIGHTLY	DISAGREE SLIGHTLY	DISAGREE STRONGLY
B) While individual effort is important, the best way for women to improve their position is if they work together.	AGREE STRONGLY	AGREE SLIGHTLY	DISAGREE SLIGHTLY	DISAGREE STRONGLY
C) Men have more of the top jobs because our society discriminates against women.	AGREE STRONGLY	AGREE SLIGHTLY	DISAGREE SLIGHTLY	DISAGREE STRONGLY
D) This country would be better off if we worried less about how equal men and women are.	AGREE STRONGLY	AGREE SLIGHTLY	DISAGREE SLIGHTLY	DISAGREE STRONGLY

Q-24. Do you think of yourself as a feminist? (Please circle the number of your response)

1. YES
2. NO

Q-25. How strongly do you feel about this? (Please circle the number of your response)

1. STRONG
2. NOT SO STRONG

Q-26. Do you usually think of yourself as a Republican, a Democrat or an Independent? (Please circle the number of your response.)
1. REPUBLICAN
2. DEMOCRAT
3. INDEPENDENT
4. OTHER PARTY (Please specify) ————————————————

Q-27. Which of the following best describes your political views? (Please circle the number of your response)
1. EXTREMELY LIBERAL
2. LIBERAL
3. SLIGHTLY LIBERAL
4. MODERATE
5. SLIGHTLY CONSERVATIVE
6. CONSERVATIVE
7. EXTREMELY CONSERVATIVE

Q-28. How much influence do you think someone like you can have over *local government* decisions? (Please circle the number of your response)
1. A LOT OF INFLUENCE
2. SOME INFLUENCE
3. VERY LITTLE INFLUENCE
4. NO INFLUENCE AT ALL

Q-29. How much influence do you think someone like you can have over *national government* decisions? (Please circle the number of your response)
1. A LOT OF INFLUENCE
2. SOME INFLUENCE
3. VERY LITTLE INFLUENCE
4. NO INFLUENCE AT ALL

Q-30. Please use the space below to describe any political, social or economic issues in which you are interested:

——
——
——
——

SECTION III – LAW AND THE LEGAL SYSTEM

Next, we would like to ask about your experiences with and attitudes about the legal system.

Q-31. Please read over the following statements about lawyers and the legal system in general and circle the *response* that is closest to your view.

A) Most people who go to lawyers are trouble-makers.	AGREE STRONGLY	AGREE SLIGHTLY	DISAGREE SLIGHTLY	DISAGREE STRONGLY
B) It doesn't do much good to go to court because the courts are biased against people like me.	AGREE	AGREE	DISAGREE	DISAGREE
C) Lawyers will not work as hard for poor clients as for clients who are rich and important.	AGREE STRONGLY	AGREE SLIGHTLY	DISAGREE SLIGHTLY	DISAGREE STRONGLY
D) I can't use the courts because legal proceedings are too complicated for me to understand them.	AGREE STRONGLY	AGREE SLIGHTLY	DISAGREE SLIGHTLY	DISAGREE STRONGLY
E) People should not call upon a lawyer until they have exhausted every other possible way of solving their problems.	AGREE STRONGLY	AGREE SLIGHTLY	DISAGREE SLIGHTLY	DISAGREE STRONGLY
F) The legal system favors the rich and powerful over everyone else.	AGREE STRONGLY	AGREE SLIGHTLY	DISAGREE SLIGHTLY	DISAGREE STRONGLY
G) The cost of getting a lawyer would keep me out of court even if I felt I had a good case.	AGREE STRONGLY	AGREE SLIGHTLY	DISAGREE SLIGHTLY	DISAGREE STRONGLY
H) The legal system is set up to deal with problems involving large sums of money and not with the kinds of legal problems the ordinary person has.	AGREE STRONGLY	AGREE SLIGHTLY	DISAGREE SLIGHTLY	DISAGREE STRONGLY
I) If I thought court proceedings could help me, I wouldn't hesitate to go to court.	AGREE STRONGLY	AGREE SLIGHTLY	DISAGREE SLIGHTLY	DISAGREE STRONGLY
J) Members of minority groups, like blacks and Hispanics, are treated fairly in the legal system.	AGREE STRONGLY	AGREE SLIGHTLY	DISAGREE SLIGHTLY	DISAGREE STRONGLY

Q-32. Please read over the following fact situations and indicate whether you think the situation described *is or is not* prohibited by law. (Please circle the number of your response)

A) Your supervisor repeatedly asks you out on dates and threatens to fire you if you refuse, but he never takes any job action against you when you decline.
   1. PROHIBITED
   2. NOT PROHIBITED

B) Your co-workers keep sexually suggestive photos of nude and partially clothed women in bathing suits tacked to the walls in public places and make graphic sexual jokes on a daily basis. You feel so uncomfortable that you find it difficult to perform your job.
   1. PROHIBITED
   2. NOT PROHIBITED

C) Your supervisor offers to promote you if you have sex with him. When you decline, you are given a negative performance evaluation and are denied a raise.
   1. PROHIBITED
   2. NOT PROHIBITED

D) Every week, your supervisor tells sexist jokes to you and your co-workers even though he knows it makes you uncomfortable.
   1. PROHIBITED
   2. NOT PROHIBITED

Q-33. Have you ever hired a lawyer? (Please circle the number of your response.)
1. YES
2. NO

Q-34. Please briefly describe the reasons for hiring a lawyer:

_____

_____

_____

SECTION IV – PERSONAL INFORMATION

Finally, we would like to ask you a few questions about yourself to help interpret the results.

Q-35. Your present age: _____ years

Q-36. Please describe your occupation:

TITLE: _____

KIND OF WORK YOU DO: _____

_____

_____

Q-37. What was your approximate PERSONAL income last year?
1. UNDER $15,000
2. $15,000 TO $34,999
3. $35,000 TO $49,999
4. $50,000 TO $74,999
5. $75,000 TO $124,999
6. $125,000 OR MORE

Q-38. What was your approximate FAMILY income last year?
1. UNDER $15,000
2. $15,000 TO $34,999
3. $35,000 TO $49,999
4. $50,000 TO $74,999
5. $75,000 TO $124,999
6. $125,000 OR MORE

Q-39. What is the highest level of education that you have completed?
       (Please circle the number of your response)
1. LESS THAN COMPLETION OF HIGH SCHOOL
2. COMPLETED HIGH SCHOOL
3. TECHNICAL SCHOOL
4. SOME COLLEGE
5. JUNIOR COLLEGE DEGREE (A.A.)
6. COLLEGE DEGREE
7. POST-GRADUATE WORK

192   *Confronting Sexual Harassment*

Q-40. How would you classify your race and/or ethnicity? (Please circle the
        number of your response.)
1. BLACK
2. ASIAN
3. CAUCASIAN
4. HISPANIC
5. NATIVE AMERICAN
6. OTHER (Please Specify)

Q-41. How would you describe your marital status? (Please circle the
        number of your response)
1. NEVER MARRIED
2. MARRIED
3. DIVORCED
4. SEPARATED
5. WIDOWED
6. LIVING WITH PARTNER BUT NOT MARRIED

THANK YOU!!!! That completes the questionnaire. Your assistance is
greatly appreciated.

As work on this project progresses, I may conduct interviews with some of
the women who completed this questionnaire to ask them more in-depth
questions. If you would consider sitting for such an interview, please fill in
the items below.

Name: _____

How can I contact you? _____

Appendix C: Measures for Gender Consciousness

POLAR POWER – Women's Influence in Society

Some people think that certain groups have too much influence in American life and politics, while other people feel certain groups don't have as much influence as they deserve. Please read the following list of groups and circle the phrase that best describes your view of how much influence the group has in American life and politics.

Women

Too Much Influence
Just Right Influence
Too Little Influence

POLAR EFFECT – Anger About Women's Treatment in Society

How often do you find yourself angry about the way women are treated in American society? (Please circle the number of your response)

Almost Never
Occasionally
Sometimes
Very Often

SYSTEM BLAME – Society Discriminates Against Women

Men have more of the top jobs because our society discriminates against women.

Agree Strongly
Agree Slightly
Disagree Slightly
Disagree Strongly

This country would be better off if we worried less about how equal men and women are.

Agree Strongly
Agree Slightly
Disagree Slightly
Disagree Strongly

COLLECTIVE ORIENTATION – The Best Strategies for Improving Women's Position in Society

The best way for women to improve their position is for each woman to become better trained and more qualified and do the best she can as an individual.

Agree Strongly
Agree Slightly
Disagree Slightly
Disagree Strongly

While individual effort is important, the best way for women to improve their position is if they work together.

Agree Strongly
Agree Slightly
Disagree Slightly
Disagree Strongly

When reading or listening to the news, how much attention do you pay to issues that especially affect women? (Please circle the number of your response.)

Almost Never
Occasionally
Sometimes
Very Often

References

Books and Journal Articles

Allen, Pamela (1970), *Free Space: A Perspective on the Small Group in Women's Liberation*, New York: Times Change Press.

Arvey, Richard D. and Marcie A. Cavanagh (1995), 'Using surveys to assess the prevalence of sexual harassment: some methodological problems', *Journal of Social Issues*, 51 (1), Spring, 39–52.

Barclay, Scott (1999), *An Appealing Act*, Evanston, IL: Northwestern University Press.

Barclay, Scott and Anna-Maria Marshall (2004), 'Supporting a cause, developing a movement, and consolidating a practice: cause lawyers and sexual orientation litigation in Vermont', in Stuart Scheingold and Austin Sarat (eds), *The Worlds Cause Lawyers Make*, Palo Alto: Stanford University Press (forthcoming).

Belton, Robert (1978), 'A comparative review of public and private enforcement of title VII of the civil rights act of 1964', *Vanderbilt Law Review*, **31** (4), May, 905–61.

Benford, Robert D. (1993), 'Frame disputes within the nuclear disarmament movement', *Social Forces*, **71** (3), March, 677–701.

Benford, Robert D. and David A. Snow (2000), 'Framing processes and social movements: an overview and assessment', *Annual Review of Sociology*, **26**, August, 611–39.

Bernstein, Anita (1994), 'Law, culture, and harassment', *University of Pennsylvania Law Review*, **142** (4), April, 1227–311.

—— (1997), 'Treating sexual harassment with respect', *Harvard Law Review*, **111** (2), December, 445–527.

Bingham, Shereen G. (ed.) (1994), *Conceptualizing Sexual Harassment as Discursive Practice*, Westport, CT: Praeger.

Bisom-Rapp, Susan (1999), 'Bulletproofing the workplace: symbol and substance in employment discrimination law practice', *Florida State University Law Review*, **26**, Summer, 959–1047.

Bobo, Lawrence (1992), 'Prejudice and alternative dispute resolution', *Studies in Law, Politics and Society*, **12**, 147–76.

Brady, Diana (2003), 'How to Prove Your Charges After the Prima Facie Case Specific: To Sexual Harassment', 9 to 5, http://www.sexharassment.net/law7.htm.

Buechler, Steven M. (1995), 'New social movement theories', *Sociological Quarterly*, **36** (3), Summer, 441–64.

Bumiller, Kristin (1987), 'Victims in the shadow of the law', *Signs*, **12**, Spring, 421–39.

—— (1988), *The Civil Rights Society: The Social Construction of Victims*, Baltimore: Johns Hopkins Press.

Cahill, Mia L. (2001), *The Social Construction of Sexual Harassment Law: The Role of the National, Organizational, and Individual Context*, Burlington, VT: Ashgate Dartmouth.

Cain, Patricia A. (2000), *Rainbow Rights: The Role of Lawyers and the Courts in the Lesbian and Gay Civil Rights Movement*, Boulder, CO: Westview Press.

Canon, Bradley C. (1998), 'The Supreme Court and policy reform: *The Hollow Hope* revisited', in David Schultz (ed.), *Leveraging the Law: Using the Courts to Achieve Social Change*, New York: Peter Lang.

Canon, Bradley C. and Charles A. Johnson (1999), *Judicial Policies: Implementation and Impact*, 2nd ed., Washington, DC: Congressional Quarterly Press.

de Certeau, Michel (1984), *The Practice of Everyday Life*, trans Steven Rendall, Berkeley: University of California Press.

Cleveland, J.N. and M.E. Kerst (1993), 'Sexual harassment and perceptions of power: an under-articulated relationship', *Journal of Vocational Behavior*, **42**, 49–67.

Cochran, C.C., P.A. Frazier, and A.M. Olson (1997), 'Predictors of responses to unwanted sexual harassment', *Psychology of Women Quarterly*, **21** (2), June, 31–47.

Coles, F.S. (1986), 'Forced to Quit: Sexual Harassment Complaints and Agency Response', *Sex Roles*, **14**, 81–95.

Cornell, Drucilla (1995), *The Imaginary Domain: Abortion, Pornography, and Sexual Harassment*, New York: Routledge.

Costain, Anne N. (1992), *Inviting Women's Rebellion: A Political Process Interpretation of the Women's Movement*, Baltimore: The Johns Hopkins University Press.

Curran, Barbara (1977), *The Legal Needs of the Public: The Final Report of a National Survey*, Chicago: American Bar Foundation.

Daniells, Lorna M. (1993), *Business Information Services*, Berkeley and Los Angeles: University of California Press.

d'Anjou, Leo and John Van Male (1998), 'Between old and new: social movements and cultural change', *Mobilization*, **3**, 207–26.

Delgado, Richard, Chris Dunn, Pamela Brown, Helena Lee, and David Hubbert (1985), 'Fairness and formality: minimizing the risk of prejudice in alternative dispute resolution', *Wisconsin Law Review*, **1985** (6), 1359–404.

Dellinger, Kirsten and Christine Williams (2002), 'The locker room and the dorm room: workplace norms and the boundaries of sexual harassment in magazine editing', *Social Problems*, **49** (2), 242–57.

D'Emilio, John, William B. Turner, and Urvashi Vaid (2000), *Creating Change: Sexuality, Public Policy, and Civil Rights*, New York: St. Martin's Press.

DiMaggio, Paul J. and Walter W. Powell (1983), 'The iron cage revisited: institutional isomorphism and collective rationality in organizational fields', *American Sociological Review*, **48** (2), 147–60.

Dobbin, Frank and John R. Sutton (1998), 'The strength of a weak state: the rights revolution and the rise of human resource management divisions', *American Journal of Sociology*, **104** (2), 441–76.

Dobbin, Frank, John R. Sutton, John W. Meyer, and W. Richard Scott (1993), 'Equal opportunity law and the construction of internal labor markets', *American Journal of Sociology*, **99** (2), 396–427.

Dolbeare, Kenneth, and Phillip E. Hammond (1971), *The School Prayer Decisions: From Court Policy to Local Practice*, Chicago: University of Chicago Press.

Edelman, Lauren B. (1990), 'Legal environments and organizational governance: the expansion of due process in the American workplace', *American Journal of Sociology*, **95** (6), May, 1401–40.

Edelman, Lauren B., Steven E. Abraham, and Howard S. Erlanger (1992), 'Professional construction of the legal environment: the inflated threat of wrongful discharge doctrine', *Law and Society Review*, **26** (1), 47–83.

Edelman, Lauren B., Howard S. Erlanger, and John Lande (1993), 'Internal dispute resolution: the transformation of civil rights in the workplace', *Law and Society Review*, **27** (3), 497–534.

Edelman, Lauren B., Sally Riggs Fuller, and Iona Mara-Drita (2001), 'Diversity rhetoric and the managerialization of law', *American Journal of Sociology*, **106** (6), May, 1589–641.

Edelman, Lauren B., Christopher Uggen, and Howard Erlanger (1999), 'The endogeneity of legal regulation: grievance procedures as rational myth', *American Journal of Sociology*, **105** (2), September, 406–54.

Egan, Timothy (1993), 'Harsh Homecoming for Senator Accused of Harassment', *New York Times*, January 29, 1993, Final Edition.

Ellingson, Stephen (1995), 'Understanding the dialectic of discourse and collective action: public debate and rioting in antebellum Cincinnati', *American Journal of Sociology*, **101** (1), July, 100–44.

Elman, R. Amy (1996), *Sexual Subordination and State Intervention: Comparing Sweden and the United States*, Providence, RI: Berghahn Books.

Engel, David M. (1998), 'How does law matter in the constitution of legal consciousness?', in Bryant G. Garth and Austin Sarat (eds), *How Does Law Matter?*, Evanston, IL: Northwestern University Press.

Engel, David M. and Frank W. Munger (2003), *Rights of Inclusion: Law and Identity in the Life Stories of Americans with Disabilities*, Chicago: University of Chicago Press.

Eskridge, William N., Jr. (2002), *Equality Practice: Civil Unions and the Future of Gay Rights*, New York, Routledge.

Evans, Sara (1980), *Personal Politics: The Roots of Women's Liberation in the Civil Rights Movement and the New Left*, New York: Vintage.

Ewick, Patricia, and Susan S. Silbey (1992), 'Conformity, contestation, and resistance: an account of legal consciousness', *New England Law Review*, **26** (3), Spring, 731–49.

—— (1995), 'Subversive stories and hegemonic tales: toward a sociology of narrative', *Law and Society Review*, **29** (2), 197–226.

—— (1998), *The Common Place of Law: Stories from Everyday Life*, Chicago: The University of Chicago Press.

Faber, Daniel, (ed.) (1998), *The Struggle for Ecological Democracy: Environmental Justice Movements in the United States*, New York: The Guilford Press.

Farley, Lin (1978), *Sexual Shakedown: The Sexual Harassment of Women on the Job*, New York: McGraw-Hill.

Feeley, Malcolm M. (1992), 'Hollow hopes, flypaper, and metaphors', *Law and Social Inquiry* **17** (4), Fall, 745–60.

Felstiner, William L.F. (1974), 'Influences of social organization on dispute processing', *Law and Society Review*, **9**, 63–94.

Felstiner, William L.F., Richard L. Abel, and Austin Sarat (1980–81), 'The emergence and transformation of disputes: naming, blaming, claiming ...', *Law and Society Review*, **15**, 631–55.

Feminists for Free Expression, 'The Free Speech Pamphlet Series: Sexual Harassment', Feminists for Free Expression, http://www.ffeusa.org/html/ statements/statements_harassment. html.

Feminist Majority Foundation (2003), 'What To Do If Someone You Know is Sexually Harassed', Feminist Majority Foundation, http://www.feminist.org/911/ harasswhatdo.html.

Fitzgerald, Louise F., Fritz Drasgow, Charles L. Hulin, Michele J. Gelfand, and Vicki J. Magley (1997), 'Antecedents and consequences of sexual harassment in organizations: a test of an integrated model', *Journal of Applied Psychology*, **82** (4), August, 578–89.

Fitzgerald, Louise F., and Alayne J. Ormerod (1993), 'Breaking silence: the sexual harassment of women in academia and the workplace', in Florence L. Denmark and Michele A. Paludi (eds), *Psychology of Women*, Westport, CT: Greenwood Press.

Fitzgerald, Louise F., and Sandra L. Shullman (1993), 'Sexual harassment: a research agenda for the 1990s', *Journal of Vocational Behavior*, **42** (2), February, 5–27.

Fitzgerald, Louise F., Sandra L. Shullman, Nancy Bailey, Margaret Richards, Janice Swecker, Yael Gold, Mimi Ormerod, and Lauren Weitzman (1988), 'The incidence and dimensions of sexual harassment in academia and the workplace', *Journal of Vocational Behavior*, **32** (2), April, 152–75.

Fitzgerald, Louise, Suzanne Swan, and Karla Fischer (1995), 'Why didn't she just report him? The psychological and legal implications of women's responses to sexual harassment', *Journal of Social Issues*, **51** (1), Spring, 117–38.

Fitzgerald, Louise F., Suzanne Swan and Vicki Magley (1997) 'But was it really sexual harassment? Legal, behavioral and psychological definitions of the workplace victimization of women', in William O'Donohue (ed.), *Sexual Harassment: Theory, Research, And Treatment*, Boston: Allyn and Bacon.

Flemming, Roy B., John Bohte, and B. Dan Wood (1997), 'One voice among many: the Supreme Court's influence to attentiveness to issues in the United States, 1947–1992', *American Journal of Political Science*, **41** (4), October, 1224–50.

Fleury-Steiner, Benjamin (2002), 'Narratives of the death sentence: toward a theory of legal narrativity', *Law and Society Review*, **36** (3), 549–77.

Francke, Katherine (1997), 'What's wrong with sexual harassment?', *Stanford Law Review*, **49** (April), 691–772.

Furchtgott-Roth, Diana and Christine Stolba (2001), *The Feminist Dilemma: When Success is Not Enough*, Washington, DC: The AEI Press.

Gamson, William A. (1992) *Talking Politics*, New York: Cambridge University Press.

Gamson, William A. (1995), "Constructing social protest', in Hank Johnston and Bert Klandermans (eds), *Social Movements and Culture*, Minneapolis: University of Minnesota Press.

Gelfand, Michele J., Louise F. Fitzgerald, and Fritz Drasgow (1995), 'The structure of sexual harassment: a confirmatory analysis across cultures and settings', *Journal of Vocational Behavior*, **47** (2), October, 164–77.

Giuffre, Patricia A. and Christine L. Williams (1994), 'Boundary lines: labeling sexual harassment in restaurants', *Gender and Society*, **8** (3), September, 378–401.

Goldberg-Hiller, Jonathan (2002), *The Limits to Union : Same-Sex Marriage and the Politics of Civil Rights*, Ann Arbor: University of Michigan Press.

Goldberg, Stephen, B.E.D. Green, and F.E.A. Sander (1986), 'ADR problems and prospects: looking to the future', *Judicature*, **69** (5), February-March, 291–99.

Grauerholz, E. (1996), 'Sexual harassment in the academy: the case of women professors', in Margaret S. Stockdale (ed.), *Sexual Harassment in the Workplace: Perspectives, Frontiers, and Response Strategies*, Thousand Oaks, CA: Sage.

Graves, Florence and Charles E. Shepard (1993), 'List of Packwood Accusers Grows; Kissing, Touching Described as Abrupt, "Out of the Blue"', *Washington Post*, February 7, 1993, Final Edition.

Groch, Sharon (2001), 'Free spaces: creating oppositional consciousness in the disability rights movement', in Jane Mansbridge and Aldon Morris (eds.), *Oppositional Consciousness: The Subjective Roots of Social Protest*, Chicago: University of Chicago Press.

Grossman, Joanna L. (2003), 'The culture of compliance: the final triumph of form over substance in sexual harassment law', *Harvard Women's Law Journal*, **26**, Spring, 3–76.

Gruber, James E. (1998), 'The impact of male work environments and organizational policies on women's experiences of sexual harassment', *Gender and Society*, **12** (3), June, 301–20.

Gruber, James E. and L. Bjorn (1982), 'Blue-collar blues: the sexual harassment of women autoworkers', *Work and Occupations*, **9**, 271–98.

Gruber, James E. and Michael D. Smith (1995), 'Women's responses to sexual harassment: a multivariate analysis', *Basic Applied Social Psychology*, **17** (4), December, 543–62.

Gurin, Patricia (1985), 'Women's gender consciousness', *Public Opinion Quarterly*, **49** (2), Summer, 143–63.

Gurin, Patricia, Arthur H. Miller, and Gerald Gurin (1980), 'Stratum identification and consciousness', *Social Psychology Quarterly*, **43** (1), March, 30–47.

Gutek, Barbara (1985), *Sex and the Workplace: The Impact of Sexual Behavior and Harassment on Women, Men and Organizations*, San Francisco: Jossey-Bass.

—— (1992), 'Disputes and dispute-processing in organizations', *Studies in Law, Politics, and Society*, **12**, 31–52.

Gutek, Barbara, A.G. Cohen, and A.M. Konrad (1990), 'Predicting social-sexual behavior at work: a contact hypothesis', *Academy of Management Journal*, **33** (3), September, 560–77.

Gutek, Barbara and M. Koss (1993), 'Changed Women and Changed Organizations: Consequences and Coping with Sexual Harassment', *Journal of Vocational Behavior* **42**, 28–48

Handler, Joel F. (1978), *Social Movements and the Legal System: A Theory of Law Reform and Social Change*, New York: Academic Press.

—— (1992), 'Postmodernism, protest, and the new social movements', *Law and Society Review*, **26** (4), 697–732.

Harkavy, Jonathan R. (1999), 'Privatizing workplace justice: the advent of mediation in resolving sexual harassment disputes', *Wake Forest Law Review*, **34** (1), 135–69.

Harrington, Christine B., and Sally Engle Merry (1988), 'Ideological production: the making of community mediation', *Law and Society Review*, **22**, 709–37.

Heimer, Carol A. (1999), 'Competing institutions: law, medicine, and family in neonatal intensive care', *Law and Society Review*, **33** (1), 17–67.

Hill, Eve (1990), 'Alternative dispute resolution in a feminist voice', *Ohio State Journal on Dispute Resolution*, **5** (2), 337–79.

Hoffman, Elizabeth A. (2003), 'Legal consciousness and dispute resolution: Different disputing behavior at two similar taxicab companies', *Law and Social Inquiry*, **28** (3), Summer, 691–716.

Hull, Kathleen E. (2003), 'The cultural power of law and the cultural enactment of legality: The case of same-sex marriage', *Law and Social Inquiry*, **28** (3), Summer, 629–58.

Hunt, Scott A., Robert D. Benford, and David A. Snow (1994), 'Identity fields: framing processes and the social construction of movement identities', in Enrique Larana, Hank Johnston, and Joseph R. Gusfield (eds), *New Social Movements: From Ideology to Identity*, Philadelphia: Temple University Press.

Hunter, Rosemary, and Alice Leonard (1997), 'Sex discrimination and alternative dispute resolution: British proposals in the light of international experience', *Public Law*, Summer, 298–314.

Jacob, Herbert (1969), *Debtors in Court*, Chicago: Rand McNally.

Johnston, Hank and Bert Klandermans (eds) (1995), *Social Movements and Culture*, Minneapolis: University of Minnesota Press.

Johnston, Hank, Enrique Larana, and Joseph R. Gusfield (1994), 'Identities, grievances, and new social movements', in Enrique Larana, Hank Johnston, and Joseph R. Gusfield (eds), *New Social Movements: From Ideology to Identity*, Philadelphia: Temple University Press.

Katzenstein, Mary F. (1998), *Faithful and Fearless: Moving Feminist Protest Inside the Church and the Military*, Princeton: Princeton University Press.

Kauppinen-Toropainen, K. and James E. Gruber (1993), 'Antecedents and outcomes of woman-unfriendly experiences', *Psychology of Women Quarterly*, **17** (4), December, 421–56.

Kihnley, Jennie (2000), 'Unraveling the ivory fabric: institutional obstacles to the handling of sexual harassment complaints', *Law and Social Inquiry*, **25** (1), Winter, 69–90.

King, Charles R. (1993), 'Calling Jane: the life and death of a woman's illegal abortion service', *Women and Health*, **20**, 75–94.

Kong, Dolores (1991), 'Sex Harassment Assailed at Boston Rally', *Boston Globe*, October 13, 1991, City Edition.

Koss, Mary P. (1990), 'The women's mental health research agenda: violence against women', *The American Psychologist*, **45** (3), March, 374–80.

Kluger, Richard (1975), *Simple Justice*, New York: Vintage Books.

Kritzer, Herbert M., Neil Vidmar, and W.A. Bogart (1991), 'To confront or not to confront: measuring claiming rates in discrimination grievances', *Law and Society Review*, **25** (4), 875–87.

Kubal, Timothy J. (1998), 'The presentation of political self: cultural resonance and the construction of collective action frames', *Sociological Quarterly*, **39** (4), Fall, 539–54.

LaFontaine, Edward, and Leslie Tredeau (1986), 'The frequency, sources and correlates of sexual harassment among women in traditional male occupations', *Sex Roles*, **15** (7–8), October, 423–32.

Langelan, Martha J. (1993), *Back Off! How to Confront and Stop Sexual Harassment and Harassers*, New York: Fireside Books.

Lawrence, Susan E. (1991a), 'Justice, democracy, litigation, and political participation', *Social Science Quarterly*, **72** (3), September, 464–77.

—— (1991b), 'Participation through mobilization of the law: institutions providing indigents with access to the civil courts', *Polity*, **23** (3), Spring, 423–42.

Legal Momentum, 'Publications and Resources', Legal Momentum, http://www.legalmomentum.org/pub/index.shtml education

Lempert, Richard (1976), 'Mobilizing private law: an introductory essay', *Law and Society Review*, **11**, 173–89.

Levine, Kay and Virginia Mellema (2001), 'Strategizing the street: how law matters in the lives of women in the street-level drug economy', *Law and Social Inquiry*, **26** (1), Winter, 169–207.

Levy, Dan (1991), 'SF Protest Against Thomas Confirmation', *San Francisco Chronicle*, October 16, 1991, Final Edition.

MacKinnon, Catherine A. (1979), *The Sexual Harassment of Working Women*, New Haven: Yale University Press.

MacKinnon, Catherine A. (1987), *Feminism Unmodified: Discourses on Life and Law*, Cambridge, MA: Harvard University Press.

Mansbridge, Jane J. (2001), 'The making of oppositional consciousness', in Jane J. Mansbridge and Aldon Morris (eds), *Oppositional Consciousness: The Subjective Roots of Social Protest*, Chicago: University of Chicago Press.

Mansbridge, Jane J. and Aldon Morris (eds) (2001), *Oppositional Consciousness: The Subjective Roots of Social Protest*, Chicago: University of Chicago Press.

Marshall, Anna-Maria (1998), 'Closing the gaps: plaintiffs in pivotal sexual harassment cases', *Law and Social Inquiry*, **23** (4), Fall, 761–93.

—— (2001), 'A spectrum in oppositional consciousness: sexual harassment plaintiffs and their lawyers', in Jane J. Mansbridge and Aldon Morris (eds), *Oppositional Consciousness: The Subjective Roots of Social Protest*, Chicago: University of Chicago Press.

—— (2003), 'Injustice frames, legality, and the everyday construction of sexual harassment', *Law and Social Inquiry*, **28** (3), Summer, 659–89.

Marshall, Anna-Maria and Scott W. Barclay (2003), 'In their own words: how ordinary people construct the legal world', *Law and Social Inquiry*, **28** (3), Summer, 617–28.

Mather, Lynn and Barbara Yngvesson (1980–81), 'Language, audience, and the transformation of disputes', *Law and Society Review*, **15**, 775–821.

McAdam, Doug J. (1982), *Political Process and the Black Protest Movement, 1930–1970*, Chicago, University of Chicago Press.

—— (1996), 'The framing function of movement tactics: strategic dramaturgy in the American civil rights movement', in Doug McAdam, John D. McCarthy, and Mayer N. Zald (eds), *Comparative Perspectives on Social Movements: Political*

Opportunities, Mobilizing Structures, and Cultural Framings, New York: Cambridge University Press.

McCann, Michael W. (1992), 'Reform litigation on trial', *Law and Social Inquiry*, **17** (4), Fall, 715–43.

—— (1994), *Rights at Work: Pay Equity Reform and the Politics of Legal Mobilization*, Chicago: University of Chicago Press.

—— (1998), 'How does law matter for social movements?', in Bryant G. Garth and Austin Sarat (eds), *How Does Law Matter?*, Evanston, IL: Northwestern University Press.

—— (1999), 'Review of *The Common Place of Law: Stories from Everyday Life*, by Patricia Ewick and Susan S. Silbey', *American Journal of Sociology*, **105** (1), July, 238–40.

McCann, Michael and Tracey March (1995), 'Law and everyday forms of resistance: a socio-political assessment', *Studies in Law, Politics and Society*, **15**, 207–36.

McCann, Michael W. and Helena Silverstein (1998), 'Rethinking law's "allurements": a relational analysis of social movement lawyers in the United States', in Austin Sarat and Stuart Scheingold (eds), *Cause Lawyering: Political Commitments and Professional Responsibilities*, New York: Oxford University Press.

McCarthy, John D. and Mayer N. Zald (1977), 'Resource mobilization and social movements: a partial theory', *American Journal of Sociology*, **82** (6), May, 1212–41.

McKinney, K. (1994), 'Sexual harassment and college faculty members', *Deviant Behavior*, **15** (2), April-June, 171–91.

Melucci, Alberto (1989), *Nomads of the Present: Social Movements and Individual Needs in Contemporary Society*, Philadelphia: Temple University Press.

Menkel-Meadow, Carrie (1985), 'For and against settlement: uses and abuses of the mandatory settlement conference', *UCLA Law Review*, **33** (2), December, 485–514.

Merit Systems Protection Board (MSPB) (1981), *Sexual Harassment in the Federal Workplace: Is it a Problem?*, Washington, DC: US Merit Systems Protection Board.

—— (1988), *Sexual Harassment In The Federal Government: An Update*, Washington, DC: US Merit Systems Protection Board.

—— (1995), *Sexual Harassment in the Federal Workplace: Trends, Progress and Continuing Challenges*, Washington, DC: US Merit Systems Protection Board.

Merry, Sally Engle (1990), *Getting Justice and Getting Even: Legal Consciousness Among Working-Class Americans*, Chicago: University of Chicago Press.

—— (1995), 'Resistance and the cultural power of law', *Law and Society Review*, **29** (1), 11–26.

Mezey, Naomi (2001), 'Out of the ordinary: law, power, culture, and the commonplace', *Law and Social Inquiry*, **26** (1), Winter, 145–68.

Miller, Arthur H., Patricia Gurin, Gerald Gurin, and Oksana Malanchuk (1981), 'Group Consciousness and Political Participation', *American Journal of Political Science*, **25** (3), August, 494–511.

Miller, Richard E. and Austin Sarat (1980–81), 'Grievances, claims and disputes: assessing the adversary culture', *Law and Society Review*, **15**, 525.

Morris, Aldon D. (1984), *The Origins of the Civil Rights Movement: Black Communities Organizing for Change*, New York: The Free Press.

—— (1992), 'Political consciousness and collective action', in Aldon D. Morris and Carol McClurg Mueller (eds), *Frontiers in Social Movement Theory*, New Haven: Yale University Press.

Muir, William K., Jr. (1973), *Law and Attitude Change*, Chicago: University of Chicago Press.

National Organization for Women, 'Women-Friendly Workplace and Campus Campaign Summary', Now, http://www.now.org/issues/wfw/summary.html.

Nielsen, Laura Beth (2000), 'Situating legal consciousness: experiences and attitudes of ordinary citizens about law and street harassment', *Law and Society Review*, **34** (4), 1055–90.

Oliver, Pamela (1984), 'If you don't do it, nobody else will: active and token contributors to local collective action', *American Sociological Review*, **49** (5), October, 601–10.

Olson, Susan M. (1984), *Clients and Lawyers: Securing the Rights of Disabled Persons*, Westport, CT: Greenwood Press.

Padavic, I. and J.D. Orcutt (1997), 'Perceptions of sexual harassment in the Florida legal system: a comparison of dominance and spillover explanations', *Gender and Society*, **11** (5), October, 682–98.

Patai, Daphne (1998), *Heterophobia: Sexual Harassment and the Future of Feminism*, New York: Rowman & Littlefield Publishers, Inc.

Phillips, Leslie (1993), 'Packwood fends off criticism; Harassment claims dog Oregon senator', *USA Today*, February 11, 1993, Final Edition.

Piven, Frances Fox, and Richard Cloward (1977), *Poor People's Movements*, New York: Pantheon.

Platt, Gerald M. and Michael R. Fraser (1998), 'Race and gender discourse strategies: creating solidarity and framing the civil rights movement', *Social Problems*, **45** (2), May, 160–79.

Pollack, Wendy (1990), 'Sexual harassment: women's experience vs. legal definitions', *Harvard Women's Law Journal*, **13**, Spring, 35–85.

Polletta, Francesca (2000), 'The structural context of novel rights claims: Southern civil rights organizing, 1961–1966', *Law and Society Review*, **34** (2), 367–407.

Polletta, Francesca, and James M. Jasper (2001), 'Collective identity and social movements', *Annual Review of Sociology*, **27**, 283–305.

Quinn, Beth A. (2000), 'The paradox of complaining: law, humor and harassment in the everyday work world', *Law and Social Inquiry*, **25** (4), Fall, 1151–85.

Robinson, Beth (2001), 'The road to inclusion for same-sex couples: lessons from Vermont', *Seton Hall Constitutional Law Journal*, **11** (2), Spring, 237–57.

Rogers, J. and K. Henson (1997), '"Hey, why don't you wear a shorter skirt?" Structural vulnerability and the organization of sexual harassment in contemporary clerical employment', *Gender and Society*, **11** (2), April, 215–37.

Rosenberg, Gerald (1991), *The Hollow Hope*, Chicago: University of Chicago Press.

Rospenda, K.M., J.A. Richman, and S.J. Nawyn (1998), 'Doing power: the confluence of gender, race and class in contrapower sexual harassment', *Gender and Society*, **12** (1), February, 40–60.

Saguy, Abigail C. (2000a), 'Employment discrimination or sexual violence? Defining sexual harassment in American and French law', *Law and Society Review*, **34** (4), 1091–128.

——— (2000b), 'Sexual harassment in France and the United States: activists and public figures defend their definitions', in M. Lamont and L. Thevenot (eds), *Rethinking Comparative Cultural Sociology: Repertoires of Evaluation in France and the United States*, Cambridge: Cambridge University Press.

——— (2002), 'Sexual harassment in the news: the United States and France', *The Communication Review*, **5**, 109–41.

Sarat, Austin (1990), '"… The law is all over: " Power, resistance and the legal consciousness of the welfare poor', *Yale Journal of Law and the Humanities*, **2**, 343–79.

Sarat, Austin and William L.F. Felstiner (1995), *Divorce Lawyers and Their Clients: Power and Meaning in the Legal Process*, New York: Oxford University Press.

Sarat, Austin and Thomas R. Kearns (1993), 'Beyond the great divide: forms of legal scholarship and everyday life', in Austin Sarat and Thomas R. Kearns (eds), *Law in Everyday Life,* Ann Arbor: The University of Michigan Press.

Scheingold, Stuart (1974), *The Politics of Rights*, New Haven: Yale University Press.

Schneider, Elizabeth M. (1986), 'The dialectic of rights and politics: perspectives from the women's movement', *New York University Law Review*, **61** (4), October, 589–652.

Schultz, David and Stephen E. Gottlieb (1998), 'Legal functionalism and social change: a reassessment of Rosenberg's *The Hollow Hope*', in David Schultz (ed.), *Leveraging the Law: Using the Courts to Achieve Social Change*, New York: Peter Lang.

Schultz, Vicki (1998), 'Reconceptualizing sexual harassment', *Yale Law Journal*, **107** (6), April, 1732–805.

——— (2001), 'Talking about harassment', *Journal of Law and Policy*, **9**, 417–33.

——— (2003), 'The sanitized workplace', *Yale Law Journal*, **112** (8), June, 2061–196.

Scott, James (1985), *Weapons of the Weak: Everyday Forms of Peasant Resistance*, New Haven: Yale University Press.

——— (1990), *Domination and the Arts of Resistance: Hidden Transcripts*, New Haven: Yale University Press.

Seron, Carroll, and Frank Munger (1996), 'Law and inequality: race, gender … and, of course, class', *Annual Review of Sociology*, **22**, 187–213.

Sewell, William H. (1992), 'A theory of structure: duality, agency and transformation', *American Journal of Sociology*, **98** (1), July, 1–29.

Sherwyn, David, Michael Heise, and Zev. J. Eigen (2001), 'Don't train your employees and cancel your "1–800" harassment hotline: an empirical examination and correction of the flaws in the affirmative defense to sexual harassment charges', *Fordham Law Review*, **69** (4), March, 1265–304.

Shoenfelt, Elizabeth L., Allison E. Maue, and JoAnn Nelson (2002), 'Reasonable person versus reasonable woman: does it matter?', *American University Journal of Gender, Social Policy, and Law*, **10** (3), 633–72.

Silverstein, Helena (1996), *Unleashing Rights: Law, Meaning, and the Animal Rights Movement*, Ann Arbor: University of Michigan Press.

Snow, David A. and Robert D. Benford (1992), 'Master frames and cycles of protest', in Aldon D. Morris and Carol McClurg Mueller (eds), *Frontiers in Social Movement Theory*, New Haven: Yale University Press.

Snow, David A. and Doug McAdam (2000), 'Identity work processes in the context of social movements: clarifying the identity/movement nexus', in Sheldon

Stryker, Timothy J. Owens, and Robert W. White (eds), *Self, Identity, and Social Movements*, Minneapolis: University of Minnesota Press.

Snow, David A., E. Burke Rochford, Jr., Steven K. Worden, and Robert Benford (1986), 'Frame alignment processes, micromobilization, and movement participation', *American Sociological Review*, **51** (4), August, 464–81.

Snow, David A., Louis A. Zurcher, Jr. and Sheldon Ekland-Olson (1980), 'Social networks and social movements: a microstructural approach to differential recruitment', *American Sociological Review*, **45** (5), October, 787–801.

Steinberg, Marc. W. (1998), 'Tilting the frame: consideration on collective action framing from a discursive turn', *Theory and Society*, **27** (6), December, 845–64.

—— (1999), 'The talk and back talk of collective action: a dialogic analysis of repertoires of discourse among nineteenth-century English cotton spinners', *American Journal of Sociology*, **105** (3), November, 736–80.

Stockdale, Margaret S. (1996), 'What we know and what we need to learn about sexual harassment', in Margaret S. Stockdale (ed.), *Sexual Harassment in the Workplace: Perspectives, Frontiers, and Response Strategies*, Thousand Oaks, CA: Sage.

Stockdale, Margaret S., A. Vaux, and J. Cashin (1995), 'Acknowledging sexual harassment: a test of alternative models', *Basic Applied Social Psychology*, **17** (4), December, 469–96.

Suchman, Mark C. and Lauren B. Edelman (1996), 'Legal rational myths: the new institutionalism and the Law and Society tradition', *Law and Social Inquiry*, **21** (4), Fall, 903–42.

Sutton, John R., Frank Dobbin, John W. Meyer, and W. Richard Scott (1994), 'Legalization of the workplace', *American Journal of Sociology*, **99** (4), January, 944–71.

Swidler, Ann (1986), 'Culture in action: symbols and strategies', *American Sociological Review*, **51** (2), April, 273–86.

Tangri, Sandra, M. Burt, and L. Johnson (1982), 'Sexual harassment at work: three explanatory models', *Journal of Social Issues*, **38**, 33–54.

Tangri, Sandra and S.M. Hayes (1997), 'Theories of sexual harassment', in William O'Donohue (ed.), *Sexual Harassment: Theory, Research, And Treatment*, Boston: Allyn and Bacon.

Tarrow, Sidney (1992), 'Mentalities, political cultures, and collective action frames: constructing meaning through action', in Aldon D. Morris and Carol McClurg Mueller (eds.), *Frontiers in Social Movement Theory*, New Haven: Yale University Press.

Taylor, Joan Kennedy (1998), *What to Do When You Don't Want to Call the Cops: A Non-Adversarial Approach to Sexual Harassment*, New York: New York University Press.

Taylor, Verta (1996), *Rock-a-By Baby: Feminism, Self-Help and Postpartum Depression*, New York: Routledge.

—— (1999), 'Gender and social movements: gender processes in women's self-help movements', *Gender and Society*, **13** (1), February, 8–33.

Taylor, Verta and Nancy E. Whittier (1992), 'Collective identity in social movement communities: lesbian feminist mobilization', in Aldon D. Morris and Carol McClurg Mueller (eds), *Frontiers in Social Movement Theory*, New Haven: Yale University Press.

Thompson, E.P. (1975), *Whigs and Hunters: The Origin of the Black Act*, New York: Pantheon.

Tushnet, Mark (1987), *The NAACP's Legal Strategy Against Segregated Education, 1925–1952*, Chapel Hill: University of North Carolina Press.

Vose, Clement E. (1967), *Caucasians Only*, Berkeley, CA: University of California Press.

Walsh, Edward J. and Rex H. Warland (1983), 'Social movement involvement in the wake of a nuclear accident: activists and free riders in the Three Mile Island area', *American Sociological Review*, **48** (6), December, 764–81.

Weeks, Elaine Lunsford, Jacqueline M. Boles, Albeno P. Garbin, and John Blount (1986), 'The Transformation of Sexual Harassment from a Private Trouble into a Public Issue', *Sociological Inquiry*, **56**, 432–55.

Welsh, Sandy (1999), 'Gender and sexual harassment', *Annual Review of Sociology*, **25**, 169–90.

White, Lucie E. 1990. 'Subordination, rhetorical survival skills, and Sunday shoes: notes on the hearing of Mrs. G.', *Buffalo Law Review*, **38** (1), Winter, 1–58.

Whittier, Nancy (1995), *Feminist Generations: The Persistence of the Radical Women's Movement*, Philadelphia: Temple University Press.

Williams, Christine (1997), 'Sexual harassment in organizations: a critique of current research and policy', *Sexuality and Culture*, **1**, 19–43.

Williams, Christine, Patti A. Giuffre and Kirsten Dellinger (1999) 'Sexuality in the workplace: organizational control, sexual harassment, and the pursuit of pleasure', *Annual Review of Sociology*, **25**, 169–90.

Williams, G.I. and R.H. Williams (1995), '"All we want is equality": rhetorical framing in the fathers' rights movement', in J. Best (ed.), *Images of Issues*, 2nd ed., New York: de Gruyter.

Yngvesson, Barbara (1993), *Virtuous Citizens, Disruptive Subjects: Order and Complaint in a New England Court*, New York: Routledge.

Yoder, Janice D. and Patricia Aniakudo (1995), 'The response of African-American women firefighters to gender harassment at work', *Sex Roles*, **32** (3–4), February, 125–37.

Zemans, Frances K. (1983), 'Legal mobilization: the neglected role of the law in the political system', *American Political Science Review*, **77** (3), September, 690–703.

Human Resources Literature

Barrier, Michael 1998. "Sexual Harassment." *Nation's Business* 86(12): 14–19.

Bohren, Jan (1993) "Six Myths of Sexual Harassment." *Management Review* 82(5): 61–3.

Brady, Teresa (1997) "Third-Party Sexual Harassment." *Management Review* 86(4): 45–7.

Fulcher, Gerry (1992) "The New Battle of the Sexes." *Industry Week* 241(9): 22–6.

Hatch, D. Diane (1999) "Employer Liable for Customer Harassment of Employee." *Workforce* 78(3): 108.

Hickens, Michael (1998) "Sexual Harassment Revisited." *Management Review* 87(9): 6.

Holyoke, Larry (1997) "Discrimination Lawsuits Spawn New Industry." *Workforce* 76(6): 26–7.

Koonce, Richard (1998) "It's Time We All Grew Up." *Training and Development* 52(8): 16.

Laabs, Jennifer (1998a) "What You're Liable for Now." *Workforce* 77(10): 34–42.

Laabs, Jennifer (1998b) "Steps to Protect Your Company Against Sexual Harassment." *Workforce* 77(10): 41.

Laurenzo, Diane (1996) "Isn't it Time to Stop Talking?" *Management Review* 85(9): 5.

Maremont, Mark with Jane A. Sasseen (1996a) "Abuse of Power." *Business Week*, No. 3475, May 13: 86.

Maremont, Mark (1996b) "Aftershocks are Rumbling Through Astra." *Business Week*, No. 3476, May 20: 35.

Maremont, Mark (1997) "Sex, Lies, and Home Improvements." *Business Week*, No. 3520, March 31: 40.

Moore, Herff L., Rebecca W. Gatlin-Watts, and Joe Cangelosi (1998) "Eight Steps to a Sexual-Harassment Free Workplace." *Training and Development* 52(4): 12–13.

Moskal, Brian (1991) "Sexual Harassment: An Update." *Industry Week* 240(22): 37–41.

Muller, Joann (1999) "Ford: The High Cost of Harassment." *Business Week* November: 94.

O'Blenes, Carole (1999) "Harassment Grows More Complex." *Management Review* 88(6): 49–51.

Reynolds, Larry (1992) "Translate Fury Into Action." *Management Review* 8(13): 36–8.

Risser, Rita (1999) "Sexual Harassment Training: Truth and Consequences." *Training and Development* 53(8): 21–3.

Seligman, Daniel (1993) "Growth Situation." *Fortune* 128(15): 195–8.

Solomon, Charlene Marmer (1998) "Don't Forget the Emotional Stakes." *Workforce* 77(10): 52–8.

Verespej, Michael (1995) "New-Age Sexual Harassment." *Industry Week* 244(10): 64–8.

Verespej, Michael (1998) "Back on the Front Pages." *Industry Week* 247(7): 7–11.

Judicial Opinions

Alexander v. Yale University, 459 F.Supp. 1 (D. CT 1977)
Andrews v. City of Philadelphia, 895 F.2d 1469 (3rd Cir. 1990)
Barnes v. Castle, 561 F.2d 983 (DC Gir. 1977)
Barnes v. Train, 13 FEP Cases 123 (D. DC 1974), rev'd sub nom *Barnes v. Costle*, 561 F.2d 983 (DC Cir. 1977)
Brown v. City of Guthrie, 22 FEP Cases 1627 (W.D. OK 1980)
Bundy v. Jackson, 19 FEP Cases 828 (D. DC 1979), rev'd 641 F.2d 934 (DC Cir. 1981)
Burlington Industries v. Ellerth, 524 U.S. 742 (1998)
Burns v. McGregor Electronic Industries, 989 F.2d 959 (8th Gir. 1993)
Caldwell v. Hodgeman, 25 FEP Cases 1647

Corne v. Bausch and Lomb, Inc., 390 F.Supp. 161 (D. AZ 1975)
Elliott v. Emery Air Freight, No. C-C-75–76 (W.D. NC 1977)
Ellison v. Brady, 924 F.2d 872 (9th Cir. 1991)
Faragher v. Boca Raton, 524 U.S. 775 (1998)
Garber v. Saxon Business Products, Inc., 552 F.2d 1032 (4th Cir. 1977)
Guyette v. Stauffer Chemical Co., 518 F.Supp. 521 (D. NJ 1981)
Halpert v. Wertheim & Company, 27 FEP Cases 21 (S.D. NY 1980)
Harris v. Forklift Systems, Inc., 510 U.S. 17 (1993)
Heelan v. Johns-Manville, 451 F.Supp. 1382 (D. CO 1978)
Henson v. Dundee Police Dept., 682 F.2d 897 (11th Cir. 1982)
Hill v. BASF Whyandotte Corp., 27 FEP Cases 66 (E.D. MI 1981)
Katz v. Dole, 709 F.2d 251 (4th Cir. 1983)
Kyriazi v. Western Electric Company, 461 F.Supp. 894 (D. NJ 1978)
Marino v. D.H. Holmes Co., 21 FEP Cases 452 (E.D. LA 1979)
Miller v. Bank of America, 418 F.Supp. 233 (N.D. CA 1976), rev'd 600 F.2d 211 (9th Cir. 1979)
Munford v. James T. Barnes & Co., 441 F.Supp. 459 (E.D. MI 1977)
Neeley v. American Fidelity Assurance, 17 FEP Cases 482 (W.D. OK 1978)
Oncale v. Sundowner Offshore Services, Inc., 523 U.S. 75 (1998)
Rabidue v. Osceola Refining Co., 584 F.Supp. 419 (E.D. MI 1984), aff'd 805 F.2d 611 (6th Cir. 1986)
Robinson v. Jacksonville Shipyards, Inc., 760 F.Supp. 1486 (M.D. FL 1991)
Rogers v. Loews L'Enfant Plaza, 526 F.Supp. 523 (D. DC 1981)
Smith v. Rust Engineering Company, 20 FEP Cases 1172 (N.D. AL 1978)
Tomkins v. PSE&G, 422 F.Supp. 553 (D. NJ 1976), rev'd 568 F.2d 1044 (3rd Cir. 1977)
Vinson v. Meritor Savings Bank, 23 FEP Cases 37 (D. DC 1980), rev'd 753 F.2d 141 (DC Cir 1985), aff'd sub nom *Meritor Savings Bank v. Vinson*, 477 U.S. 57 (1986)
Walter v. KFGO Radio, 518 F.Supp. 1309 (D. ND 1981)
Williams v. Saxbe, 413 F.Supp. 654 (D. DC 1976), rev'd on procedural grounds 587 F.2nd 1240 (DC Cir. 1978), on remand sub nom *Williams v. Bell*, 487 F.Supp. 1387 (D. DC 1980)
Yates v. Avco Co., 819 F.2d 630 (6th Cir. 1987)

Index

212   *Confronting Sexual Harassment*

Katz v. Dole (1983) 42
Kearns, Thomas R, and thinking legally 122
Kihnley, Jennie 144
Koonce, Richard 83

Laabs, Jennifer 81
LaFontaine, Edward 91
Langelan, Martha
  and *Back Off!* 28
  and collective action 67–8
  and examples of sexual harassment 64
  and male power 65
  and social change 68
Larana, Enrique 2
Laurenzo, Diane 81
law
  and collective action frames 19
  and collective identities 19
  and conflict resolution 20
  and construction through social practice
    12
  and perceptions of 20
  and resistance to inequality 2
  and sexual harassment 169
  and social change 1, 2, 15, 170
    dispute-centered approaches
      4–6
    judicial impact studies 3–4
  and sources of information 124–8
  and symbolic aspects of 4
  see also legal consciousness; legal
    mobilization
lawyers, and social movements 5
Lawyers' Committee for Civil Rights Under
    Law (LCCRUL) 37
legal consciousness 7, 10–14, 170
  and criticisms of 13
  as a cultural practice 10–11, 166
  and development of 145
  and frames and schemas 11
  and grievance procedures 145–6
  and institutions 23–5, 170–1
  and legal environment 21–3
  and legal rules 21–3, 170
  and legality 11–12, 145
    flexible definition of 122
    legal norms 122–3
  and perceptions of law 20
  and politics 16–21, 170
    absence from research 16–17
    collective action frames 18–19

collective identities 18, 20
  individual resistance 17
  realignment of personal identity 17–18
  and sexual harassment 16
  and situating in social problems 14–16
  and social practice 23, 166
  and types of 13
legal innovation 33
legal mobilization 7–10, 32 n3
  and conflict resolution 7–9
  and definition of 7
  and legal rules 123
legal norms 122–3
legal remedies, characteristics of effective
    22
legal rules 15
  and legal consciousness 21–3, 170
  and legal mobilization 123
  and re-negotiation of 24
  and sexual harassment 16, 22–3, 121–2
    naming of 124, 128
legality 11–12, 170
  and flexible definition of 122
  and legal consciousness 145
  and multivalent nature of 15
lesbian family rights
  and debate over 15–16
  and legal rules 22
'lifestyle' politics 61
litigation strategies, disadvantages of 4–5

McAdam, Doug J 62
McCann, Michael W 4, 21
  and rights-based arguments 19
MacKinnon, Catharine 36–7, 40, 42, 69
  and effects of sexual harassment 65
  and *Sexual Harassment of Working Women*
    36
management, *see* employers
Management Review 76, 78
Mansbridge, Jane J, and oppositional
    consciousness 88
Marino v. D H Holmes Co (1979) 56 n8
mass media, as source of information 126–7
Mauro, Thomas 37
meaning, social influences on 110
Merit Systems Protection Board (MSPB) 89,
    142, 143
Meritor Savings Bank v. Vinson (1986) 42–3,
    45–6, 124
Merry, Sally Eagle, and consciousness 10